CW00455666

Vile Pathetic specimen

Written by

Kes Davis

Antony Rowe
Publishing Services

This book has been printed digitally and produced in a standard specification in order to ensure its continuing availability

Published by Antony Rowe Publishing Services in 2005
2 Whittle Drive
Highfield Industrial Estate
Eastbourne
East Sussex
BN23 6QT
England

ISBN 1-905200-33-1

Printed and bound by Antony Rowe Ltd, Eastbourne

This book would have stayed under my bed gathering dust had it not been for my wife Alison who has been a support beyond belief, and my wonderful children Amelia, Ellie, Kirsty and Ashley.

To all the people lost in addiction,
and the people who knew them.

The events in this book are based on my life as I went from child, alcoholic, homeless drug addict, to a qualified drug and alcohol therapist, in a respected private hospital in rural Sevenoaks in Kent. This is my story....

A special message for Nick from the cottage, of which I hold lovely memories of, and his dog the one and only Kick Start. Please contact the publishers Nick so Alison, my wife and I know that you are safe and alive.

<u>ACKNOWLEDGEMENTS</u>

I deeply wish to acknowledge the encouragement and support I have been given from my friends whilst writing this book. On the top of my list would be my beautiful wife Alison who I first met at the cottage twenty years ago, the kindness she showed me then has not diminished over the years, since Alison became my sounding board she has up built up my self esteem and confidence to a level that I thought not possible, all this she has done through her consistent unconditional love. Thank you Ali, I love you.

The journey of this book has been shared with my good friend Jamie Burdett, through good times and bad we have remained friends and using a combination of our skills we have managed to put print on paper. Jamie is one of the survivors of life and has a book hidden in amongst the pages of his own metaphorical recovery, I hope that he will one day share his journey with us. The people I have worked with have been my proof readers, editors and critics, I thank all of you, with special thanks to all the staff at Godden Green Clinic and an extra special thank you to Dr Slime, Harry, Salmah, Joe, Eeva, Tina, Carlos, Steve, Mina, Joan, Rose, Liz and another special thank you to Dr John and Dr Royds.

To Joy, Tracy and Hayley there is help out there. Thank you Kate and Sandra for being so patient about my constant, can you just do this for me, requests.

Introduction

My name is Kes I am a thirty seven year old addiction therapist, I enjoy my work and am happy in what I do. I am married to the love of my life and have four wonderful children, two that live with me and two that don't but I'll explain more about that later. All in all you could look at my situation and think I was just an every day bloke with an every day family, I have an ordinary house an ordinary car, pretty much Mr ordinary, I am definitely happy. What I have now I call my second life.

Not so long ago I was dying; I had three weeks left to live. My first life, ruled by my addictions, finished when I was thirty and the controlling forces from that life are now dead to me. I began writing my story during my recovery from alcoholism and drug addiction. In the first year of recovery I became part of a recovery programme and during that stage wrote down my life to see it more clearly and work out why I drank and took drugs and who I affected. I found that once I started writing, I couldn't stop and the result is this book. My recovery continues every day of my existence and will continue until the end of my second life.

I am both alcoholic and drug addict. I began my drinking at a very early age and continued to the point of almost no return; the choices I made were erratic, misjudged and destructive. My addictions took me to dark places in my mind and even darker places in reality. The scenery on my journey of life was pain, abuse, confusion, crime, and death. Now this may sound weird but all the way through this terrifying bus man's holiday there was lots of fun and excitement.

Alcohol became the emotional crutch and crux of my existence. The understanding of how to form relationships and have a healthy understanding of self was missed and replaced by an all-consuming desire to drink and in subsequent years use drugs.

For thirty years I escaped from the pain, truth and reality that had been my entire life in either alcohol or drugs. In doing so I lost sight of who I was and became a vessel for abuse and that alone. I am not going to say that I am one of the lucky ones for getting through this, because the lucky ones don't get abused in the first place. I alone clawed my way back from certain death and insanity, yes people gave me suggestions but it was down to me to take them, I hope that I can help as many people as possible achieve the same, through my work and this book.

1
Drink

I was ten and standing in the pantry of my home during one of our regular family piss-ups. In my hand I held the most important thing in my life. A bottle of whisky. I took three giant gulps of the aromatic liquid. I had been waiting for over an hour for this moment, getting increasingly tight, fractious and obsessed. I felt out of place and uncomfortable and knew that there was only one thing that would make everything right. With the whisky flowing through my system I could breath freely again. In five short minutes I could walk back into the crowded room full of confidence and bravado, exactly what I needed in this company.

During the party I returned to the pantry every time I felt the alcoholic edge wavering. By the time everyone had left, the bottle would be half-empty and hidden away. It wouldn't be missed. My family were drinkers and always had been. Alcohol was a way of life, so why should I be any different.

However, there were still rules and drinking whisky at ten was unacceptable. I was fortunate that the pantry was always well stocked. Along the fraying wooden shelves a whole host of alcohol choices stood waiting for my indulgence. I took great pride in choosing the relevant bottle for my needs. On some days I simply felt a bit down and needed a hit, then it would be spirits, the bottle carefully picked and then placed at the back behind a full bottle of the same type. For more adventurous excursions, when I'd roam the local woods, lost in childish imaginings, beer, cider or my uncle's homemade wine was best. Filling my bicycle bottle full and taking off for long drunken rides was a favourite pastime.

I can't remember the first ever time I drank but the story of my first drunken exploit, I've heard many times over. I was two and managed to drink enough of the contents of a bottle of sherry from the fridge to send me into blackout. On return from the doctors, my Mother retold the story with hilarity and never failed to bring it up at parties, almost proud of her son's alcoholic capabilities. It was stories like this when I was a bit older and drinking with purpose that helped me convince myself that nothing was wrong with my actions.

Not that I had too many difficulties on that account. Watching all the adults around you regularly drink to a drunken state leaves you thinking that this is an acceptable thing to do. Lack of communication in an emotionally cold house contributed to this, as feelings were never discussed. This left me angry and confused on many occasions and then I'd turn to my comfort blanket. Not quite a crocheted square of material but effective all the same. The feelings I felt I was plagued with were topped off with a good portion of loneliness and I remember being pre school age, say three or four and playing day after day with whatever insects crawled about on the floor. I would play with the insects knowing that there was no other person in the house to play with, that was the way it always was day after day alone sitting on the cold tiled floor wearing only my vest and pants, my friends the insects and I kept each other company until my loneliness turned to anger and I squashed them with the palm of my hand, and how I felt guilty and sad after they had gone, then I really was alone. I would try to amuse my self and draw for most of the time, leaning on a small glass coffee table, one day however I leant a little too hard and the coffee table twisted and smashed into a thousand pieces, shards of glass littered the floor and cut my feet. Even though I was terrified of waking up my dad I knew I had to. I was scared and my feet were bleeding, after only just whispering Dad he awoke and I told him what had happened, he just said "wait till your mother gets home" and rolled back over and went to sleep. Even at the tender age of four I knew what to expect when mother got home, my feet were not bandaged, I was not cuddled, I was beaten, told I would never be forgiven as I was a "fucking liability" and was told to get out of my Mums sight, that was every day stuff to me.

My anger never truly lifted and bubbled under the surface at all times, kept just in check on most occasions although violent outbursts occurred regularly. Violence was another family trait.

My Grandfather was the boss of the family and I adored him with the respect I thought appropriate. However it was always from a distance. No one was close in my family. The only times it appeared that we even liked each other was during the drinking parties. The rest of the time, it was heads down and mostly work, moaning and eating. My Grandfather ruled by violence and fear but I was only to learn that at an older age. Under the influence he had managed to be barred from every pub in his local area when he was young and old come to think of it. He brought his violence into the house as well and managed to beat seven children to death whilst still inside my Grandmother, leaving my Mother as one of four instead of eleven.

He was six foot tall, had a bulging, muscled body, white hair and a bushy moustache nestled under his five-times-broken nose. He was a fighter by nature and at times showed amazing courage. One of the best stories was of him walking from the South of France to Dunkirk carrying two kids during the war. He also worked in bomb disposal, after the war, and had a reputation for great bravery, including carrying a bomb from a burning pub, although not till the booze had been rescued first.

His tales when told as a child amazed me and they cemented my hero worship. There were other stories, however, that were missed out at the time. I wasn't told the story about him ripping all the doors off the house and making his wife and young children sleep outside night after night because one of the kids had not closed the living room door; or the fact that he would regularly eat steak whilst the family had watered down tomato soup or nothing at all. He was feared, not respected, and when he died there were no tears, at least not until the fake ones bubbled out through drink- fused false emotions at the wake, which was just another justification for a three day piss up.

From a young age my mother became the maternal carer for her siblings. She tried to protect them from her father and sometimes got the shit beaten out of her for this. She was, and still is stronger than many men. She was built more for comfort than speed and at five foot five is square and stocky. Her face was usually set hard against the world and there was little humour or joy in her expressions. This only changed at the parties when, laced with booze, she would erupt into a tuneless rendition of 'knees up mother brown' or something similar.

She had a finger missing on her left hand from a factory machine accident and scars all over the rest of her hands from her heavy work, potato picking, Christmas tree uprooting or some other manual labour; she was frightened of nothing including hard work. Hard work was what she mostly did, that and feeding her brood. Mum was either shouting most of the time or totally silent, a silence so intense you were scared to break it for fear of getting a punch in the face or at least having your head ripped off verbally. She had terrified me for as long as I could remember, she would call me a pathetic specimen and the look she gave me would confirm she must be right.

She met my father when she was sixteen; he was thirty. He was an honest and old-fashioned fellow. He worked hard and provided all she wanted. There was no violence about him and he became a human doormat for her to walk all over for the rest of their lives. He never really complained and she ruled the roost. He was happy to have a wife and she had found the escape she needed from her tyrant of a father. Their marriage has stayed solid throughout their lives albeit appearing loveless and full of resentment.

They had four children, with me the last. I was the only boy and suffered at the hands of my sisters. Most sibling relationships are fraught but hopefully they are founded on love, I doubt that mine ever was or will be, as it's difficult to give love if you don't know what it means. My sisters were all very different but each one fucked-up in their own way. The most difficult one was Suzi, the second child. She was destructive, nasty, would bully me when ever she had the chance. In short, she was a young female version of our grandfather. Some of it was the way she was nurtured but a lot of it was her nature, I feel.

She dressed and acted like a tomboy and lied all the time. Out of the three she was the most physically abusive towards me and would take her anger out on me whenever she felt like it. She had short dark hair, a bit stocky like my Mum and was the first to smoke and drink. She turned into an alcoholic. My Mum wasn't shy of beating her when she ran out of patience and as she had little patience to start with, the beatings were often and at times brutal. I remember one instance when Suzi staggered backwards down our street as Mum punched her repeatedly in the face screaming a selection of obscenities.

Cathy was the youngest girl and the closest to my age as she was only three years older. She had long blonde hair that was often styled in plaits down her back. She was incredibly moody and cried every time she didn't get what she wanted. To keep her quiet my parents gave in to most of her demands so she became a spoiled little brat. She was the prettiest and most feminine of the three and played on her looks. She also had a tender side and would hold my hand occasionally but could then turn in a split second so although I craved her affection, I never trusted it.

Nicola was the eldest and left home as soon as she was sixteen. As she was seven years older, I didn't get to know her too well. She had normal brown hair, was quiet and plain. She kept to herself a lot and was the only one I didn't hate.

In our flat on a notorious estate, life was difficult and challenging. My early years were full of neglect and at times abuse, both physical and mental. It felt like it was constant. I was an angry child and remember feeling a lot of frustration. I had no affection from my mother. To this day I can't remember a single hug or ever hearing her say, 'I love you'. My father was different and gave me hugs but he was never around, as he worked such long hours. Our house was a lonely house where everybody had to walk on eggshells for fear of upsetting mum, which could result in a beating.

One afternoon my feelings became difficult to ignore which was understandable in that atmosphere. I felt an explosive energy building in me and wanted to scream but knew I'd only be beaten or shouted at if I did and in frustration at not finding an outlet lifted my arm and bit down hard. The pain was severe and sharp but somehow helped. My feelings of anger dispersed and although I was left with red and blue teeth marks with blood seeping out of the indentations, I felt better. As soon as I found this release I used it regularly, biting as hard as I could whenever I felt I needed to be in control of the emotional pain and loneliness I remember feeling most of the time. At times I could feel the skin between my teeth on the verge of breaking and would clench my jaw, holding my skin right at the limit knowing I could tear my arm if I chose to.

The need for control but the dysfunctional methods of obtaining it permeated our entire family. It started with my Grandfather and his fear- inducing violence, which was passed to my Mother. At any family gathering he would rule the room with his menacing presence. She used violence in a similar way and it wasn't uncommon for me to be bounced around the kitchen by my hair, I can remember being around four and some how being accused of breaking a plate in the kitchen. Straight away the bellowing that nearly broke my ear drums started as my mum stormed into the kitchen like a tornado, I have such clear memories of her grabbing the hair on the top of my head and pulling me off the ground. I tried to hold on to her for arms so that my arms would take my weight as it felt as if my scalp was going to be ripped from my skull, she would be shouting into my face, her nose almost touching mine, her hot breath stinking of cigarette smoke blowing over my face and me breathing it in as she shouted, "What have you done you fucking little bastard?" with such force that she covered my face in spit at the same time.

With all her might she slammed me down on the floor and I hit the lino with the base of my spine. The indescribable pain shot up my spine and in to my scull, instantly knocking the breath out of me. To my horror she lifted me again to repeat the process, I yelped like a young puppy unable to beg for mercy as I felt like vomiting because of the pain, my arms and legs had lost all their power to resist her and a sick feeling resonated through my very bones robbing me of any hope I had of lessening the blow on my spine by putting my feet down first, Mum repeated this action six, seven maybe eight times, I can't be sure as I could not think straight through the fog of sickness and pain. She finished her onslaught by throwing me across the kitchen and I vividly remember sliding across the cold lino head first into the cupboard door, and then silence.

I lay there not able to move my legs or arms, not able to cry, not able to do anything except lay still and play dead much like a wild animal does when it is attacked by a larger animal, laying there hoping that the attacker will leave it alone and not deliver the killer blow. I don't know how long I lay there but I do know that nobody came to my rescue, nobody cuddled me, nobody tried to make things better. I also don't know how long the pain seemed unbearable and I was unable to even sit down, it did however seem like an eternity.

Being around mum was like walking through a mine field whilst playing Russian roulette, I don't know what was worse, the beatings or the mental torture.

My sisters used bullying tactics maybe to help themselves release their own anger and frustration, most of the time I was the butt of their abuse. On one occasion, which stayed with me for many years, they made me stand in the corner of our kitchen and taunting me and laughing, made me strip till naked. As I stood there crying and thinking of a way out, they brandished a broom and poked me with it until they were bored of their bullying. Suzy was the instigator and the others went along with it. When I was finally naked, they laughed and made fun of my genitals until I couldn't bear it any longer and burst out of the room crying and screaming. I ran upstairs jumped into my bed and tore into my arms, wishing my sisters dead. This was the sort of thing that went on as we were frequently left in the house alone as mum and dad worked night shifts a lot of the time.

I look back now and can see just how messed-up they must have been to behave like this. Looking at the environment in which we lived it was hardly surprising, but at the time all it did was engender a deep level of anger and hatred for people I should have loved. The house in which we lived had to be kept spotless, not by mum, but by us the kids and if I didn't do my chores my mum might just stab me as she had told me so many times, "don't make mess, don't drop any thing, don't do this, don't do that, do as you are told, or I'll kill you, DON'T BREATH". Mum would stare at me and whoever of my sisters was there, for ages and growl in a voice not much more than a whisper "I'm gonna kill you whilst you are asleep". Thinking back now as an adult, I hope she didn't mean that literally but back then as a child I believed her.

That was a normal evening for us, we were ordered around like servants clearing up for mum, making tea for mum, trying our hardest not to annoy mum, just in case she flipped.

In the same way as my Mother took after her Father, my Dad took after his. He was a lovely old man and on the trips up to London I would hum inside with anticipation. I loved being curled up on his lap breathing in the tobacco and whisky aromas, acquired from his lunchtime down at the local. He was a cuddly man who smiled a lot, a rarity in my life. On the day he died, the family trip to London ended at the hospital instead of his home. Nothing was explained to me and as I sat in the car outside on my own, I felt angry and confused at being left out. I was only about five but remember my Dad coming out through the doors of the hospital, getting into the car and everyone driving home in silence. I desperately wanted to know why my Dad was crying but no one spoke. When I asked the question later at home, Nicola my sister said that Granddad had gone to heaven and then she went out with her friends. I was confused and sad that I was not going to see granddad anymore but I never cried, in fact I can't remember crying about anything ever after that.

This was often the way at home, nothing was dealt with healthily and my young pain and confusion turned to resentment and anger over time, although I was unable to show it to anyone but myself as any show of emotion if at all negative would cause me to be branded a pathetic specimen by my mother. That was one of her favourite phrases.

Dad never seemed to be at home as he worked nights in a factory, he was a slim man, strong and very quiet he didn't argue with mum at all. No matter how she treated us he would just go along with it, his name was Frank and when mum was too tired to hit me herself, the phrase, "Frank, hit the boy" would bring me to a sigh of relief as he only ever hit me on my body and never hit me in the head, later on he would hug me and say " don't do it again". The trouble was I didn't usually have a clue what it was I was not meant to do again but I would just say "Ok dad" and accept that I must have done something wrong as I didn't want to be branded as even more of a trouble maker and annoy mum enough to hit me. I had never experienced any real healthy affection or seen any, the only affection I ever heard was mum and dad having sex late at night. I knew what I was listening to wasn't for me to hear, but it was hard for me not to listen as my room which was shared by the golden child youngest sister and was right next door to their`s.

In those early years we moved house more times than I can remember So much so that we were nick-named the gypsies by our relatives. It was when we moved to another rural area that the torture went up a gear.

Identifying my feelings in some of these memories I have uncovered has been difficult to say the least. I have always had two base feelings, one of impending doom and one of overwhelming anger, these feelings were made stronger whilst living at our new home in the country side. I would have nightmares every night. There were three reoccurring nightmares I won't go into every detail of what was in the night mares because the content of them was so far over shadowed by the feeling of an all engulfing impending doom. So severe that the death of everything beautiful that was ever created could not have generated a feeling to match the despair I drowned in during and after my

9

nightmares. Like I have already said, when it came down to showing love in my family I might as well as been trying to imagine what the weather was like on Saturn, the nearest thing that I knew to love was the noises that came out of mum and dad's bedroom sometimes, but I wasn't the only one in this emotional void, there were four of us kids all in our different states of emotional starvation.

I was 4½ when my eldest sister started to sexually abuse me, the first time it happened we were alone in the spotless front room of our house It is all very clear, every thing from my age to the polished wooden floor to the orange nylon nighty with white frilly cuffs she was wearing. I concentrated on every thing in that room except what was going on, I slipped out of this reality and into the reality that I visited most of the time in order to avoid whatever was going on in my life and on this particular occasion it happened to be the start of sexual abuse, a different pain but I used the same method of escape. At the time all I felt was confusion, shame and fear of being caught by my dad who was sleeping in the next room as he had been on night shifts. My sister did what she did and made me do what I did, maybe in some twisted attempt to gain some shred of love and affection, as she had experienced about as much love as I had, and was using the only example she knew of to try and quell the yearning for closeness that must have burned inside of her as it did me. That example must have been a more sinister version of what I would hear some nights coming from mum and Dad's room, Like I said, my method of escaping that reality is the very reason I remember other details so well, and the very reason I remember the shame, guilt, anger, helplessness and hopelessness of my life then. The impact of the sexual abuse that my sister put me through has followed me throughout my life even to this day, but at least now I'm in control of what memories and feelings do to me and not the other way round. I feel sad that my first sexual experiences were so painful and marred all of my relationships with women sexually and on a level of trust. The feeling that all females were pretty sick and nasty was not helped by the fact that given an opportune moment when we were alone my mum would take off her t shirt if she was wearing one or undo her blouse, then take off her bra exposing her breasts to me and invite me to play with them, fondle them, the colour of my face would always change to beetroot red and I would shy away, she would giggle and then make derogatory statements about my penis.

If I were reading this as the reader now I would be saying to myself, "why didn't you tell your Dad," and asking the question, he will do something now wont he? But you see the trouble there was that dad put me on too much of an edge to talk to him about anything sexual as he used to grope my buttocks as I ran upstairs from him to get to my bed room and dive into bed, knowing that I would be unavoidably groped if he tucked me in, my Dads abuse reached its crescendo on a family holiday when he took me into the shower with him. Again I slipped into my own reality and memorised every inch of the stainless steel shower and wooden slatted floor, I remember him moving towards me naked and then thank goodness just blackness, my memory has spared the rest from me. I was such an easy target for all manner of abuse. In my mind I was a stupid, pathetic specimen, my parents had seen to that. I knew no different and thought that was just the way it is, it didn't seem unusual for my sister to abuse me and five minutes later be hovering whilst I carried on drawing, or watching a cartoon. I had never been allowed round to visit a friends house and no one was ever allowed to visit mine, so you see I had no frame of reference to go by unless they were family.

Apart from the physical, verbal, sexual and emotional abuse, I had to learn to deal with the feeling that all of this caused me to have. Sex was deemed to be something disgusting and vile so in my mind if mum found out what I had been doing with my sister she would surely kill me like she had threatened to do so many times, or if dad found out what I had done with my sister he would tell mum and if mum knew that dad was touching me up or worse the punishment would be unimaginable. The pressure I was living under was immense and the only relief I had was to abuse myself be it through biting or stealing alcohol from the cupboard or punching myself in the stomach or head to numb the pain I felt inside. Throughout all of this the main thing that stopped me from killing myself was the farm that my aunt and uncle lived on. I would lose myself for hours and hours in the woods in a world of my own, playing with my cousin who was about the same age as me, although he was nothing like me we were great friends. My cousin's name was Mark and when it was just him and me together I was allowed to let my body work as a body should work. You see at home any bodily function was deemed to be totally disgusting and unacceptable, Burping was punishable by being told what a vile disgusting bastard I was, and being made to feel less than human by having to leave the room and apologise over and over and over and so on and so on. On leaving the room you would probably receive a slap for good measure. Now a fart was deemed worse than a burp and any one who ever farted was called a filthy animal and was ordered out of the house. The repression of breaking wind from an early age has caused me constant painful gastric and overall stomach problems, I grew up feeling ashamed of the very way me, as a human being worked, Mum never to my knowledge has ever passed wind in any way shape or form in her life. What used to annoy me though is the fact that we always had a family dog that farted constantly and shit upon the floor with not so much as a 'you are a bad boy'.

All of these traits of holding in any bodily function were taken to school with me and when I was at school I suffered immense pain through my mums conditioning. That conditioning didn't stop there. Meal times were a hideous experience for me, we always had to eat at the table as a family at every opportunity which is nice in a healthy family, but lets not forget that this one was run by a mad dictator, Mum would pride herself on her cooking skills and we had to go through the ritual compliments a thousand times over every mouth full, like it was the first time we had ever tasted food, the portion sizes were so big some times we would have to have two plates each as the amount of food we were given would have fed three families. I know this must sound ungrateful but believe me, I am not, the food was good but there was no way any of us could even dent the amount we were given, at the end of meal times the three girls were allowed to leave the table but I had to stay and watch as the leavings off of every plate were scrapped on to my plate, and I was ordered to eat. I would start eating as I would rather do that than be bounced around like a rubber ball. I ate and ate being told about starving people in other countries and how ungrateful I was if I didn't eat it all, if I did manage to eat it all by some miracle I was then told what a "greedy fucking pig" I was, I could not win and after nearly every meal I would have to sneak off to the loo and stick my fingers down my throat in order to vomit and relieve the agony I was in, I would then feel guilty thinking about the starving people mum had told me about but relieved because I was now in control of the pain.

As a child and adult I carried on the vomiting process that I came to know as bulimia and have been left with permanent gastric problems and hardly any enamel on my teeth as my stomach acid has worn it away over the years. Bulimia was one of the tools I used for getting through my miserable existence. I didn't have to binge on food to try to make me feel better, I was force fed it and in later years I carried it on as it had grown into a coping mechanism. It was just something else I had to hide at school.

As if school wasn't bad enough I was already having to try to avoid sitting next to people because I smelt of dried urine. That fact had been spoken of by other kids who avoided me and I didn't want to go through the embarrassment of it being brought up again. The reason I smelt of urine coming from such a clinically, spotlessly clean home was because I couldn't stop wetting the bed. It was down to me to change my sheets and keep my part of the room clean so I would rinse my underwear in the bathroom sink and dry them behind the radiator so no one could see them. I went through a constant process of turning my mattress, sleeping in a wet bed with wet sheets and drying what I could by stealing my eldest sister's hair dryer and using it when it was safe, Some nights I would not sleep at all for fear of wetting the bed, I learnt over time to drink just enough booze to help me relax so I didn't wet the bed, but too much would make the bed wetting worse. My sister who shared the same room was also a bed wetter, but how she dealt with her wet bed I didn't know. I hated the embarrassment of wetting the bed as it confirmed what my mum had taught to me, that me and my body were foul and disgusting. Personal hygiene was never taught me, I learned it through being made to feel embarrassed and belittled, I first started using a tooth brush at around the age of seven after being bullied and taunted called names like yellow teeth and enduring agonising tooth ache, Mum or dad never showed me how to use it or showed me if I even had one. Every morning I would just use whatever one came to hand first, I didn't know everyone had their own personal tooth brush. I thought you were to use any one like you would a hand towel. On some level just about everything that I learned I taught myself, my parents introduced me to booze but I taught myself to drink it.

I started to drink seriously at around seven. I was always given a little beaker of beer by some relative or other, usually one of my Uncles. At first I hated the taste and didn't drink much but as the party's which were weekly grew more raucous I would be encouraged to drink-up. I always felt ashamed of who I was and unimportant so when given the opportunity to do something that the adults were doing I went straight at it. It made me feel older and that I belonged because all of a sudden mum was not calling me a pathetic specimen. When I was drinking I was told I would be just like my granddad which in my eyes was a compliment, Mum would praise me and smile at me during these bouts of drinking, I felt loved and accepted, that warm feeling of the alcohol was mixed up with the feeling of me being accepted and these two feelings together gave me all the motive to drink as often as possible. I soon found that if I got passed the taste and gulped it straight down I'd feel a lot better and begin to laugh and muck around and telling jokes, entertaining the crowd. I found that the more I drank, the better I felt and all my insecurities melted away. Although this really took off at around seven I remember my first experience of it at around four, when I was plied with gin by my aunt whilst she repeatedly pushed my head in to her large breasts in a sexual manner, this was thought to be most amusing by some of the men at the party whilst I was just embarrassed. I was also so drunk that I blacked out, that too was thought comical.

At first I only drank at the parties and took what little was given to me but after a while I wanted more as it occurred to me that the thing that made life better lived in a bottle. The older I got the more frequently I drank. It made me feel like I had a friend, something I could rely on. When I drank, the feelings of anger and hatred boiling away inside me shrank and the drink or booze as it was known in our household allowed me to feel how I wanted to be, free and happy. With booze inside me I could escape; escape from my family, my feelings and my true self. When I hadn't had a drink the only thing that helped me sleep at night was the thought of never waking up ever again, the thought of dying cheered me up enough to relax me into a broken sleep, I fantasised about dying daily. For me it was a way of hiding, just a variation on the way we would hide behind the settee when the rent man or milk man called, or the way I would hide from my mum when she would stare at me with mad eyes at night some times and threaten to strangle or stab me when I was sleeping. That didn't do much for me when it came to trying to get a good night's sleep. In fact sleeping at night is something that I have never been able to do properly due to her causing me to be terrified pretty much all of the time. So you could say that hiding was second nature to me. Be it in a bottle or in the wardrobe under a pile of clothes trying to sleep and listen at the same time for footsteps in the bedroom.

This wasn't the only way I escaped and I think the other main interest of my life gave me the physical strength to cope with the booze at such an early age, exercise. I was a bull- headed child and developed into a bull- headed adult. I threw myself into things with great enthusiasm and with exercise I pushed myself regularly to my very limits, completely exhausting my body at times so my mind would be quiet. By an early age I could run a marathon and ran many miles each week. I didn't do this because I knew it was good for me. I did it because I knew that pushing myself to the point of collapse over shadowed the dark pain in my life, and gave me a buzz I wanted. I would push and push myself proving to some part of me that I was strong and invincible.

After one particular painful experience of my childhood I vowed to myself to become as big and strong as my body would allow. It was party time again. The whole family and assorted friends had come round to our house. I can't remember what the occasion was although mum and dad didn't need a reason. It could have been an anniversary, a birthday or just because it was a sunny day, any excuse would do.

The party had all the usual suspects. My Uncles and Aunts were all on good form. Auntie Doris was singing away at the top of her voice to a Patsy Cline record, being cheered on by a crowd of drunken supporters. I had been slyly drinking, not picky about what I got my hands on, taking sips from people's glasses when they weren't looking. I felt great and was running around telling jokes and generally being 'a kid'.

Boxing was a major part of the family's life; all the men were connected to it. Some were actual boxers and others merely scrappers who watched it on the telly. Whatever level of expertise, they all liked a fight, preferably involving themselves. In the early evening, following many hours of drinking, my Uncle Josie bumped into me as I was playing with my cousins and jokingly threw a few play punches at me. With a high level of booze inside me and on instinct I threw some play punches back, a few striking him. My Mum's Dad threw his head back and said in a gruff voice.

'Good on yer boy, I can see you're gonna be a fucking heavyweight when you grow up, enchya' he rasped and ruffled my hair. I smiled, chuffed to pieces that I had been welcomed into the boxing fraternity. I felt fantastic that my Granddad had taken such pleasure from me and ran off with a huge smile on my face.

About half an hour later, Uncle Josie came and found me in the garden. He had a pair of boxing gloves in his hand and as he approached manoeuvred me into a corner between two walls. He had his lips curled in an awkward smile, showing nicotine stained teeth and as the wall touched my back I felt trapped. Although I was drunk I was also scared. He leaned towards me and said, 'so, let's find out how tough you really are then.' His breath smelt boozy and he swayed slightly on his feet.

I wasn't sure what was happening as we squared-up. In the purple corner stood me, wearing a tank top and Bay City Rollers trousers, weighing in at six stones. In the black corner my opponent put on his gloves. He wore what looked like undertakers cast-offs, was grinning a piano keyboard snarl and weighed a good seventeen stones.

'Put your dukes up then my boy', he snarled and put his hands in front of him to 'touch gloves'. I hesitated and then stepped forwards. I sparred with my cousins regularly and although there was occasional blood spilt, it was all done with fun. This felt different and I put up a front, I felt like the child I was. Things started off gently enough with me pushing out my left hand in soft jabs, stabbing at his torso. He laughed and let me hit him. He gently punched my shoulder and I smiled, relaxing as I realised he was only playing. We traded blows for a while and I ducked and hopped around starting to enjoy myself. The padding of the gloves meant I wasn't getting hurt and I upped my strength punching him harder.

With no warning he threw a proper punch. It hit me on the cheek and knocked me tumbling across the ground. My face felt numb and instant tears welled in my eyes. I was so shocked I couldn't react and just sat in a heap. 'Oh dear, is that it all you've got sunshine?' he said patronisingly and tutted, shaking his head. I tried to crawl away but he blocked my movements and snapped at me to get up which I did with difficulty. He punched me a couple of more times either side of the head so the second blow counter-acted the first but I didn't fall. It felt like my head had been put in a vice and I cried out. The noise of the party meant I couldn't be heard and my Uncle, a man whom I respected and liked, laid into me with enough of his strength to leave my face bloodied and my body bruised. After only a couple of minutes, which felt like an hour, he stood back and I fell to my knees groaning with pain, 'Ah, come on lad, don't be such a girl, remember, big boys don't cry'. He was laughing as he took his gloves off. 'If you're gonna be a boxer, boy, you need to learn to take punishment.' He winked at me and stood back to admire his work. I fought desperately to keep the tears at bay. I knew I mustn't show pain or weakness. That was the golden rule and had been drummed into me from the time I could speak by all the members of my family.

I knelt in the dirt, confused and in pain. Although this feeling was familiar and I had had it from my Mum, this was the first time I had received it from someone I had once respected and a boxer to boot. My body ached and my head throbbed, feeling like it was ten times bigger than it was. Fearing he might dish out some more lessons, I knew I had to escape and using adrenaline to fire my muscles I jumped up and ran away, struggling out of his outreaching arms as I fled past.

I ran to a quiet bit of the garden and hid behind a tree. Slumping to the ground and unable to contain all the pain, confusion and fear any longer, I gritted my teeth and shook making the kind of noise you would make if you were pulling a six-inch nail out of your foot. It wasn't long before someone heard the noise and soon concerned relatives surrounded me. They stood in a circle bleating useless things like, 'What happened?' and 'Come on boy, don't cry now,' as blood ran down my face and dripped onto the ground from my chin. My breathing was strained and I was shaking uncontrollably, I must have looked quite a mess but it was all I was capable of. One of my Aunts got out her hanky and started to wipe my face. I let her do it, as I couldn't move.

As she wiped she repeated the family mantra, 'You're a big boy now, Kes, come on dry up those eyes. She helped me to my feet and took me to the front room. I was put in a chair and left. On the way out she said nothing and closed the door. I felt like I'd been punished and sat in silence, not knowing how to feel or what was going on. I was left in the chair for about three hours and during that time I moved from feeling disgusted at myself for having shown my feelings, broken down and cried, to forming a belief that I was going to become as strong as I could and work hard at building myself into a prize fighter no matter what it took. I also confirmed a belief that became so solidly ingrained in my mind it still sticks firm today, never show pain and never show fear. I never wanted to feel weak again and I never wanted to loose another fight.

That night as I lay in my bed, moaning from the slightest movement, I asked myself why I'd been beaten. On the way home nobody mentioned it and it was just another event that went undiscussed, brushed under the family's emotional carpet. The only answer I could come to was that there must be something wrong with me; none of my cousins were beaten. I felt disgust and shame and crawled into a foetal position desperately wanting to bite my arms, but as my jaw still ached as if all the teeth needed filling's, I couldn't.

In the morning I awoke battered and bruised but carried on with the day as I had done many times before and put it down as just another bad day, the only difference was there was another name on my beware list. At breakfast the following morning I asked my Dad if he could make me some weights and two days later I received them. With the weights and my running I embarked on a training regime that would be difficult for most adults. I ran or cycled many miles each day and lifted weights both morning and night. I was soon the strongest in my area for my age and joining a judo club helped me learn how to fight. I also kept up the sparring with my cousins whenever they were around, although the fun was replaced by a need to fight for me. Before long I was a right little scrapper although I was still too young to go looking for fights. In time, that would change.

The farm where we now lived was a perfect place for me to grow. I could escape after school, if I bothered to go and during the holidays, worked in the orchards, picking apples and hops. Getting a head full of twigs and earwigs wasn't pleasant but at least it meant I got money in my pocket, another family necessity. Hard work and lots of it was a trait that the whole family adhered to and I started young. I was encouraged to work from the age of six or seven and if that warranted not going to school then I didn't go to school. Laziness was frowned upon and was the second worst thing in the world you could possibly be, the first being a coward. The most horrible job I can remember doing at that age was a job called screw pegging. It consisted of walking up and down every row of a hop garden banging in or replacing the metal rods that stuck out of every hop mound, there might have been five thousand of these in one hop garden, the replacement metal rods were carried on my back and banged into the ground with a huge wooden mallet that I also carried, all of this was done during the winter, the wind blowing though the hop gardens sounded horrible and frightening as it whistled and wailed, my hands would be freezing and split with the cold and walking through the manure that fertilised the hop gardens just made the whole job harder. I look at my six year old daughter now and cannot imagine her ever having to work anything like that, but fear of my mum and recriminations from other members of my family stopped me from giving in and saying I couldn't do it. I just carried on regardless of the pain and cold, plenty of adults do that work but as far as I know I'm the only child that had. Apart from this physically demanding work building my constitution, there was another knock on effect.

With cash I could indulge my growing addiction and the local shop was more than happy to take my money for booze although I claimed it was always for my Dad. With the pantry stock and the shop, I could get booze whenever I wanted and it soon became a regular occurrence. I would never drink at home but would gather provisions and head off into the woods or sit by a local reservoir and drink till I felt better. When I wasn't drinking or exercising I'd feel unhappy and the gaps between these pleasures became times I had to tolerate just to get to my next fix.

I was aware that my behaviour was unacceptable but didn't realise how dangerous it was. I knew I had to keep what I was doing away from prying eyes and became as good an expert in hiding my actions as I was at hiding my emotions. Long sleeves were worn when my arms were covered in bite marks, damage from rage outbursts was quickly covered up, my drinking was a solitary past-time and I always had some mouthwash or chewing gum to cover the smell on my breath.

My true self became more distant with each year and my understanding of emotions and how to deal with them was put on hold before I was ten. Fear, pride, inadequacy, resentment and false grandiosity, like the layers of sediment in rock formations, separated me from the truth and I became a human ball- bearing pinging through a destructive pinball machine, bouncing from one disaster to another.

2
Granddad.

By ten, I was drinking four or five of times a week and earning. School wasn't getting much of a look in and in my mind that just made me feel more grown up, but I also had my child times. A warming memory that still brings a smile today is a time when my father and I built a toy fort together. I had seen one on the T.V. and pestered my Dad to get it. With funds always tight he decided to construct his own, and together every night for a week, we set about making the best fort I've ever seen. His attention to detail was amazing, above the fireplace in the main hall were little swords made from bent pins. It was the most time I ever spent with him alone and each day I'd be waiting by the window, full of excitement as he returned from work. Although delighted with the end result I was also disappointed as it meant a return to only spending snatched snippets of time with him, when he wasn't working or running errands for my Mum.

My main happy memories of this period are linked to the freedom I had on the farm. It was a giant playground with no supervision, which led to me learning to ride a motorbike by the age of six and drive a car by eight. I used to go on adventures with my younger cousin and during the years leading up to adolescence we would scour the land as cowboys and Indian's, setting-up camps and throwing our bowie knives around, occasionally into each other. The freedom I had on that farm definitely saved my life whether I was working or playing at least I was not in the house, choking on the ever thickening atmosphere of depression. My aunt and uncle who lived on the farm had an old cottage there and that lovely old run down place became my sanctuary.

I spent as much time as possible out of the house as the atmosphere inside was usually very heavy as if the walls were made of lead. I find it difficult to remember a time when my Mum wasn't in a bad mood of some sort. She would be forever shouting at my Dad for something or other and the only times she would communicate with my sisters or I was when we needed to do jobs or had forgotten them. I took regular trips to the chemist to get her prescriptions for Valium or Mogadon and each time hoped in vain that the pills would turn her into the mother I wanted, but that never happened. I don't think that a chemist would give a months supply of valium and sleeping tablets to a ten or eleven year old boy now, Mum would shout her orders at me and I would toddle off to the shops like her little soldier, every time I collected her pills I thought about disappearing into the woods and taking all of them with as much booze as I could get down me, I was just grateful to be out of the house again as the longer I was out the longer I could avoid being hit again, or ridiculed or worse.

I always felt awkward around her, as if I was in the way. This left me feeling uneasy in my own home and escape became my main priority. When I was excited about something, once or twice I ran into the kitchen to share my news. She would respond with grunts and never take her eyes off what she was doing. I would stand in the kitchen or living room and feel embarrassed for feeling happy. My sister's were a bit better and would listen for a while before turning away and finding something more interesting to talk about. I felt as if I wasn't important and that nothing I did meant anything to them. This created a feeling of rejected isolation and as I grew older I increasingly spent time away from the house on my own, apart from when I was in school. I tried to understand my mum, but there were times when she would ignore all of us completely not for a day or two but for one month, two months, three months, and when I say ignore I mean not even acknowledge that we were alive. The depression in the house was unbearable and the only thing that seemed to make it better was money, and I wasn't going to earn money being at school.

School was a place I dreaded. There were only a handful of kids I spoke to properly and found it difficult to make friends. I was terrified of doing anything that made me stand out so avoided new things and anything that included a group. One of my constant companion fears was looking stupid. The only confidence I possessed was a false bravado nurtured through my exercise and drinking. This resulted in me creating a defence system of a mean and moody personality. It was designed to keep people away as I had no understanding of how to allow them to get close. That two year period of being ten and eleven was one of the turning points in my life, I was becoming physically bigger and it was becoming harder for mum to hit me so most of the hitting was being done by dad. "Hit the boy Frank" became a phrase I was not as scared of any more. Frank would try to smack me but that was futile as the effect didn't touch me, so he would inevitably punch me repeatedly in the back trying to wind me, by the age of eleven I was a tough cookie and remember saying to Frank "didn't hurt "as he punched me. Then he'd repeatedly punch me "didn't hurt ", I would say again, hardly being able to breath. Mum started to concentrate on hurling hurtful insults at me. And it seemed that each one would be more cutting than the last," I know what you're fucking like you dirty bastard" was one of her favourites, I thought she knew what was in my very soul and that meant that I must have been some useless vile sub human, worth less than dog shit, that's how she made me feel with her words, I would rather have a beating any day than the torture that she put me through making me feel that I was the result of some mistake that should never of happened, she made me feel like I was made out of all the crap that God should have thrown in the bin but instead he made me. I could be in a crowd of a billion people and feel lonely because of what she had said.

At secondary school along with my cousin, I made a couple of friends and we became a little gang. The week leading up to the first day of 'big' school, I struggled with sleep and woke in cold sweats during the night. I was still wetting the bed but not as often, it was just the nerves of starting a new school that made the bed wetting worse that week, The morning of the first day arrived and I remember feeling sick the whole way there. I had my defence mechanism set to full and walked to the classroom with my head down, glaring at anyone who came into my line of vision. As I sat down at my allotted table, I was relieved to see at least one friendly face, my cousin's. Along with him and myself there were two other boys. Mum had brought me a new school uniform and I was so grateful that I fitted in, Mum laying out good money for a uniform didn't go without me paying a price, I had to endure three months worth of moaning and being made to feel like she was throwing her money down a drain and it was my fault, before it was bought and what seemed like constant moaning after, I had put what money I had towards the uniform but that meant nothing to her. Most of my money was borrowed by my dad. A couple of quid here, a couple of quid there, I never got it back and didn't care as I felt sorry for him because of the constant nagging and moaning he had to go through at the hands of my mother. He was working six twelve hour shifts a week and that wasn't enough for her. I would slip whatever money I had in his back pocket whilst he was sleeping, if he would have known about it he would have probably felt worse than he did already. The two other boys sitting at my new school table became good friends of mine.

John was a natural born joker and he was always cracking jokes or playing tricks. He wore a mischievous grin permanently fixed to his face, was a little shorter than me, had bushy black hair and, like many boys his age was a scruff. His shirt was never tucked in and how he avoided tripping over laces that spent most of the time following his shoes like a train amazed me. From that first day, being with John always meant fun, even the teachers couldn't help but giggle at his constant humour. Whether he was blowing-up condoms on his head or telling jokes, John was always laughing.

Joe was different but came to be the brother I had never had but desperately needed. Initially however, I was wary of him and put my moody defence shield up. He fell outside my criteria for what was 'acceptable' so I ignored him. He was taller but thinner than both of us and was the opposite of John. His mum was a proud woman and this

25

had transferred to Joe, he was smart and always smelled of soap. His shirts were the cleanest white in school and he spoke with clear concise words in a posh home-counties accent. However, underneath and away from school a different side to Joe emerged, he was wild and adventurous and was always the first to start planning whatever harebrained scheme we were into. He was fitness obsessed like me and we ran and ran together, Joe enjoyed the run whilst I enjoyed winning, we always collapsed with smiles at the end of a run no matter who won.

The last hour of each day would be my favourite, as I knew I'd soon be back on the farm testing out our newest contraption, be it an attempt at making some sort of flying device or the latest go-cart, which was held together with string, gaffer-tape and hope. On some evenings we would go back to Joe's house instead of the farm and I loved these times. Joe came from a wealthy family, and his house was a palace compared to mine. It had loads of bedrooms and a swimming pool. His Mum always put on a great spread whenever I went round and we even had things like pizza, which I had never even tried. Joe was the first person I felt close to. We liked the same things and although he lived a few miles from the farm, which meant I didn't get to see him as much as my cousin, he was the one person I missed. Those first few weeks in secondary school were a revelation to me, I had friends all of a sudden and they thought I was cool as I could drive, RIDE A MOTOR BIKE, was as hard as nails and could drink. My life at home started to become a secondary thing and being out and about was more a priority than ever before, Mum and dad never seemed to be bothered how much I was out or what time I came in. By the time I was twelve I was like an independent adult.

Finding a refuge from my home life, round at Joe's became something I added to my list of escape routes. His Mum always asked me how I was and even gave me occasional hugs which I enjoyed albeit uncomfortably. We became firm friends quickly and the four of us gelled into a little gang within a month of meeting. It felt great to feel part of something and I loved being the leader. It was always me that set the tone for our adventures. Being the 'top' man, or boy as we were still only twelve or so, made me feel important and I loved the sense of control it gave me.

They didn't drink like I did though and would sip at whatever concoction they brought along to join in. That was fine with me as it meant I always had more than my fair share. As I developed a fledgling confidence, through my interaction with the gang, I found that I enjoyed the feeling of being part of something and sought out other opportunities at school. It didn't take me long to find the 'bad' boys and I was soon in the experimenting group, that congregated behind the gym building at lunchtimes. The boys were all older than me but because of my size and reputation I was never bothered. I'd sidle up to the group with my favourite tipple, a bottle of my Uncle's homemade wine topped off with a few slugs of vodka and sup from it as they shared a single can of lager between eight of them. I never shared and would spend frequent afternoons in class, half cut and blissfully unaware of the lessons, in a daydream world all of my own. When I was at school that was an average school day.

In the lead up to the summer holidays of secondary school my parents were planning a holiday. I did what I thought to be my fair share of work, and bunked off school on many days, to work on the farm. As hard work was believed to be more important than an education this was never seen as something wrong and the money I earned certainly helped. I was looking forward to the holiday more than anything and couldn't wait for it. It became my focus and earning the money to help pay for it was hard work. Because of this and the fitness regime I had increased, I laid off the booze for the first time since I started drinking. It simply became something I didn't need as I had a focus and purpose.

The only time during a three-month period that I drank was after an accident at my Dad's work one afternoon. The factory where he worked had closed down for the summer and he and the other workers were earning some extra cash by clearing a large area of waste-ground. It was mainly rough scrub, half-broken trees and scattered rusting dustbins. Dad gave me a long billhook, which is like an axe but with a short handle and long blade shaped like the bill of a seagull.

Everything I did, I attacked like a bull in a china shop and this was no different. I went at the scrub and trees with great gusto, raising the billhook high above my head and bringing it down with all my force. As I aimed into the stump of a tree with one of the giant swings, I misjudged it. The curved side of the blade bounced off the stump and the billhook was sent flying towards my leg. It buried itself deep in my shinbone and a surge of pain was sent rushing through my body. I sank to the floor like a dropped sack of potatoes, in total shock. My heart was racing and I was sure I was going to be sick as I eased the point of the billhook out. I had my back towards the group that was working and I sat quietly, biting my lip, with my hand pressed hard against the wound.

It was big enough to put my thumb into but there was hardly any blood. It hardly wept apart from a yellowish, whitish liquid that filled the hole. My Dad called over to ask me if I was ok,.I leaned round and yelled to him that I was all right and just having a rest, smiling through gritted teeth. I ended the day without having done much more work but I had managed to hide the hole in my shin without being found out. No one had seen my pain.

When my Dad asked me why I had a cloth wrapped round my leg and was limping, I lied saying I had scratched my leg on some bushes and twisted my ankle. For the whole of the drive home I couldn't think of anything but downing a bottle of medicinal booze. As soon as we arrived home, I made my limping way to the pantry, removed a bottle of wine, filled it more that usual with the extra vodka, slung it into a rucksack and gingerly cycled to the reservoir. With my leg, up to my knee, sunk in the cold water I drank back the booze.

As I hadn't drunk for a while the feelings of drifting off in anaesthetised bliss felt wonderful. As my leg went numb and the pain dispersed with each slug, I felt a rush of pride as I reflected on my achievement. Nobody had witnessed my pain and I hadn't cried. I had stayed firm to my belief and all the work I had put in over the time between my beating and the current incident had paid off. I hadn't shown anything of my true feelings and had dealt with it on my own.

The fear that the adults might think me weak and the fact that I knew I had to be accepted made me remain tight-lipped and I kept thinking I had to tough it out. After last time when I was left alone, I remembered that I promised myself that from then on, whatever trouble I got into, it was down to me and me alone to get out of it, and at all costs I must never show my true feelings. From that moment onwards I believed that a tough exterior was paramount and all feelings should be buried beneath this veneer. As far as I was concerned, feelings were a weakness. I had proved to myself I could do it and from that point on would always be in control of my feelings no matter how painful they were. Because of my injury I couldn't work for a month nor

do much running so for the six weeks left before the holiday I concentrated on lifting weights.

Mum and Dad had booked the holiday months in advance and had grafted doubly hard to be able to afford it. They had been working twelve-hour shifts, seven days a week for months, we hardly ever saw them although that wasn't unusual and it suited me down to the ground. I had spent a large part of the winter screw pegging. The money I saved up, combined with the summer's work seemed like a fortune, about eight hundred pounds in today's money. I gave my Mum two hundred towards the holiday, which she accepted, with little fuss. I felt very grown up to be contributing to the holiday as my sisters hadn't and they were all older, although I got no credit from my parents for it.

The holiday morning arrived and as usual there was lots of shouting as we organised ourselves but everyone was in a good mood and we drove off with my sisters and me all sitting in the back seat.

The gates of the holiday camp finally loomed in front of us after a journey that seemed to take hours. I was really looking forward to a magical time and that feeling stayed with me all the way to the first night when my Dad, of all people ruined everything. My Mum and sisters were sitting at a table and Dad and I went to the bar. When ordering the drinks he asked me if I wanted a beer and I said that I'd prefer an orange. He laughed and told me that as I was on holiday he'd buy me a pint. I couldn't stop him as he thought he was doing something special, little did he know that I'd been drinking like a fish for years and was trying to stay dry. I was really angry but as I couldn't exactly explain why. I took the glass and downed it in one right in front of him. In my mind, my actions were saying, 'Look what you've made me do', although in reality all I was doing was spiting myself.

After that my dry spell was over and for the rest of the holiday I threw as much booze as was humanly possible down my neck. When I had that first beer in the pub, I had the feeling that everything was ruined. 'What's the fucking point?' I thought. To teach my Dad a lesson I wanted to make myself as ill as I could. I succeeded in achieving this and drank to the point where I *had* to stop as I had reached a stage where even the smell of booze made me heave.

I thought that I was drinking under duress and although I wasn't, that's what I convinced myself. In protesting against someone else I was actually fulfilling a need within myself and inside, a part of me, my addict, revelled in the chance to tighten its grip.

On one evening we went out as a family to the resort's nightclub, which was like a workingman's club but with more tinsel and flashing lights. I was drinking Guinness to prove that I could drink like a real man, as it was my Granddad's favourite tipple. I wasn't drinking sensibly; I was necking as much as could right in front of my Mum. She said something that confirmed in my mind that all I was doing was correct. She said the immortal line, 'You're just like your Grandfava, you are'. To me that was all the justification I needed. If she thought I was like him then I had become 'a somebody' and would be finally listened to.

I look back at that time and wonder why I was never stopped. It must have been clear that something was wrong with my emotional state and my drinking. After all I was twelve and was not behaving like most twelve- year-olds. However, with everyone around me so busy and most of them dealing with their own problems, combined with my excellent ability at hiding things, the truth of what was happening was impossible to see, especially by me.

We returned from holiday to a shock announcement. Nicola was getting married. She'd been seeing a guy for about a year and had jumped at his proposal as if the emergency doors had popped open on a plane. She saw her escape route just as mum had done when she married dad and within three months was saying, 'I do' to the wrong man. The marriage pretty much bankrupted my parents as they laid on a fantastic party, way beyond their means.

There was a horse and carriage, the most amazing flowers everywhere, the church looked like a page from a story book and a massive piss-up with endless flowing booze to top the day off. It was a great event and went without a hitch, apart from a couple of inter-family fights. As we waved off the happy couple, I remember feeling so jealous I'm surprised I didn't turn green. I thought she was so lucky to be getting out of our home. The following day as the hangover settled on me like a giant black cloud, I wallowed in self-pity, knowing that the only person in the family who treated me remotely like a human being had left and I was now completely on my own.

The post-wedding week was a nightmare at home, with arguments every night about money and the lack of it. Mum and Dad had got themselves into considerable debt and would have to repeat the seven-day shifts for weeks to come just to keep their heads above water. My Dad's rationale was that it was important for Nicola to have had a special day and that it was all worth it to see her so happy.

So, when the telephone rang a fortnight later heralding the news that the marriage was over, the roof almost blew off with the rage spewing from Mum. She was livid, storming around the kitchen banging pans and smashing plates. She ranted about how useless Nicola was and then turned her anger on the rest of us. We were all useless apparently and she wailed about how she shouldn't be surprised, as this was what her life had always been like. I hid on the stairs, hugging my knees, sitting on the top step; there was no way I wanted to be within striking distance on this night.

Following the rage, the depression, and it lasted for months. She barely spoke a word and shuffled between work and the kitchen as if in a daze. She upped her intake of pills but her face never moved from a fixed expression of blank pain. Although never receiving the affection I craved from her, I never stopped loving her, an almost impossible thing for any child to do. Her mood infected the whole house; it was as if even the furniture was depressed. It was agony to see her in such a state. All my efforts at making conversation were ignored or greeted with unenthusiastic nods and grunts. Helping round the house didn't make any difference and dinner times became silent affairs apart from synchronised eating noises.

The only time she spoke was to moan about how skint we were and we were all reminded constantly. After a month of this as a constant I couldn't stand it any longer and knew it was down to me to save the situation. It seemed to me that the only thing that would make her happy was money so I set my little mind to finding a way to get it and in larger amounts than farm work would provide. From this thought my first big plan formed in my head and from that, 'The Musketeers' were born.

3
Big wide world

Although my family had a sense of honour, that sense of honour was twisted and in my family stealing was dealt with using blind ignorance as long as no one was hurt. Things would quite often appear in the house that had been liberated from an undeserving source and given over to those in real need. It didn't take me long therefore, in my quest for money, to decide on crime as an obvious solution.

I called a meeting of the gang and the three of us sat in an old, unused barn on the outskirts of the farm as I presented the problem to them. I didn't want my cousin involved, as he might be a weak link and let something slip to the family. We immediately discounted any house or local shop, as robbing from people who didn't deserve it was a definite no-no. An hour of brainwork and a few drained wine bottles later, the obvious target sprung at me from my drunken mind, the school.

The boys loved the idea as we all hated school with equal disgust. Our plan was to rob the safe of the lunch money. Our rudimentary maths just stretched to working out that if there were eighteen hundred kids at school and at least half of them had a school lunch at a pound a go, that meant serious booty. We named ourselves 'The Musketeers' and excitedly began to make a plan.

There were only four classes at school that Joe, John and myself enjoyed, P.E, metalwork, woodwork and art. Although woodwork played no part, the others came in very handy. The metalwork teacher, Mr Ross, wore inch thick glasses, had one lung and not much control over the class. After setting tasks at the start of each lesson he would return to the front of the class to read the Daily Mirror, answering questions with brief unexplained rasps.

This was perfect, as within a fortnight we had fashioned a highly accurate grappling hook. We were very proud of our work and combined with a stolen pair of bolt croppers, glasscutters from the art room and ropes from P.E, we were all tooled-up and ready for Operation Sherbet Mountain, named by Joe after watching an advert on T V one night. The base of operations was an unused barn on Joe's parent's land that we had checked out two nights before our daring plan.

The school was about five miles from the barn and we knew every path like the back of our hands. Five miles was nothing to us and a gentle jog would see us there within an hour or so, with me and John on foot and Joe on his chopper we decided to meet at the Sherbet Mountain. Once there we planned to throw the rope and hook onto the main building roof, climb up, break in through the glass windows in the ceiling and descend to the central office where we'd already established, lay our reward, the safe.

Under the pretence of illness, as the sickroom was in the same place, Joe had already scoped out the safe. There was a smaller key-safe next to the big safe and it was easily broken in to. We knew that the money was put in at the start of each week and decided by Wednesday it would be full so our plan was to go in on Thursday night.

The day of the raid came and the three of us walked round school with smug grins and must have winked at each other a hundred times. We were discrete but the knowledge that we were going to rob the school and no one had a clue was almost impossible to contain We were like special agents and when we spoke about the impending robbery we used our code words like Sherbet Mountain and H Q. We are blood brothers and I reminded them of that as Joe looked like he was about to bottle out. We had used the usual staying at each other's houses excuse and met at the barn at seven sharp. We had camouflage cream, stolen from the local army surplus store, the grappling hook, ropes and cutters, three balaclavas, three torches and black rucksacks for the loot. It felt like a real mission and taking it very seriously, we synchronised our watches, including Joe's Action Man special and put our hands on each other's. In serious tones, our voices as low as they could go, we said 'One for all and all for one', then packed and set off. I don't know about the others but I certainly wasn't scared, I just felt very excited and couldn't wait to get there.

We had previously agreed on a 'speak only when necessary' policy, so jogged in silence using a half-moon and flashes of light from the torches as our guide, Joe of course insisted on using his chopper so he was lookout up in front, I loved every second of the run, imagining I was in the SAS. We arrived at the school five minutes ahead of schedule and gained access to the school grounds by cutting the huge padlock attached to the dimly lit side gate. Then quietly opened the ten-foot-tall galvanised steel gates and crept silently past the floodlights towards the main building where our prize awaited us. Once there, I swung the grappling hook in a wide circle above my head and launched it upwards. It landed on the felt roof near an air vent cover and as I pulled gently on the rope it snagged the vent and got lodged firmly, it was a great shot and the rope felt totally secure. We climbed up the rope and were soon all in place on top of the building.

Once we were on the roof, we found the skylight and got the glasscutters ready. We planned to cut a nice clean hole, through which we could get down. However, we weren't exactly trained, this being our first robbery, and we smashed the glass. The whole lot went and landed with a loud 'smash' as it splintered into a thousand little pieces. We all held our breath and sat there, frozen, waiting for a reaction to the noise. After an agreed safe period, we decided no one had heard us, so we continued.

We dropped through the broken skylight and faced our next task. We had to break into the secretary's office. By now, our air of professionalism was starting to wear a bit thin and after trying to pick the lock for half an hour we gave up and brawn taking over from brains, broke the glass in the door. So there we were, with the safe in front of us and all we needed was the safe-key from the smaller key-cupboard. The loot was ours, or so we thought. The key cupboard was in no mood to go quietly and we spent nearly an hour whacking and banging it trying to prise it open. Eventually it opened and we stood there flabbergasted; "Its fucking empty" I exclaimed. The secretary must have taken the keys home with her each night.

After this bitter blow we were a bit stuck and weren't sure what to do. However we weren't beaten. After a heated discussion a decision was made to take the locked safe back with us to the barn and work on it there. We managed to slide it into position under the skylight and tied a rope round it. Lifting it however was another matter. The bloody thing must have weighed half a ton. Myself John and Joe were on the roof puffing from strained effort, John and Joe accepted they were staring into the face of defeat, dejected they reluctantly gave up on the safe, but I wasn't ready to give up " Get out of the bloody way" I said to John and Joe, my voice straining under the weight of the safe hanging on the rope that my grip was struggling to hold on to, it felt like my shoulders were coming out of their sockets and sweat was dripping off of my nose as I stood hunched over the sky light struggling , pulling, heaving at the safe that had beaten John and Joe put together, every time I pulled the safe another inch nearer the sky light it felt like my bones were going to snap, I refused to give up, John and Joe looking at me like I was mad, which to be fair, to a certain degree, I was, The safe was at the sky light but as much as my effort and madness pulled at the rope that was now drawing blood from my hands I couldn't get it through as the sky light was too small, a slight mistake on our part, we should have made sure that the bloody thing would actually go through the sky light in the first place. It was no good I had to let go of the rope . The safe fell and went crashing down onto and through the secretary's desk, wood, paper, phones and pens flew into the air with a cloud of dust, a deafening noise vibrated throughout the school. The safe heist was over. However, having come this far we knew we had to do something. So we decided to rob every teacher's desk we could get into and after an hour's hard raiding, we had amassed the princely sum of nine quid and forty fags. By now we were tired, disgruntled and thirsty, so we looked in the fridge for something to drink; even that was barren.

Needless to say, that was one of our less fruitful missions. However it had given us what we needed, a real taste for liberating goods from the capitalist pigs, as our justification allowed us to believe. We knew that with better planning and foresight we could pull something off and before long were presented with the perfect opportunity. Looking back I can see that at that stage in my life at around twelve or thirteen there wasn't much in the world that I was scared of, I wasn't even scared of death, in fact I welcomed the thought of death like an old friend, what frightened me was at home indoors.

It was early December and the whole school was full of Christmas spirit, the holidays were virtually upon us and the teachers had their annual Christmas party planned. It was going to be held in the canteen and through innocent discussions with our teachers we established it to be a big deal. The tables had been arranged to create a dance floor and a stage had been built, with a makeshift bar adjacent. That was what we were interested in, because I had my eyes set on the alcohol.

The three musketeers met in the usual place, Joe's barn, about an hour before the robbery. We went over all the details with a fine- toothcomb. This time the venture was going to be a success. We knew we needed to be mobile and seeing as we never used the roads, a car would be no good, which was a shame as we had one. We decided that we needed a dirt bike and a quick one. We knew where one was to be had so we went and hot-wired it, placing it in a thicket behind the school the previous evening, ready for our getaway. We justified our stealing of cars and motorbikes by saying to each other that every one had insurance.

We arrived at the school at two- thirty in the morning and got into it in the usual way. We broke into the canteen via the roof after some dextrous moves with the grappling hook. After climbing down the rope we were confronted with a King Solomon's mine of booze. There was everything a good bar should have: gin, vodka, brandy, lager, wine and so on. It took us twelve trips to get it all out and back to the bike. It was like winning the lottery and the thrill fizzed through my bloodstream, as sure as some of the booze would later. John and Joe wanted to pull out and call it a day after a couple of trips but I couldn't stop. I wasn't finished until we had lifted every drop of booze from the place. With panniers and rucksacks bulging, we made trip after trip until all the booze was back in the barn, home and dry, so to speak.

John was scared to take any of the booze home and I don't blame him, as his Mum, a devout Christian would have hit the roof if she had any inkling as to where it all came from, so me and Joe split the rest.

The shed that was built onto my parent's kitchen looked more like the stockroom of a pub, bottles of differing spirits, about thirty bottles of wine and a couple of hundred cans. My Mum and Dad couldn't believe their eyes when they saw it. When they asked me where it had all come from, I used the expression they did when stuff suddenly appeared and said, 'It fell off the back of a lorry', and feeling very grown-up, winked at my Dad. There was no fuss made, as with the family in dire straights, any unpaid for extras were warmly received and I actually got a pat on the back for it. Receiving loads of attention, I lapped it up like a starving dog. For a short while I felt like the person I wanted to be, respected and revered. It was doubly sweet, as my sisters were really jealous of all the attention.

High from our success the gang spent more time together coming up with grand plans, although very few ever came to fruition, but that never mattered to us as. Joe had an older brother who we felt was pretty crazy. He taught us how to make homemade gunpowder. We were fascinated by it. Now the musketeers had some real firepower. The three of us were very ingenious and we soon developed a single shot pistol that worked on the same principle as a flintlock. The barrel was fixed to the handle with insulation tape and the ammo was a four-inch nail. It was lethal. We also made a hand-held rocket launcher and homemade grenades. They were pretty powerful and could easily have taken someone's hand off if used incorrectly. We were seriously playing with fire and every day we were covered in small burns or cuts and bruises. We weren't bothered; to us it was a natural part of being the dangerous gang we were and wore our scars like battle medals. Life at home dragged on in the same depressing way, I was getting hit less as I wasn't there much, the gang had become my family and me theirs.

Convinced we were a private army of mercenaries, we built an underground shelter that was furnished with a month's supply of food and water and enough gunpowder to rival Guy Fawkes. We felt really let down when the nuclear war that everyone was talking about never happened and even worse when Argentina didn't invade; we were ready for anything. Forever adding to this madness was the constant cocktail of booze and exercise. When we were pissed we'd sometimes shoot apples or tins off each other's heads with makeshift crossbows, and when we weren't pissed we continued training for our imaginary Olympics.

It wasn't natural for fourteen-year-olds to be exercising the way we were. Mind you it wasn't natural for fourteen-year-olds to be doing much of what we were getting up to. I had started schoolboy boxing and continued my judo and combined with my weight training was turning into a scrapper to be reckoned with. I could bench-press two hundred and fifty pounds and run a marathon. I was fit and strong and I knew it. I really lived up to the reputation it gave me, happy to fight anyone who said the wrong thing. For the first time in my life I felt powerful and strong. The main thing it gave me was confidence, but it was a false confidence betraying my real fragile state underneath. I was still vomiting after eating and now I wasn't at home much I had started my own binge eating without mum to force the food into me, in fact the only time I really concentrated on not vomiting was when I was on the booze, after all booze is a valuable commodity and I wasn't going to waste it.

Inside, I was laying down problems that would become the foundation for my destructive life for years to come but I had no idea of the difficulties that lay ahead and indulged in all the wrong things with reckless abandon. I kept all this hidden, I now know how well I hid it, as my eldest sister would comment on how lovely I was when I was younger and how well behaved I was. In general, people thought I was a nice and pleasant young man. Little did they know that away from my personable exterior, I was a closet anarchist, burglar and drunk?

Although life outside the house had improved dramatically and the gang gave me a feeling of belonging, inside the rot continued. Mum didn't miraculously improve with the addition of a shed of booze and our schemes dried up with regards to the riches I set out to acquire, mainly because I was having too much fun with the gang and forgot about 'saving' the family. I spent less and less time at home and frequently slept in our camp if the weather was good enough.

I spent as much time with the gang as I could and my drinking was increasing slowly but surely, as the drinking increased so did the crime. We never did mindless crime like vandalise anything, what we did we felt had a good reason and that was either booze or money. Motorbikes had always been a strong focus and by fifteen we all had our own but what we all lacked was the paraphernalia that went with it like decent boots, leathers and so on. We decided that as we didn't have enough money, we'd have to rob a motorcycle shop. We were getting used to robbing and it was becoming second nature to us. I guess as we'd never been caught and didn't know any better it was the natural way for us to get things. We targeted a showroom that was just a few miles from where we lived. We went and checked it out and although there were no cameras there were alarms on the windows and doors. We knew that the only way in was through the roof. As luck would have it, the night that we chose to go in, there was an almighty thunderstorm.

It was the usual technique and we were soon up on the roof. After moving a couple of flimsy asbestos sheets, Joe smashed through the ceiling with his Dr Martin' size elevens. Lowering ourselves down, we soon found all the things surrounded us on our list. We quickly started filling the army surplus rucksacks we'd brought, as we had to work fast. Joe couldn't find the switch to turn off the lights the shop used to illuminate the front display so, me and my cousin, who by now was confirmed as a solid member of the gang, were lit-up and on show, if anyone had walked past. We ended up filling as many bags as we could carry and were soon away into the night. I guess our booty totalled a couple of grand's worth of stuff, plenty for ourselves and some left over which was sold on.

Any pangs of guilt that we felt were quickly squashed by a conversation about insurance. As far as we were concerned it wasn't as if we were breaking into someone's house and stealing personal stuff, in fact we had *some* ethics and thought that type of stealing was deplorable. We thought we were much better than that and despised the people who nicked stuff that way. Of course, we were wrong but were comforted by lying to ourselves, a trait I became such an expert in, in so many ways. I lost sight of any semblance of truth, internally or externally.

We had become a pretty reckless band of brothers, nicking from school, warehouses and joyriding bikes around the countryside. We became a law unto ourselves and revelled in it. We were questioned at school, along with everyone else and told that the police would be watching but we weren't bothered, we felt safe. The bond between us unbreakable and there was never any question of betrayal. There was no way any of us would grass the others up; we relied on each other totally. It was a great feeling. The only other thing that made me feel as good as this was booze.

Joe and I were like Siamese twins and we did everything together. I even went on a family holiday with them once and it was great. We joined the air-training core together but that was for one simple reason, we wanted to fire live ammunition from a real gun. The rifles we got to use were Martini 303's and we got as much target practice as we were allowed. For Joe and me every day was an adventure of some sort.

He and his family became substitutes for my own and being with them in their relaxed, laughing and loving home only served to make me hate mine even more. Sitting at dinner in my house I would wish I were a few miles down the road, joking with Joe's Mum and being praised for stories of success from school, usually connected to sport of some kind. If I tried speaking at dinner in own home, I was over-talked as one of my sisters launched into their usual one-upmanship and regaled some tale that put mine to shame. Whatever I did was never enough but I swore to myself repeatedly, that one day I'd show them all and then they'd have to listen to me.

Although Joe and I were thieves, we had a bizarre sense of right and wrong and using a twisted logic we tried to balance all our wrong doings with good deeds. In our minds it was a fair compensation, as far as we were concerned and as long as we were balancing the morality scales, on our terms, we were all right.

Part of the balance came through our work with the pensioners from the bit of town surrounding the school. It was the school that came up with the idea of letting some of the kids get involved with the local community. The idea was we'd go out into the community and do odd jobs or a bit of shopping for the elderly who had trouble getting around. The old boys and dears loved us to bits and we thoroughly enjoyed it too, sitting for hours talking with them and listening to all their stories. There was one particular old couple that I couldn't wait to see each week. They made their own wine and sherry and weren't averse to getting it out to offer me a little tipple. When they had a drink so would I, they were just being hospitable. I didn't just go round there to drink though, I did all they're gardening and shopping too. The drinking and gassing were just great bonuses.

One old boy was fascinating. He would have me mesmerised for hours with his tales about the war and how he became a professional footballer. He had lost both his legs in a car crash when he was fifty but that didn't stop him from still being full of life. I lost count of the afternoons we spent together talking and playing nine-card brag. He would always let me have a couple of bottles of Guinness as well, which to me was the cherry on the cake.

It must have been around this time that youngest sister golden child and nasty piece of work middle sister left home. I was relieved they had gone but was then left alone to deal with the burden of the ever increasing pressure and depression at home .I often though that the blokes that married my sisters must have been mugs and that my sisters were out of order deceiving them into marrying them like that, but then again they were doing what they had to do to get out the same way I was doing what I had to do.

About this time, at about fourteen, I started work in a fish and chip shop. That may be surprising but one of the main things that had been drummed into me from a young age me was the importance of work. I took the same attitude to work as I did to most other things; I ripped the arse out of it. Like many addicts, whatever happens to be your point of focus, you go at it one hundred percent. The money I was getting at the chip shop was crap but the benefits were huge. I would start work at five in the morning and prepare the fish, defrost the chickens and fill up six dustbins full of chips ready for the day ahead.

All this took me a couple of hours and around seven am, I'd take advantage of the benefits. I'd fill my rucksack with pies, sausages, chips and lots of fish, basically whatever I could nick. Then I'd be off on my rounds visiting all the pensioners I knew, dropping little presents on their doorsteps; a nice bit of cod here, a couple of sausages there. One old girl used to say to me, 'Cor blimey Father Christmas was 'ere again this morning', and give me a cheeky wink. I knew she knew but nothing was ever said.

After starting work at five and working hard for two hours I was knackered and was often half asleep on my feet at school. Sometimes I'd go back to the Chippy after school and work the evening shift. About six months passed before I got the inevitable sack. He told me the profits had gone downhill since I'd started, he didn't accuse me outright of stealing but it was pretty much what he was saying. He couldn't prove anything, as I was the only one working during the morning shift. At the time I didn't understand the position of trust I was abusing, as I didn't really understand trust as a basic concept. Except when it came to trusting the gang and my booze.

In the last year of school I became seriously involved with a girl, who was in the year below. It was my first taste of love, although it was probably a mixture of jagged hormone fuelled emotions wrapped in a superficial cover that people call love when they don't know any better. She was called Stella and I think she felt the same way. She was about a foot shorter than me, had blonde curly hair to her shoulders, grey blue eyes and a pretty freckled face. She was quiet and reminded me of my eldest sister which freaked me out because the thought of my sister being my first sexual experience would make me feel ashamed of who and what I was. That in turn made my first healthy relationship with a female feel dirty and sick. All of this made me feel more worthless and easily manipulated by her, I thought that if I didn't do what she wanted to the letter she might leave me and the thought of rejection from another female was too painful to comprehend.

We went through all the motions of slushy, mushy, teenage romance and as Joe was going out with Stella's best mate, we went everywhere together, the musketeers and their maidens. She laughed at my jokes, held my hand when we walked and made me feel important. Although I really enjoyed being with her and didn't want to lose her I felt awkward around her so I would go fitness training, or blowing things up with Joe. We didn't talk much and she never asked me how I felt about anything. As that was nothing new it suited me fine.

The relationships were good for us though and curbed our thieving antics. I cut right back on my drinking as she didn't approve, although all I was doing was swapping one addiction for another and nicking and drinking became necking, for a while anyway.

Stella was my first proper girlfriend but not the first person I slept with, that pleasure belonged to three- fingered Ros. She was so-called not because you could fit three fingers inside her but because an ex-boyfriend in a fit of jealous rage had cut off two of her right hand fingers with a bread knife. Although the punishment was a bit too severe for the crime, she wasn't exactly an innocent. Ros single-handedly fulfilled the role of a local brothel and was more than happy to take the cherries from the local boys as soon as they felt ready. A significant percentage of the boys in our area had used Ros as part of their rites of passage into manhood. It was something you looked forward to as a guarantee of your growing maturity, like your first drink or voice breaking. Although I'd managed the drinking way ahead of schedule my time with Ros came at a normal age, I was fourteen.

Joe had already had his go and kept urging me to make the hallowed trip to her caravan to join the ranks of 'men' Ros had liberated from boyhood. My mother's brain washing about sex being disgusting and me being a vile pathetic specimen had left its scars but with Joe's continuous talking about it, I became jealous and one Friday night decided my time had come. Arrangements were made and the following night I made my way to the gypsy site on the outskirts of town.

Ros was thirty-nine, had never been to a dentist and saw exercise as a threat to her health. She had rolls of fat under drooping breasts and a bush that needed a touch of explorer to conquer, however, she was willing and able and overly welcome.

I should have felt full of confidence as I walked through the site, considering the amount of 'Dutch courage' I'd consumed during the hours before but I flinched at every shout and dog bark. Smoothing down my hair and taking a deep breath I rapped on the white rusty door and stood still, scared and nervous about what was going to happen next.

The door opened and a haze of cannabis smoke spewed out and swirled into the sky. Ros grinned through the few remaining teeth she had left and beckoned me inside. She wore a once-white apron style dress that had two buttons on the front that once undone released her breasts. 'So, handsome, what's your name then', she said, in what I presume was an attempt at a seductive drawl. Stammering I got out my name and sat beside her. In a well-practised movement she took my hands and made me undo her buttons. The dress fell forwards and her breasts fell into my nervously grabbing hands as I looked down I realised the pictures I'd seen in magazines, were an unrepresentative advertisement for the real thing. If this was the real thing then those magazines were definitely false advertising.

As Ros hitched up her skirts and slowly opened her legs, I felt myself ready to explode with anticipation. She lay back on the pullout sofa bed and simply smiled at me. I whipped off my lower clothes as fast as I could and climbed aboard. With a half bottle of whisky sloshing round my system and the clumsiness of unpractised youth, it was hardly a 'Hallmark' moment and I was pumping away well before she expertly slid me in with her three fingered hand. It was over briefly and that was that. I could hold my head up high in sexual conversations, greatly exaggerating what had been an unusual experience into a highly competent sexual achievement, as far as my mates were concerned, I was a sex god.

4
Pipe dreams

My life at school was drawing to a close and exams were looming on the horizon. I had no intention of taking any even though I was in 'O' level classes and my teachers were talking to me about Art College. My art teacher was insistent that I stay on but I hated school and I hated most of the teachers. As far as I was concerned, school was a prison, preventing my moneymaking genius to fully flow. I wanted to get as far away from the place as fast as I could. It's a decision I look back on with regret, knowing that it was a real turning point in my life. But seeing as mum and dad were encouraging me to leave and go out to work full time the decision was kind of made for me, thanks to my parents.

I left school with one attitude over-riding all others, to make money and lots of it. To start with I did what I knew; I went to work on the farm where I'd worked before, screw pegging. I was fifteen and roaring around on a motorbike with no license. Working meant money in my pocket and freedom to indulge in whatever I fancied; I felt like the king of the hill, well occasionally anyway.

With the advent of young adulthood, my problems became harder to handle and my anger, frustration and low self-image and worth all worsened, resulting in frequent moments of fury. At other times a catastrophic feeling of doom hung over me and I felt suicidal. Whenever either of these feelings became too much to handle I turned to the booze to take the pain away, which was becoming second nature to do so. The planning was as important as the piss-up and I'd spend hours thinking about it and looking forward to it. It was the only thing that would keep me going. I know now how counter productive it is taking lots of liquid depressant when you feel depressed, but back then alcoholic oblivion was the only place I felt safe.

My delusional self-lying desperately tried to keep me convinced I was happy but I actually hated working on the farm and wasn't that bothered about Stella when I was feeling really low. The other feeling I had been experiencing for as long as I can remember was being desperate to leave home. Nasty piece of work middle sister would come back home out of a twisted sense of misplaced loyalty sometimes and when I was around she used me to let out her own trapped emotions by verbally attacking me with great spite and vile belittling. She got great pleasure from seeing me squirm and I rarely came back at her as I was so used to being bullied. I would hold on to all the anger she created within me keeping it in a tight knot in my stomach and then go out and get drunk, I didn't know any better and on the flimsiest of excuses I would go out and start a fight pummelling someone or being pummelled till I felt the knot in my guts unravelling. I had found it easy to be a violent thug towards males but they were always of the same ilk as me.

My Dad was never at home and still worked every hour he could. My Mum had never recovered from her depressive days and stayed in a permanent grump. I knew I had to escape and started to save money, although with a drinking habit to keep up and a girlfriend to take out, my savings were forever being raided. Away from the house I felt like an adult with my job and steady girlfriend, but inside despite my size and age I still felt like a four or five-year-old who had only just been abused and the anger simmered away constantly. I was always open to new escape routes so when I became friendly with the hippies on the farm and was introduced to cannabis, I welcomed it with open lungs.

I was apprehensive about the hippies at first as once again they fell outside my acceptance parameters but after a few cider and pasty lunches I got to know two of them well and one afternoon they made the necessary introduction and I befriended cannabis. Lunchtimes would involve the motley working group breaking off into various huddles, each one with a different identity. Having no handle on my own identity, I morphed into whichever one was closest or had booze with them, I would settle in for an hour of bullshit or silence, drinking and sandwiches.

It was the cider and pasties that attracted me to the hippies first, a change from the beer, bread and cheese I was used to with the local farm regulars. The cider was made with real apples and I knew it would be very strong. At lunchtime the hippies asked me to join them on a walk to *their* spot and having spotted the cider and made friends with one of them during the morning, I was eager to join. I hadn't quite reached the stage of regular morning drinking yet so the prospect of an alcohol-laced afternoon was an opportunity not to be missed.

After eating lunch, the usual tobacco came out, but the hippies had large handmade leather pouches, containing all the necessary elements for perfect joints. As Moony, or Clive as that was his real name, rolled the first joint I became enthralled. I'd heard talk of weed and seen its effects at school but as I never hung out with the smoking gang I had never tried it. This truth I kept hidden from the hippies as the joint came round my way. I wasn't quite sure what to do and watched Clive closely. It appeared to me that all you did was smoke it like a cigarette but take larger inhalations and hold on to the smoke in your lungs for a much longer time.

My insecurities constantly with me and now, being on new ground, I wanted to show my mettle, so when the joint was passed to me, I inhaled till I could go no more. An inch of paper, tobacco and weed consumed, I held on to my breath till I was ready to pass out. The smoke erupted from my mouth in a long plume, immediately followed by such a violent coughing fit that even the hippies looked nervous. When I finally stopped, smiled then giggled it had a ripple effect that bubbled through the small group till we were all rolling around with laughter.

I couldn't wait for the next joint to be lit and focused on nothing else; watching it being passed round hoping not much was smoked before it reached me. On my second attempt I was much less gung-ho but still managed to smoke half of it before the guy waiting for his turn had a word about 'hogging the tube'. I passed it to him, embarrassed but content that I'd got a good amount I lay back revelling in the effects.

It was a different experience to drinking and one I wasn't expecting. I found everything around me funny and giggled relentlessly. Things looked different and my mind wandered through a maze of questions that normally would never have occurred to me each one more ridiculous than the last and adding to my increasing hilarity. Things I touched felt more intense and all other sensory stimuli had the same effect. It was like things were normal but in a softer, less threatening and funnier way.

By the time I lolled behind the hippies on the way back to work, puffing on the end of the last joint till I inhaled paper smoke from the burning roach, I was well and truly stoned. My whole body and mind were relaxed, floating in a new world, where worries and insecurities melted away as I wafted through the next few hours mechanically and automatically doing my work but always thinking in new and funny ways. I sort of retreated into my own head and played with my thoughts as they entertained me whilst my body just went through the actions it was so used to it could achieve this without conscious interaction. My consciousness was elsewhere, musing on why hops existed in the first place and where they went afterwards, how the colours were brighter and why they smelled lovely.

Slowly the effects decreased until I came back to reality with a bump. I had been temporarily removed from my crap job, loveless relationship, depressing and abusive family and all the other shit elements that made up my life, and now without the cannabis fog, I had to face them again and the misery returned, heightened by my mental mini-holiday. These feelings swamped me during the remaining two hours of work and I longed for a return to the giggling, pain-free thought playground that I'd just been frolicking in.

At the end of the day I sidled up to one of the hippies who had a pouch and asked if I could get some gear off him. He smiled knowingly and gave me a few joints worth. I cradled the gear in my hands and wrapping it in a few papers placed it gently in my wallet. It was all I could think about on the way home and the time spent eating and waiting was passed tortuously.

When everyone was in bed I took out my wallet and undid the little parcel. I was used to rolling my own cigarettes so simply added the weed to the tobacco and rolled a little cardboard tube to go in the end. I had no idea how much you put in so divided the weed in half and made two joints. I then went to my bed and opening the window next to it lit up and leaned out a bit. The joint softly placed between my lips I brought the lighter flame closer, I was more excited than I'd been in a long time and as the joint lit, I breathed in the aromatic smoke till my lungs were filled to bursting.

I held on for a count of thirty and then slowly exhaled, coughing a bit but proud that I hadn't repeated my first fit. I smoked the rest of the joint in the same way and within a few minutes my body turned to jelly and I slumped onto my bed lost in my own happy little world again. Still dressed I pulled the covers round me as my imagination reeled off lovely dreamlike thoughts, extinguishing the present and creating fanciful futures where happiness existed and life was good. As with all addicts, I wanted more and after half an hour of bliss I smoked the second joint trying to hold the smoke for even longer. I lay back in smiling relaxation. Nothing mattered any more and everything was going to be all right.

The next morning I still felt pretty good and now I had found a new and exciting way to escape I walked to work with a spring in my step. I found the hippie that had given me the weed and asked if I could buy some from him. I gave him fifteen quid and that afternoon received a full bag the size of two cigarette packets. With the weed in my pocket I relaxed that afternoon. I had a new friend who would help me walk through life, a source of escape I could return to whenever I needed, another helping hand to ensure I never had to face the truth of my life or who I was. Along with the ever-constant booze, my escapist arsenal was growing strength and with it I strode out purposefully on a life path that took me quickly towards my own demise, but that was a long way from happening yet.

Whilst working on the farm I harboured thoughts about finding my true purpose, as I new there was more to life than farm work. I'm not sure who I thought I was but the monotony of boring work and the addition of lunchtime smoking meant the afternoons became mental playgrounds, when my body would act out its job, as if on automatic pilot and internally I lived in my dreamscape.

To break up the monotony of the week I would sometimes visit my grandparents on my mother's side as they only lived a couple of miles from the farm. My Granddad had been in and out of hospital for years waging his personal cancer war. He had four operations in all and each time they'd cut a bit more of his lungs away until he ended up with only a quarter of one lung left. Because of this he always had an oxygen bottle by his side. I'd be greeted with the same scene every time I arrived. My Nan would be reading the paper or watching the telly and my Granddad would be sitting at the table coughing, his bottles of Guinness set out in front of him and his tobacco ready to be rolled.

With her raspy voice, which sounded like her throat was made of sandpaper, Nan would offer me a cup of tea, which I always accepted, even though the sterilised milk in it made me feel sick. Sam, the dog, would peer out from under the settee and would always be greeted by Granddad's loving words, 'Get back under there you fucking bastard', as he swiped at him with his walking stick. I don't really think that Nan and Granddad were animal lovers.

One time still shines clearly in my mind. I was round for lunch as usual and Granddad was all suited and booted with a red tie on and a pork-pie hat perched on his head. He always wore that hat whenever he went out. Nan gave me my cup of tea and I asked my Granddad if he was going out, just to make conversation. He didn't turn away from looking out of the window and told me that his mate Jim was turning up, to take him to the Walnut Tree, a local pub. He kept straining his neck to look up and down the road with his oxygen mask planted firmly on his face as he took great gulps of oxygen. Nan sat and watched him with a face like thunder, she said, 'I hope your fucking oxygen runs out, you bastard!' Naturally he ignored her.

I don't blame her for talking to him like that, considering the way that she was treated. I'd been round on countless occasions when Nan would have a black eye or a split lip. You might be wondering why nothing was ever done to stop it, but it was impossible to interfere. The question of 'Why?' has to be answered with another question, 'What could we do?' Nan had been with him for the best part of her life and had made her choices, including staying with him. She had become a victim a long time ago and had played the role for so long, she didn't know any different and no one was going to change her mind. In a twisted way everybody had accepted it like she had and I went along with everyone else as that was all I knew.

It must have been a couple of months later that the cancer returned with a vengeance. As granddad had only a small bit of lung left, there was nothing that the surgeons could do, so the inevitable occurred, he died.

I couldn't really understand why everyone was so upset; he had been a complete bastard to almost everyone including my Nan, especially her. As I've mentioned, she lost seven potential babies through his beatings whilst she was heavily pregnant. I felt nothing, as I'd spent so long developing a system of burying anything close to emotions, that my reaction to everything was numbed. It had been such a long time since I'd allowed myself to feel any pain, when I should have felt it, I couldn't. All I felt was confused and guilty for not having any feelings of sadness when everyone else around me was crying. Naturally, these feelings were buried deep in a place in my mind.

The wake was a far from solemn affair and the drink flowed freely. I took part in this wholeheartedly, after all I might not know how to cry but I certainly knew how to drink and what better justification than the wake of my grandfather. After drinking three quarters of a bottle of scotch with my cousin, we were elected to walk my Uncle Eddie home. Eddie had been drinking heavily; he could have floated a battleship with what he'd consumed. He had also been a middleweight golden gloves boxing champion years before. He was good enough to be known for miles around as a hard man and that was an understatement; Eddie was as hard as nails. Luckily he wasn't in full fighting mode that night but did manage to take on a couple of cars, head on, in the middle of moving traffic. As we were there, nothing happened, apart from a bit of tyre screeching, some swearing and a great rugby tackle from Mark my cousin.

After the funeral, it was back to our home routine. I was still seeing Stella and she was around quite a bit. For some reason, my Mum couldn't stand Stella. Mum spoke snappily to her when she was round and was even nastier behind her back. One day she was having a particularly bitchy tirade and Suzi, who had sided with my Mum, joined in with glee. The two of them together made quite a bitch team and I was getting increasingly wound up. This treatment had been going on for quite a while and I had reached my limit.

I snapped and shoved Suzi up against the wall in the passageway. I held her against the wall with my arm across her throat and yelled in her face, 'Shut the fuck up, you useless stupid bitch!' My Dad ran in from the lounge and instantly threw a punch that landed right on my jaw. I fell to the floor in total shock but instinctively staggered back up, in all the confusion and the stupid bitch screaming her head off, dad managed to punch me several times in the face, each punch making me madder. The pain created a flash of anger and I drew my fist back ready to give my Dad the hiding of his life. Something inside snapped and although I was on the verge of giving him the hiding of his life I managed to control my actions. How, I don't know. I guess some misplaced honour wouldn't allow me to hit him with the venom I wanted to, after all, he was my Dad.

I was furious, angrier than I'd ever been in my life, years of frustration exploding inside and rushing to the fore. I screamed at the top of my voice, kicked a door off its hinges and stormed upstairs. I grabbed my army rucksack and threw it on the bed. I began ripping my draws out of the desk, flinging them against the wall and then picked up the scattered clothing, thrusting each item deep into the rucksack with white knuckled fists. When the rucksack was full I turned and still full of rage, kicked the doors off my wardrobe, smashed my fist into a mirror and then ran downstairs and out of the house in rage, mum and dad keeping well clear while this was going on.

There were some abandoned hopping huts a few miles away that I had used a thousand times before so it was no skin off my nose to bed down there for a while. I sped to the huts on my motorbike and once there slumped to the floor. Some time later, when the rage had left and I had a fire going, I stopped to think about what had happened. I was out, out of my family's life for good.

I was glad I'd done it and knew I wouldn't return until I was who I wanted to be. I rolled a joint and got a bottle of whisky from my rucksack. I sat in front of the fire getting drunk and stoned, mulling over all the crap that had gone on for years.

The following morning I woke with a thumping headache and a rumbling stomach. I reached out for the whisky and took a great slug, shivering in disgust, as it was only seven in the morning. Reality hit me hard, as I was cold and hungry. I relit the fire and warmed myself up. I felt like death warmed up and went to work. All day I thought about how I would cope now I was on my own, the solution was simple and I started spending most dinner times at Joe's house. His mum was more than happy to feed me and never questioned why I was there, although I think Joe must have told her the bottom line for me was that I was fifteen and free.

Joe's Mum made the best homemade pizza ever and she was very generous, I never went hungry. Along with my visits to Joe's I went to see Stella everyday as well. More often than not these visits were made to keep her happy and I'd always leave in time to pop into the local boozer for a skin full. Nightly pub drinking was becoming a daily habit and with my anger never far from reach, I had got a bit of a name for myself as a drinker and scrapper. I got into lots of fights. I think I went looking for them. They'd usually start at closing time outside the pub when I was full of booze. I won more than I lost and always enjoyed myself. Well when I say enjoyed myself what I mean is I felt like the feelings that the booze couldn't touch was released a little by the violence, so I guess it was a sense of satisfaction rather than enjoyment. Fighting for me seemed a natural release of frustration at a life I didn't want to be living and it didn't take much to get me started. When I was being hurt I felt like I was alive, when I was risking my life I felt like I was alive, other than that the rest of the time I was without booze and drugs I felt suicidal and the thought of death cheered me up.

At this time Joe was waiting to go to college, we were both sixteen or so by know. He wasn't sure what he was going to do but he was very bright and could have done anything. By the end of the summer, he had started to get a bit moody and sullen and spent lots of time in bed not wanting to do anything. He didn't want to go out riding the bikes or anything else that we had loved doing together for as long as I could remember. He had split up with Sarah, Stella's mate, and had been seeing an American chick. He'd been having lots of rows with her and so I put the moodiness down to the rows.

I had acquired a new motorbike from a guy in the pub that was selling it cheap and after work one day, picked it up and couldn't wait to get round to Joe's to show him and give him a go, as I knew he'd love it. I was full of excitement the whole ride over and on arrival ran up to Joe's room. He was standing by his window looking out across the fields with a hundred-yard stare fixed to his face. This had become one of his favourite pastimes and I thought a go on the new bike might shake him up a bit. This time his face was different and I knew that something was wrong. It took me ages to wheedle it out of him and when he told me the shine on my new bike faded instantly and I was struck dumb. Joe had a brain tumour.

He told me that it had been growing for a while and couldn't be operated on. It was pushing on a part of his brain that made it too dangerous to try and take out. He had been in agony for ages but hadn't told anyone. I felt really guilty for telling him he was a moody git and needed to snap out of it. I wanted to stay and spend as much time with him as I could but that was impossible as the one thing he needed was rest.

One day he came back from one of his appointments at the hospital full of hope. He was going to be put on a treatment that was said to be very successful. Joe had always been a skinny geezer and was only nine stones soaking wet, but that all changed with the treatment. He ballooned to seventeen stone, I hardly recognised him and he could barely walk. He got to the stage where he couldn't move very much and was in pain all the time. He would just sit in silence with his head in his hands. This was the guy who had run a local amateur marathon with me only eight months previously. I'll never forget that marathon; we had ended up getting pissed in a pub singing rugby songs.

Even though Joe was gravely ill, we did manage to go out for a short walk once. He had to stop every few paces and a hundred yards must have taken an hour or so to cover. He was in a lot of pain when we got back to the house but he had enjoyed it and said he would go out again when he felt a bit better. The next time Joe went out, it was to the hospice.

He knew that he wouldn't be coming out of their and so did I. His room in the hospice was permanently dark and eerily quiet, you could drop a pin and hear it clearly. The last time I visited him; his voice was so quiet I could hardly hear him speak. He just lay there, totally still. I'm sure he knew I was there and I hope that it brought him some comfort. I just sat in silence next to Joe's bed and looked at him, I wasn't allowed to speak as even the noise of speech was to painful for him to bear. He was dying before my eyes and there was nothing I could do. Why him? he wasn't a pathetic specimen, I was, it should be me shouldn't it? .The most important person I had ever had in my life was leaving me. Joe had never hurt a fly and I loved him like a brother, but he was dying, why, why, this is so unfair, "Please don't die Joe " I said in my mind, he was the person that had stopped me from topping myself for the last few years, I knew that what I was wishing in my mind was as useless as I thought I was myself. I cuddled Joe a loving cuddle and left as quietly as I could.

I had started the process of buying a flat, with Stella, in a town called High Brooms and in the evening of the day that I last saw Joe his Mum phoned. We had returned to Stella's house, I picked up the receiver. She was crying and through the tears told me that Joe had died. I took the news as if I'd been told that next door's cat had been run over. I was totally devoid of any emotion and my instinct was to instantly shut down inside. Once again I had feelings of terrible guilt because I couldn't feel sadness, I tried to cry but couldn't and turned to the only solace I understood, the only thing that had never let me down, my faithful booze. That night I sat in the hut on my own, hardening my resolve not to show any fear or pain, firstly to myself and more importantly to others. I drank and smoked till I passed out and when I woke, started again.

I tried to keep my drinking away from Stella as much as possible but it was inevitable that she would see me pissed out of my head sooner or later. The day of the funeral I put on my best suit, my only suit, sat in the hut slowly drinking a bottle of whisky and then went to the church. That's the only bit I remember, the rest of the day disappeared in a blurry alcoholic fog.

The service passed me by except for one bit. I remember the vicar saying that the Lord moved in mysterious ways, to which I loudly exclaimed, 'What a load of bollocks'. I wish I had managed to bite my lip, but the booze had sapped my self-control. As soon as the service was over I walked silently out of the church; my eyes fixed on the floor and went in search of the nearest pub to start drinking. I didn't stop for the next two days, only out of the pub for the hours it was shut.

I sat at the bar on my own, drinking and trying not to think. As soon as any thoughts about Joe or death entered my head I automatically ordered a double whisky and downed it. I had to carry on drinking till the thoughts stopped and I believed I had forgotten about Joe. If he was going to leave me, then 'fuck him'. Joe was the only person I think I really loved and he had gone and with him went my capacity to care about anyone or anything. I didn't know how to grieve and there was no one to comfort me, apart from that which was always there, so I did what I knew best and drank till I couldn't think or feel anything.

5
Russian Roulette

With Joe and my grief successfully buried, Stella and I
continued looking for our flat. Stella's parents thought it
was wrong for us to live together before we were married
so, out of respect to them and under constant pressure
from a pleading Stella, getting married became something
of paramount importance. Stella couldn't wait to get away
from her parents and there was this huge void inside me
that I had to fill and getting married seemed like an
opportunity I couldn't miss; maybe that would do it. I was
also rudderless in my life and getting married seemed like
the right thing to do as other people did it. I liked Stella
and we had an all right time together but I don't think I
ever truly loved her. The sex seemed more mechanical
than anything else and I got much more pleasure from
drinking, getting stoned and fighting than I did from being
with her but she really wanted to get married and I had no
major problems with it so it just happened.

Stella and her parents did most of the planning and within
three months I was walking down the isle of a little church,
making commitments in the eyes of God and swearing to
love her for ever. It just happened and it was just another
day for me. I wore a suit, was on my best behaviour and
played the role of loving husband. I was well practised in
playing roles when necessary and sailed through the day on
false charm and a bottle of Barcardi.

The reception was a teatotal affair as Stella's parents were
so religious. I kept making excuses to 'see people' and
nipped outside to find my bottle and take a few giant slugs.
Then I'd pop a mint in my mouth and return to the
'party'. In fact it was far from a party and consisted of
Stella's friends and family drinking tea and eating finger
food whilst they stood around gossiping and cooing over
the bride. The day passed in a blur for me and I don't
remember it in great detail.

My relationship with Stella had widened the huge rift
between my family and me and I hadn't hardly spoken two

words to them since I'd stormed out of the house when I was fifteen. They didn't come to the wedding which added to my anger against them and my resentment towards them gave me another justification to tend to my addictions as subconsciously, all addicts use their external anger and resentment to give reason for their poisonous intake and I was no different, why I should have been so bothered about my family not coming to the wedding. In hind sight I don't know, I guess in some way there must have been a distant corner of my mind harbouring the hope that my mum would be happy for me and we could be a normal family.

After the wedding, Stella and I moved in to our little flat and settled in to married life. Nothing really changed as far as I was concerned apart from finally having a solid roof over my head. I went through the daily motions of being a newly wed but Stella did most of the decision-making and I simply agreed with her. She made the house into a home and on the surface we were a normal married couple.

One afternoon, work on the farm came to an abrupt end. Whilst working on the apple-grading machine somehow my left hand became involved in the process and got severely crushed. Needless to say, with several breaks and dislocations I was waiting for the court date as I was suing the owner and recuperating at home encased in plaster and popping painkillers like they were smarties. I was taking strong painkillers as I was in agony and it wasn't long before I became hooked, especially mixing them with booze.

Stella wasn't impressed and would blow her top at me each evening when she returned from her job. I explained to her that I was in so much pain that the only way for it to become bearable was mixing the booze with the pills. Although I wasn't out of it all the time, there were a few occasions when I was and Stella never knew what state I'd be in when she came home. She found it very difficult to understand why I got so trashed, but then she had been brought up quite religiously and so didn't really drink, whereas I had been brought up on the flipside of the coin and drinking *was* my religion.

She nagged at me constantly and it had a pretty good effect as I laid off the booze a bit. Eventually the plaster came off and the combination of boredom and being skint meant I went looking for a new job. Although the nerves in my left hand were damaged and I was still in lots of pain it didn't stop me, as pain was something I never took seriously. I looked around and found a job in a local warehouse. It was a weird place, a storage facility for beef and butter. I was told we were building the biggest beef-mountain in Europe. That all went over my head, all I was concerned about was the money and what you could nick. They were both good so I started Monday.

The contract was a good length so I was set. It turned out to be the hardest work I've ever done, lifting huge sides of beef, weighing three to five hundred pounds each for nine hours a day. As you can imagine, there were very few long-term workers as people gave up on it pretty quickly. The mix of employees was weird to say the least. There were ex-cons, gypsies, drifters and lots of other unsavoury types. There was one bloke who was a survivalist nutcase. Because the work was so physically hard, loads of blokes came in the morning but didn't return after lunch. Those that came back for more were either as hard as nails or mad as fucking hatters. We all had one thing in common though, going on the piss.

It wasn't just the work that was extreme, the environment matched this. After the sides of beef had been unloaded from the trucks they were taken into a cold store to be frozen down. It was the coldest place I'd ever been, the beef had to be kept frozen at all times and so the whole place was freezing. Some times, if the weather was warm outside, the temperature would be set lower to compensate; it went as low as minus 60 degrees. As you breathed in, the moisture would freeze on the inside of your nose and the gas in our lighters would go solid. If you were lucky and were one of the first to arrive in the morning you'd get a thermal suit, otherwise you'd just have to make do. It wasn't the sort of place that took health and safety seriously.

Naturally, like all tough environments, there was a strong sense of camaraderie, especially amongst the regulars. There was the odd fight but we mostly got on very well. During the morning we'd work hard and after shifting a hundred tonnes of beef between us we'd escape to the pub for lunch. I normally went to the pub with a bloke who was obsessed with American cars. He had a massive eight-litre Camero. The other bloke that regularly joined us was the survivalist nutter; he was into guns.

One day, the survivalist bloke, whose nickname was Hunger seemed a bit het up. Without warning, he pulled a grenade out of the top pocket of his camouflage jacket and shouting, pulled the pin out with his teeth and lobbed it behind the bar. Half a dozen people, who didn't know him, jumped up screaming and ran for the door with wild eyes in a state of panic. The landlord calmly picked up the grenade and gave it back to Hunger with scowl and said, 'For fuck's sake, if you do this once more, you're barred for good!' Apparently he was well known for this little trick, one of his favourites. I thought it was hilarious and my stomach hurt from laughing so much. From that point, I took a real shine to Hunger. Sometimes the pub would get the better of us and we'd stay there most of the day, phoning in all sorts of excuses, like we'd been in an accident, or turn up late with engine oil smeared on our faces claiming we'd broken down.

When we got to work we went through the usual routine of nearly being fired but we knew the boss would never do it. It was impossible to get people to stay in the job at the best of times and we were 'stickers'. On one occasion, the madness of my addiction came to the fore in a shocking way. We had been to the pub as usual and were spending the afternoon in the yard office which was a garden shed tucked away in the corner out of sight of the main office. We were all quite drunk and as we drank more and took the piss out of Hunger. He produced a revolver from his inside pocket, we knew he had issues and the gun caused a fair amount of interest, he emptied the bullets out of their chambers and just replaced one, he then quickly put the barrel to his temple and pulled the trigger, the click was deafening and we gave a huge sigh of relief, he slid the gun across the table to me as if to say, I bet you wont do it. I picked up the revolver and spun the chambers "This is fucking stupid said one of the other blokes, don't do it". My heart was racing as I pushed the barrel of the gun to my temple. There was no way that I could let Hunger beat me. I pulled the trigger and the silence was broken by the loud click, I then did it again click the gun sounded."Don't do it any more "Hunger said. I had beaten him. That evening I reflected and knew that I had a few screws loose. The foreman of the cold stores hated us and I can't really blame him. When we were working, we just got on with our job and worked bloody hard but as soon as there was a lull in the lorries we were like a bunch of unruly school kids. Instead of firing us he did the next best thing and gave us all the crappy work in the cold store.

It was the most dangerous bit of the job, but that never bothered us. We just turned up and did what we had to. Sides of beef would be brought into the store and we'd have to tie a rope around one of the legs and pull the whole weight off the pallet from the forklift truck and get it onto the nearest stack. These could be as high as forty feet and there was always a gap between the pallet and the stack. You had to take the whole weight of the beef as you pulled it across. Standing on top of the stacks with thousands of sides of beef, frozen solid, with ribs and other bones sticking out, each one as sharp as a razor, you were given little room for error. There were no second chances. If you slipped, that'd be it. The higher we got, the more dangerous it became, with a broken limb or possibly being impaled one mistake away. As the stacks got higher, they took on a pyramid shape, which meant the higher you went, the bigger the gap between the pallet and where you needed to get the beef to.

As the gap increased, you had to pull harder and harder on the rope. The instinctive thing to do was to wrap the rope around your wrist so you'd get a better pull. However this was clearly the worst thing you could possibly do. If the beef didn't make it, it would crash down through the gap, on its way to the floor, forty feet below. If you didn't want to follow it, taking a trip through all the ribs and other bones, getting cut to ribbons, you'd have to let your arm go it alone.

I was working with a geezer we called 'Little Legs', for obvious reasons. He was a funny little bloke and always covered in scratches and scabs. He wasn't the nicest chap you'd meet and gave the impression he'd sell his Grandmother for half a pint. One day, Little Legs made the golden mistake and wrapped the rope round his wrist. Inevitably, the worst happened and one of the sides of beef didn't make it from the pallet to the stack and fell in between. It pulled him off his little legs and he hurtled towards the edge of the stack smashing his face and shoulders on the frozen carcasses. He looked like a cowboy being pulled behind a horse in an old western. He came to an abrupt halt just near the edge, his face lodged against a frozen carcass. One of the jagged bones pierced his cheek and pinned him by the mouth. The beef, all four hundred pounds of it, swung off the edge and was doing its best to obey the laws of gravity.

The weight, all on Little Legs' wrist, was too much and with an unearthly popping sound, similar to a branch cracking in the wind, his shoulder came out of its socket. The screams could be heard throughout the building. I scrambled forwards and grabbed the rope to take some of the weight off, until the forklift driver could reach and cut it.

An ambulance came and carted him off soon enough and surprisingly he never returned to work. From what I heard he recovered, albeit with a few more scars for his collection. The rumour was the boss paid him off to keep his mouth shut about conditions.

The boss was a horrible piece of work. He was an ignorant, obnoxious, nasty git, which in this company was saying something and I gave him as wide a berth as possible. He stood just over six feet with scars all over his face and arms, one starting from the middle of his cheek and stretching down to his chin through his lips. It gave him a permanent snarl and his personality matched this. A few years before he had been in Africa working as a big game hunter. The story that went around was that he had shot most of a pride of lions when one caught up with him and managed to give him a good mauling before dying right on top of him. He was in a right state apparently and had to be driven three hundred miles across rough desert to the nearest hospital. He still managed to survive even though he needed a couple of hundred stitches. Fair play to the lion I say.

Life at the warehouse had its daily routine. After working like maniacs during the morning, dealing with the constant lorries coming in and out, then taking some well-needed refreshment, the afternoon would be our playtime. We weren't really needed between three and five pm and set about finding some distractions to pass the time. Hunger had a more than worrying obsession with guns and would bring in a sawn-off shotgun, one of his favourites, to work with him. During the afternoon lull he put it to use and indulged in his hobby.

Behind the warehouse, the huge fans used for the cold-store, made a whole world of noise as they worked hard at keeping the temperature a long way below freezing. We'd all troop round, collecting empty paint tins and other cans on the way and then set them up. Hunger would then show off his toy with passion and proceed to blow away the cans one by one. As it was so noisy, no one would ever hear us.

After a while I got bored with watching Hunger and decided to do something to amuse myself. Because of my previous experience with gunpowder, I enjoyed making little incendiary bombs out of shotgun cartridges and tins of Easy Start. They may have looked pretty innocent but you really didn't want to be anywhere near them when they went off.

The guy with the Camero had left our little gang and had been replaced by a geezer we called, 'Obie', due to his weight, or as we joked, his height problem, if he'd been 15ft tall, then he'd have been the right height for his weight but as it was he was only 5ft 10. He was so fat that he was pulled over by the police on the way to work one day and was charged with overloading. He was on his moped. One day we put him on the industrial scales, for a laugh, to see how heavy he was as he said he'd been on a diet. He was chuffed as we all stood around emitting a mixture of laughter and amazement; he weighed 32 stone. He never went anywhere without his comfort blanket; a family sized Swiss roll.

One winter's morning we were working in the cold store and so had to come out every half an hour or so for a warm-up, although it was around freezing outside it felt warm out side. We were still pretty much frozen ourselves, and bits were starting to go numb so we knew we needed a fire to warm-up. We looked around and found an old 45-gallon drum that Hunger had used as a target for shooting and with a bit of ingenuity soon had a fire going. As we began to thaw, the warmth felt like the sun beaming down on us on a beach somewhere so we rigged up a hammock to complete the picture.

We were taking it in turns to 'sun' ourselves and on my go I jumped in a little too heavily and the bloody thing split right down the middle. I spilled onto the floor, as the fantasy evaporated, and rolled towards the fire. The frays at the end of my jeans met the flame and got on so well that my right leg was soon ablaze. After the shock had dissipated, just long enough for a good burning, Hunger threw his coat off and on to me. I could never thank him enough as I could have been in serious trouble. As it was the skin on my leg had gone all crispy and the flesh below the burn wept transparent liquid.

As always, I had to rise above and bluff out the pain. There were shooting pains running up my leg and I wanted to wince but I knew I couldn't. The little voice inside was stronger than the pain. 'Don't show it, don't you dare show you hurt'. I gritted my teeth and tried to make jokes. With gritted teeth turning into a gritted body, I applied water and then petroleum jelly, then found some of the only pain reliever I knew; booze. It was always a great justifier, pain. Drinking to get over the physical hurt meant that at least I was drinking for a good reason.

I had started to accompany Hunger to his local quite a bit, well every night, sometimes all night, as the barman had a flexible attitude to the licensing laws. It was a hard drinking pub so I felt completely at home. We'd turn up and start the drinking at about eight and finish sometime a long way over the yardarm. The pub was in the middle of nowhere and so we couldn't walk home.

I had always been mad on motorbikes. I loved the neat adrenaline they provided when ridden at speed. The sensation of rushing past static scenery at ridiculous speeds with the wind rushing all around you, as far as I was concerned you couldn't beat it. The part I loved the most was finding a small hump or little bridge and running at it straight as a die and sailing into thin air for a few seconds. To me those seconds lasted hours and I was free, flying. Most nights, the journey home was quite an adventure. Hunger had a bike that was pretty quick, and we'd always race each other home down the country lanes in the middle of the night, pissed out of our faces. Copious amounts of alcohol led to no fear and no fear equals no comprehension of risk and we embraced this equation most nights.

At one time I had got my hands on a specialist Yamaha that had been used in 0-60mph trials. It was a serious piece of kit and the throttle allowed you to enter warp speed. We had both been drinking heavily but Hunger had had a lot more than me. He could hardly stand, let alone ride, so I knew I had to give him a lift home. However, it was going to be a bit tricky as the bike, being a racer, only had one seat. I had to half lift Hunger onto it. He slumped onto a metal plate behind the seat and when I got on used my back as a place to rest his drunken head.

With Hunger holding on limply round my waist, we roared off. We went the usual route heading towards the railway bridge that I used as my launch pad. I shouted to Hunger to hold on, as neither of us had helmets on. With the bridge in my sights, I opened the throttle full and the valves screamed for mercy. I knew I was showing off and I loved it. We reached the bridge and flew into the darkness; lighting up the hedge walls on either side of us with sparks as the exhaust bottomed out. The feeling was fantastic, like riding a rocket. We were airborne for what seemed like ages and my attention suddenly turned from exhilaration in flight to trepidation for our landing.

I was virtually sitting on the petrol tank as the bike started to nosedive. I thought I was going over the handlebars; Hunger was no help wriggling about on the back like a demented jellyfish. The bike thundered back to earth and as the front hit the ground the shock absorbers bent before we bounced off into space again. On the second landing Hunger's body was above mine, screaming, but still holding on under my shoulders. His body crashed back onto the bike like a sack of spuds and with legs sprawled out behind we headed for the left-hand hedge.

The brambles and thicket whipped around us as we careered forwards. The hedge took most of the energy out of the crash and we finally came to rest about a hundred yards down the lane covered in bits of the hedge and scratches all over us. We looked back to see bits of the bike scattered in our wake like a breadcrumb trail. We both had inane, or perhaps insane, grins on our faces. 'Fuck me', we both said together. 'What a rush!' The next night we were in the pub bragging about our escapade.

I tried to hide my drinking and drunken exploits from Stella for most of the time, but as it was a pretty regular occurrence I didn't always manage it. When she found out or caught me drunk she made it pretty clear that she was not impressed. We didn't really have much of a relationship and I hardly saw her, the marriage was a mistake. I was too drunk most of the time to be bothered with it and as long as I had a bed to go home to each night I didn't really care. All she had wanted was to get out of her parent's house and all I wanted was a roof. I had neglected her, I was never physically, verbally, or mentally abusive but I had neglected her big time.

Hunger and myself were thoroughly enjoying our lifestyle but unfortunately our income and outgoings weren't compatible. On our wages we found that we couldn't enjoy our passions to the full: daily heavy drinking, cars, motorbikes and weed. I certainly wasn't going to give any of it up and not being averse to a little skip to the other side of the law we started looking for a criminal solution to the finance problem.

After some pub discussions we decided to do a warehouse job. We had been looking around and had found the perfect warehouse with a dazzling array of stuff. It was a storage facility for local traders so there were lots of different things available for lifting, from dartboards to mechanical diggers. We knew the place was alarmed but that didn't particularly worry us; what we were concerned about was the huge halogen lights opposite the warehouse shinning down on it. Trying to rob with those things blaring down would've been like trying to nick the FA Cup from a floodlit playing field.

Hunger had a solution. He said he could hide in a huge bush near the lights and after dark shoot them out with a high-powered air rifle. Give him his dues; Hunger really could shoot the balls off a gnat at a hundred paces. He took out the lights in three shots. Then we were darting amongst piles of wooden pallets and 45-gallon drums, using the shadows as our friends, we reached the door we had set as our target.

The door, which was a huge metal roller type, must have weighed a ton or more but all we had to do was lift it up about a foot, then Hunger could slip under it and open the access panel from inside. We got a scaffolding pole and used the flat end, edging it under the bottom. Once it was under the door we could lever it up by using a breezeblock. It took every ounce of strength I had to lever the door up enough but after much effort we were there.

I had to hold the door open with all my strength focused on the pole, the strain rippling through my muscles. I could just about keep it open by a foot. Hunger started to scrabble through on his belly. He was about three-quarters of the way through when I started to feel the pole slipping. I hissed at him, through clenched teeth, 'Get a fucking move on'. I was at the end of my grip and started to panic as I could still see Hunger's head sticking out just as I let go. The door came crashing down with the sound of a hundred dustbin lids, magnified by the preceding silence. I looked down tentatively, with racing thoughts flowing through my mind tackling the imagined problem of a severed head. There was nothing. He must have moved like lightning to get out of the way.

From behind the still vibrating door came a muffled shouting. Even though the sound was deadened I could clearly hear swearing. Hunger opened the access panel. He was clutching his head and looked none too pleased; still we were in. We got to work quickly and started our scout. There really were all manner of things in there; it was an Aladdin's cave. Any anger in Hunger's face had drained away and he now smiled despite nearly losing his head.

He turned to me and smiled, 'Fucking hell mate, we've hit the jackpot'. We made countless journeys back and fro to our waiting car. We collected electronic dartboards, which we already had buyers for seeing as we were such professional salesmen. There were TV's, stereos and videos, which always sell well. I don't think there was a pub in all East London that didn't have a new dartboard that summer.

For a while we were flush, all the selling netted us enough cash to feed our habits for a little while but nothing lasts forever, especially if you have a voracious appetite. Before long the money well had dried up and we were back to accruing debts, a slate at the bar and promises to drug dealers. Having got the taste of life without them we knew it was time to go back to the warehouse.

This time we got cameras, clothes, clocks and whatever was around. We took loads of Marks and Spencer's gear. The problem with thieving, is that you have to then flog the goods and that creates a lot of work, setting-up deals then chasing the money and so on. It also makes you a bit of a 'known man' and not in a good way. After a while the heat got too hot and we decided to cool off and the warehouse stealing died a natural death. Still, we got what we wanted out of it and our addictions were fed for a while.

The character I'd created for myself by this time was so full on that I never thought about being the second man.

Everything in life was a competition. I'd always have to go at least one better than the last bloke. If he drank eighteen pints, I'd drink twenty; if he smoked 10 spliffs, I'd smoke 15; if he ran 5 miles I'd run 10. It really didn't matter what it was. I had to run on as much adrenaline as possible and always made sure I won. I was renowned for it.

I knew that we had to find an extra source of income again and this time, go one better than the warehouse. The solution popped into Hungers head one afternoon, simple, an armed robbery. In his mind it was the easiest solution and he had all we needed, a sawn-off shotgun, a fast bike and a target. At the time as I had no understanding about consequences was only interested in feeding my habits and being as reckless as possible.

Hunger supplied the weapon, and for my liking he looked too keen to use it. In his case, his cut from the robbery via the use of his gun would pay for a couple of Uzi machine guns he'd been offered through a new arms dealer 'friend' of his. The scoping had been done and he had picked a perfect place. It was a busy garage in a town that housed the day's takings in an over night safe and we knew that the money went in at 10pm.

I didn't really think about what I was doing before hand but as we were getting ready to set off I knew that this was wrong, not because it was stealing or anything as moral as that, what rubbed me up the wrong way was the fact that we were going to at least terrify some poor sod half to death and I wasn't prepared to go through with that. "Sorry mate " I told Hunger. "I can't do this, this could really fuck someone up bad, someone who ain't done nothing wrong". Hunger and me spent the next twenty minutes arguing about the rights and wrongs of the whole situation, in the end it was plain to him that I wasn't going to back down. We stood in the living room of his pokey flat and Hunger became more agitated that I was pulling out, there was just no way I was going to involve an innocent person in my madness, that was totally unfair in my mind, Hunger, was shouting, angry and pissed off, he threw a punch at me, I managed to avoid it and it was then gloves off time, I don't remember him actually hitting me but I guess he must have as I was swallowing blood and the taste was unmistakable. We were rolling about on the floor, arms punching, hands scratching and gouging, legs kicking, there were head butts, bites and swearing. Hunger was on top of me and I launched him across the room with my legs, he fell against the table knocking it over. Everything that was on the table came crashing to the floor , including the sawn off shot gun. Me and Hunger were both on the floor in half sitting positions, me at one end of the room and him at the other, staring at each other, the gun was by Hunger and he picked it up looking at me with blood running down his face, blood also pouring from his now broken nose, he pointed the gun at me, pure adrenaline was running through my veins and beads of sweat were making track marks down my face, "If your gonna do it, then fucking do it" I snarled . My heart was racing in my chest as I thought he was really going to do it, he lifted the shot gun and pointed it at me with more conviction, he was blinking all of the time because of the blood running in his eyes from a cut on his forehead. "If you ain't comin' wiv me I'll fuckin' go it alone" he shouted. "Don't do it man, this is crazy" I replied. He pulled himself up on the edge of the upturned table and put the sawn off in a large inside pocket, he walked out slamming the door behind him, I sat in silence and heard his motor cycle start up and roar off. A sigh of relief came over me that I hadn't gone with him, not that I had just nearly been killed - that didn't seem all that important at the time.

On automatic pilot I went to the pub after cleaning myself up at Hunger's before I left. It took me about half an hour to get to the pub and to my surprise as I walked in there was Hunger sitting at his usual table looking none too impressed with an empty bag by his side. I sat down and had a pint, I felt strange, Hunger looked at me confused and flabbergasted, "it had all been so easy in my head, go in, shout, get the money and leave" he said in a sorry voice not much more than a whisper. "What happened?" I asked him. "I just couldn't do it after what you said about fucking someone up who had not done nothing wrong, I just couldn't do it". As I sat there reflecting and listening to Hunger explain this revelation in his life, I realised that I had done the right thing and not the easy thing. I felt good about myself at that moment.

This was a whole new feeling to me. I'd never felt like this over anything before. I'd stolen lots of things and been a complete arsehole to many people and never felt anything. All the fights and violence seemed natural and I loved it, but this was something new. For once I wasn't sitting in the pub trying to justify to myself what I had done, I was sitting there feeling good about myself because I had done the right thing.

I'd never inflicted my violence on someone innocent. They'd always started on me one way or another and they always knew what was coming. In my world, violence was a way of life, I relaxed into my chair and did what I knew best and slowly drowned myself in a sea of alcohol. I never spoke of that night to anyone.

Work at the warehouse was coming to an end. It was getting boring and tedious and the volume of trucks coming in was decreasing as the beef had found a new home, Russia. It was sold for something stupid like 10p a pound but then I suppose that was a fair price for something so rank, some of it was green. Still we found ways to keep ourselves amused, 'Mad Max' was out at the pictures and we decided to re-enact the famous Thunder Dome. The warehouse pretty much looked like it, with 60 ft ceilings and beams everywhere. We took it in turns to hang from the ceiling using lorry straps. Flying across the space each armed with long insulation pipes we'd try and beat the shit out of each other. Well, it passed the time.

Stella's Dad worked for the railways and as his new son-in-law, I thought that he might be able to help me out with getting a job for British Rail as it was then, As with all changes, I didn't really want to leave the warehouse but the new job was more money so I went for it. My leaving prompted a monumental piss-up, not because I'd be missed, it was just a good excuse. We drank a good chunk of the pub dry that night and ended with a hilarious trip home in the back of a transit driven by an ex-army tank driver. He'd been given a dishonourable discharge and still thought that any vehicle he was in was a Chieftain. I had bruises for weeks from being thrown around the back of his old van. After that night I turned my back on the glamorous life of beef hauling and opened my arms to the dazzling world of British Rail.

The phrase 'birds of a feather flock together' is very apt for drinkers. And as it turned out, the guy I started work with on the railways was a total piss-head. For me it was a right result. The job had become available because the previous guy had fried himself on the electric line; something I was aiming not to emulate.

After about a week of work, I found myself in a familiar position, sitting in a pub, aptly called, 'The Rivers of Blood'. We whiled away the time drinking, playing pool and swapping stories. It was not uncommon for this to take-up a large part of the day and so we consumed a great deal of beer, sometimes as much as fifteen to twenty pints. At some point the call would go up and we'd all leave and do the bit of work we'd been given for the day.

With the drinking and fooling about that ensued, it didn't take me long to feel the full force of the electric line. I had grabbed hold of part of an electric cable that we were repairing after our usual pub lunch; unfortunately I grabbed hold of the wrong part. Seven hundred and fifty volts shot up one arm and down the other. It was quite a shock in all ways and threw me back on my arse. Luckily I had broken free, so the current was broken. I felt a bit dazed and confused to say the least but I had to keep face and laughed it off. Never would my stiff upper lip approach be broken.

This approach to pain had been instilled in me from an early age and then re-enforced at many times through my life to the point where it was all I knew, at the warehouse I had been crushed by a lorry whilst driving a forklift. The forklift was small and the lorry big and it doesn't take a genius to work out how I came out of that one. My leg was smashed up and my ankle broken. The bloke who took me to the office, cut off my boot and as I winced in pain, he looked me in the eyes and said, 'Pull yourself together man, you're British'. It made me think about how many unnecessary deaths are down to the British stiff upper lip.

The railway job was pretty boring, as there were little of the extra curricular activities that had made the warehouse so much fun. There was the drinking of course but there were no shotgun afternoons and there was very little to nick, except copper cables that we would collect and have enough to sell at Christmas.

For a while I focused on my marriage. During the warehouse times Stella and I had hardly seen each other so I thought I'd better put some time into our relationship. A couple of months into married life and I looked to all intense & purposes like a fully paid up responsible member of society. I started doing stuff around the house and even did a little gardening. I really started to buckle down and settle into a routine. I stopped drinking during the week; in fact I stopped all my shenanigans and left them for the weekend blowout. I woke at six every morning and worked as hard as I needed to. I changed my lunchtime drinking to a game of nine-card brag and became a bored zombie living in a world of tedium.

I hated everything. My life was becoming something I despised and I was slowly sinking further and further into the doldrums. Sunday lunches with the in-laws, discussing the latest advances in vitamin pills or the terrible plight of sub-Saharan Africa. I couldn't give a fuck, I wanted to be tearing down a lane on my bike, or pissing it up in a pub somewhere.

In the midst of this new boredom there was one single outlet. A geezer I met on the railways, Dave, was a real drinker and we had struck up quite a friendship. Although the drinking had been cut down, the need inside me didn't diminish and it burned, churning around like molten lava looking for a weak crack in my exterior, just waiting to explode and be quenched with copious amounts of alcohol.

Stella and I used to go out with him and his wife and the girls would talk and we would drink. At least that was the plan. Although Stella didn't drink, Dave's wife would and soon it became clear to me that all was not well. For some people booze can be like a series of keys unlocking parts of you, normally kept hidden away. The more you drink, the more locks open. Dave's wife was one of these people and after about three drinks the first lock would be well and truly open, and the nasty bitch would vomit out one vile word and action after another.

It's only now that I know she must have been an alcoholic. The booze would start to seep into her blood and then as the blood went round her body and passed through her brain it would trip all the psycho switches until she was in full madwoman mode. We must have met her at some point down her personal destruction path, as it wasn't long before Dave left her. Soon after, I was round there helping him pick up stuff and she came on to me. Shocked isn't the word. From that point on I thought it would be best to keep well away, I had enough of my own problems without her adding to my list. Top of that list, as usual, was money. During a discussion with Dave about this, it turned out that we had something in common, moneymaking ideas. To be fair, his were a little more on the entrepreneurial side and mine on the criminal, but still he wasn't averse to a little step over the law and I was never afraid of hard work so we thought we could meet in the middle. Some of his ideas were straight out of 'Only Fools and Horses'.

We decided to buy an old beaten-up commer van, just like Del and Rodney's but with four wheels. It did however have the bad paintwork, chronic rust and belching exhaust. First we started doing some rubbish removals: Office, house and garden. The rubbish usually ended up over a hedge somewhere. The first office we tackled had all the usual stuff, chairs, filing cabinets and so on. The desk looked solid oak to me and had a leather top, definitely antique.

There was a problem, how to get it out. During the office's history a prefab wall had gone up and so the desk was too big to go through the door at any angle and we tried them all. We pushed and shoved it in all directions getting more and more frustrated. Eventually we stopped and fuming, searched for a solution. After a good swear up we decided that the only way the stupid thing was leaving the room was seven inches shorter. So we took a saw to it and removed the seven inches from each leg, then stood back proud of our ingenuity. It slipped through the door like a well-greased piston.

We had previously done some business with a local second-hand dealer and he'd been pretty fair to us so we set off in the crap mobile to pay him a visit. Before we went, we'd discussed the transaction and had decided that he would scrutinise the desk and chair carefully and it would be painfully obvious that there was something amiss with the height differences. Then genius struck, cut the same length off the chair legs. The brilliance of the idea at the time evaporated when we were in the shop. When we set them both up in front of him we stood back and looked at the ludicrous creation. Three sets of eyes took turns to search the others and we tried to keep our poker faces solid. He sat down and moved the chair forwards. He didn't fit under and looked up at us confused. The laughter that had been bubbling inside burst out and the three of us erupted in hysterics. We laughed our bollocks off for a good while and when the humour was drained, I tried to concoct a story about a midget stockbroker which set us all off again. He gave us a tenner, probably for giving him the best laugh he'd had in ages.

We decided antiques weren't our things, so we moved into the fast food business. We worked the boot fairs and the markets and had a healthy trade going. We were on one of these excursions when the crap mobile failed us. As is the way, when brakes fail, they choose to go at the worst possible moment. For us it was on a hill heading towards a roundabout. We were doing about fifty miles an hour, loaded up with books, plates, assorted other junk, a petrol lawnmower and a couple of hundred rolls and sandwiches. Dave squealed and said; 'Fuck me, the brakes have gone', and we both looked ahead and started to feel panic creep up our backs. He tried to change down but the knackered gear stick was having none of it. Stella was with us and as she was screaming, 'The roundabout, we're going to hit the roundabout' I was screaming, 'the fucking sandwiches'. My priorities as usual, arse about face.

Dave was struggling with the dustbin lid sized steering wheel as we careered into the curb of the roundabout, black smoke bellowing out behind us. We hit it head on and the cars all around screeched to a halt, as we bumped over it, the van on two wheels, cucumber, cheese and pickle flying everywhere. The plates smashed on the van walls and the lawnmower crashed through the side door taking it off its hinges. We flew across and hurtled round a right-hand bend. Three quarters of our load took the path of least resistance and parted company with the van through the door. I yelled, 'keep going, keep going' to Dave, as we couldn't afford to be caught as we had no MOT, tax or insurance. We sped off down the road trailing bits of sandwiches, broken plates and an array of condiments. We finally made it home and collapsed in a fit of laughter. We were safe albeit covered in cheese and pickle.

That was the last outing of the van and I scrapped it the next day. They don't make 'em like that anymore...thank God! We tried a variety of other moneymaking ideas but they never amounted to making us the millionaires we knew we wanted to be.

Stella and I were both working hard and had reverted back to seeing very little of each other. She was working in an insurance agency but hated it and soon packed up to work for her brother-in-law in his burger van. I couldn't see the appeal at the time but it made her happy and therefore quiet so that was enough for me.

Every Friday night I would get home and relax with a couple of bottles. She started to come in later and later until eventually she walked in dressed up to the nines and declared our marriage over. I was shocked as it came out of the blue. I knew that things could have been better but I didn't realise they had got this bad. I suppose it wasn't totally unexpected but the simple declaration of fact, without discussion, hurt a bit. I thought I'd done the right thing by her and was always there when she needed me. It didn't take long for me to work out there was someone else. Then I moved onto the logical conclusion, she was seeing the brother-in-law; so it wasn't just the burger buns he was filling.

After the initial shock I actually felt quite relieved, like a weight had been lifted. Now I was on my own again I was free to drink and take as many drugs as I wanted. I didn't answer to anyone but myself. I went round to where the burger bun Romeo lived and gave him the hiding of his life. I got all my possessions together, loaded them into the back of a railway van and set off for new horizons. It was around that time that my compensation money from the accident I had on the farm came through, so I left the marriage with a few quid in my pocket. I got ten grand from her; my half of the house, had a few thousand from the accident payout and that was it, marriage over.

For some reason I felt that if one thing went wrong then it all went wrong and so I jacked in my job on the railway as well. This wasn't a bad idea anyway as the split made work difficult because of the father-in-law. So there I was, financially buoyant, no work, free and single. It was time to indulge myself in the things I loved best, drink, drugs and self-destruction.

6
Hell and fire

With my new found freedom I set off on a serious wrecking mission. To those around me it would have been an unforgettable time and apart from the booze and drugs blackouts, it's burnt into my memory too. I moved into a rundown eighteenth- century cottage with three guys, all good fellas that I'd met in a local pub. It was a great place, a real bachelor's pad, exactly what I was looking for. It was surrounded by acres of farmland and had a small reservoir nearby, which was perfect for swimming. The place was idyllic and reminded me of my childhood environment. The other three guys were as much into bikes as I was and of course, booze.

Every night seemed like a celebration of something and nothing. Wild parties were frequent and we had a riot. There was always a bonfire going and bits of bike were everywhere, including the bathroom. Still, as I hardly washed, because we'd only get covered in oil again, that didn't bother me.

One of the geezers was called J and he was a real joker. He loved motorbikes and with his help it didn't take him long to turn my old Matchless into a purring gem of a machine. We got on really well and had a running joke about my leather jacket, as it had loads of badges on it. If it was ever missing I knew where to find it.

The youngest of the bunch was a guy called Nix, so called because he didn't have anything of his own so all his possessions belonged to someone else. Nix wasn't averse to the array of narcotics available and it would be a rare day if he weren't floating round the place as high as a kite. His idea of a good meal was half an ounce of puff, a few lines of speed and a half bottle of tequila. He was a quiet soul and if you did get him talking it became clear why. He was completely mad.

He went missing one day but we didn't think anything of it. The next day the Old Bill turned up and we knew that something was wrong. They told us that they'd found him goose-stepping up the local high street, naked, with a daffodil sticking out of his arse singing the national anthem. He'd been sectioned. Bless him; he always loved the royal family.

The place acted as a local hive/hotel for various vagabonds. There were all sorts, from bikers to travellers and the odd crusty. The price of admission seemed to be a big bag of gear or crate of booze and we didn't mind what it was; we weren't discerning drug users. We were so out of it most of the time we didn't know who they were but they were always welcome.

I had been introduced to the wonders of speed by now and used it regularly. Its a foul chemical tasting powder and does what it says on the tin. For me the main reason for taking it was so I could drink more and stay awake for longer. It joined the weed and booze as the cornerstones of my daily activities.

Work wise, I had taken to hod carrying and basically anything else on a building site. The gang I was with was more demolition than anything else and I wasn't fussy as long as there was a few quid in it. With this money coming in plus my house money I was free of financial worries, a first for me and a dangerous situation.

The morning journey would always involve a stop off at the local garage, whether we needed diesel or not. This particular garage had a special lure for us as it sold booze along with all its other goodies. We would stock up on provisions and fill our bags with Red Stripe, then head off to the site for a day of hard graft. Once, we were working on a site during the winter and the temperature was so low the cement kept freezing. We kept ourselves warm with plenty of rum, not simply a slug in the tea but whole bottles. I lost count of how much I'd had but managed to stay competent due to the numerous grams of speed in my system. One of the effects of speed is that it cancels out the 'drunk' effect of alcohol. That's not to say you aren't pissed, it just means you don't fall over. It also means you can keep drinking, which I did,

a few slugs here, a line there. The mix isn't conducive to efficient work however and I was in quite a state. We decided, through addled thoughts, that adding lots of anti-freeze to the cement would fix the freezing problem and set about making our own concoctions. It seemed to work but we subsequently found out months later that the building inspectors had condemned the site. Still we got paid and had a laugh so no harm done in my mind.

This wasn't the only disaster we created. Building, fucked out of your mind, doesn't produce brilliant results. I went to work one Sunday morning still out of it from the activity the night before. I had to bump out the bricks ready for Monday and had the idea to put a pallet on the top of the scaffolding so we'd be ready to go. I wasn't in a fit state to take them up there manually and there was a rough terrain forklift on the site that was perfect for the job This fork truck was four tons of shear power and there it was with a half drunk, half hung- over mad man behind the wheel.

I'd never driven one before and the ground was both rough and muddy because it had been pissing down all night. With all these factors in place, a wise or sober person would have had serious second thoughts, but not me. I climbed aboard and gunned the engine. I don't know how much a pallet of bricks weighs but I'd guess quite a bit. With the combined weight of bricks and machine we were a ground-to-ground semi-guided missile travelling across an uneven surface with no sense of control or sanity.

I'm not sure if there's a site-driving manual but if there is I bet the braking distance when approaching a house with a full pallet of bricks is a bit more than ten yards. Still, this was my estimation of the gap I needed to slow down, tilt the forks and deposit the bricks. It may well have worked if the brakes were working to full capacity but like most things on a building site, they didn't. A piercing reality suddenly parted the fog in my brain and I realised what was about to happen. My thoughts gathered themselves and concluded that if I put the tilt forward and slammed the machine into reverse, at the same time, I might be able to pull off a miracle.

However, God must have had his eyes elsewhere at the time as nothing happened apart from a loud crunching and then a huge smash. The machine, with me as an idle witness, crashed at full speed straight into the front of the house. The forks, with bricks acting as a wrecking ball went through the wall and into a top bedroom. With reverse finally engaged I pulled back which had the effect of the pallet of bricks swinging out. It pulled most of the front wall away with it.

I pushed the panic stop button, perhaps a little too late, and sat there motionless, with dust swirling all round me staring at the devastation. What was left of the front wall stood at an angle that at best could be described as precarious and part of the roof didn't look too clever. It might take a few weeks and lots of graft to put a house up but it only takes one idiot, still off his head from the night before, to bring it down. After the shock had sufficiently abated I climbed gingerly out of the cab. I was mumbling to myself over and over, 'Fuck, what am I going to do?'

'Right' a voice said inside, 'off to the pub'. On the way it became clear to me that I could neither rebuild the house by the following morning nor come clean to the boss. Therefore I'd take the obvious route, deny all knowledge. After a few pints in the pub this seemed fine to me, no one had seen me do it and everything was going to be fine. And sure enough, it was. The following day I turned up at the site to find the boss in a complete fury, his face a mixture of disbelief and pure anger. He turned to his crew for some sort of explanation and asked, 'Well, what the fuck's happened here?' All he got was a line of raised shoulders. I found my voice and mouthed the possibility of kids mucking around. It sounded plausible enough and everyone joined in. So that was that.

Although I enjoyed the work, my favourite times were when we let loose at the weekends. We spent the whole time drinking and playing darts; cards or pool and I loved the regular snorting to keep the momentum going. The card sessions were usually fairly peaceful but there was one session that went a bit awry. We had been playing for quite a few hours and puffing loads. We all had the munchies and there was only a loaf, jam and butter to eat, so I made a load of toast and we ate away whilst playing. I'd been doing quite well. In fact I'd been doing really well and although I wasn't cheating one of the guys suspected that my luck wasn't all down to good fortune. He had been making sarcastic comments occasionally and at first I said nothing. However he kept at me and the odd sarcastic remark soon led to accusations, which led to raised voices and before long the pressure blew.

He went off his nut and grabbed the bread-knife and thrust it towards my face. I flinched and instinctively grabbed his arm. One of the problems with being off your face is that if your mood swings into temper it can make you crazy, unpredictable and dangerous. I was suddenly facing such a situation. I knew that if I didn't get the knife off him then his anger might take over and I could be in serious trouble. As I went for the knife handle he brought his wrist round and the serrated edge ran along my index finger and cut deep down into the joint on the main knuckle. The knife went forwards then backwards and into my flesh. The table, cards and money went flying and blood splashed across the room.

I was well anaesthetised from the booze and drugs so we just kept struggling with blood going everywhere. It wasn't until the other guys stopped us that we realised how much damage had been done. I looked down at my hand and realised I was almost minus a digit, plus there were gashes all up my arm. 'Fucking hell, look at that', I said, more out of amazement then anything else. It didn't hurt and it felt like I was looking at someone else's hand, not my own. I sat down to think things through. It was payday the next day so I had to go to work and I couldn't be bothered to go to the hospital. I drank some scotch and stared at the bleeding hand. Then I drank some more scotch and by the time the bottle was almost empty I had decided that the kitchen towel I'd wrapped round it was a good enough solution and that it wasn't so bad anyway.

After some more booze and a couple of spliffs, I collapsed and passed out. I woke up feeling weak as a kitten. There was blood all round my hand and the sofa was red and wet. My head ached so much it felt like it would fall off. I got to my feet, swayed and fell back down. 'Fuck I need a drink', I said to myself and drained all the dregs I could find. Feeling a bit better I put a new towel bandage on and got ready for work. The cut opened again and began to bleed heavily although all I did was wrap the towel tighter round it. We went to work as usual and I don't know how I made it to lunchtime. We went to the pub and whilst we were playing pool the landlord told me to go to the hospital as my hand was leaking everywhere. The blood had run down the cue and there was a red line all the way to the tip leaving spots on the table I must have looked horrendous.

I gave in and went to the local casualty. The doctor was astonished that the cut was nearly twenty-four hours old. He looked at me in disbelief and just sighed. I guess it's a testament to the blanking out power of drugs and booze.

My drug intake up to this point had been, I felt on an even keel. I had stuck with puff and amphetamine and washed them down with liberal quantities of booze. As far as I was concerned at the time, this worked for me. The only change had been the regularity as it was now a daily routine. The reaction from these drugs when taken in large quantities produced the effect I was looking for, personal annihilation and regular passing out. However I was always pretty sure of what I was seeing and thinking and had a rough grasp on my surroundings. It was time to take a different drug and I was more than ready. The combination of the three stimulants hadn't taken me as far as I wanted to go.... I'd never been on a trip.

I'd been on the piss one evening, as usual, and spotted a familiar face, an old mate from school. He came over and we went through the usual bullshit of how well we were doing and were having a good old natter. He then broached the subject of drugs that immediately put us on both on familiar ground. After a short discussion he suggested that I buy some acid from him and, me being me, was hardly going to turn it down. In fact after his sales pitch I couldn't wait to get it down my neck.

It was fortunate for me that evening that for my first trip, I was in a good mood and in relatively good company. It was a magical experience and something I was totally unprepared for. The world spun with new colours, sounds and sights. Everything seemed much more intense and distorted at the same time, quite literally like being in another world. Even my six hands didn't freak me out. I wondered and wandered round in a dreamlike state seeing everything with new eyes. In short, I loved it. Once I'd found this new path to an altered perception, I wanted to walk down it as often as I could. It was a revelation to me that I could change everything around me without heading towards the drink-laced oblivion. Still I wasn't about to let an old faithful friend down, so instead of swapping one thing for another, I added another drug to my list. I'd opened a new door but wasn't about to close any others.

A big day was coming up on the calendar, October 31st and we had a huge Halloween party planned. We didn't bother inviting people, as we knew the news would get out and the gathering of bikers, hippies and other of the like would begin a couple of weeks before. After all, there were a lot of mushrooms to be picked, dried and sampled.

In case you're not familiar with natural hallucinogens, I am referring to mushrooms of the magical variety. I learnt that there's quite an art to picking, drying, preparing and consuming. Once found they shouldn't be picked immediately. First you have to go around the patch flicking the tops so that the spores will spread and ensure a full crop for the next two months. The gang from the cottage had found a huge patch that would generate a massive crop, enough for everyone and much more.

One of the guys at the den had brought himself a Triumph Spitfire. Of course it didn't work and needed a new engine but that didn't stop us thinking we could get it going and use it to go harvesting. I soon found myself, one of a group of twelve putting in a new engine. We were standing around with spanners, screwdrivers and lots of gaffer tape and after the requisite fuel, booze and drugs, we started at 1am. By 5am the engine was in and running, brakes worked OK and we were mobile.

It was a struggle getting everyone in the car but we somehow managed it and with six aboard in various contortionist positions, we were ready. I had decided that being 6ft 2inches, I'd take up too much room so opted for the roof. This was also the most reckless place to be, so naturally I had to have it. With a roar and a cheer we were off to our field to collect the crop.

The rest of the morning went by with military precision. We were quick, efficient and businesslike and had soon achieved our aim. My personal objective was slightly different. I followed the plan and flicked and picked with the best of them. However, I relapsed into childhood mode and for every one picked, ate two, as if I was picking strawberries. Before long I was off my face and as we made it back to the car I realised that I wasn't the only one, everyone was high. People laughed as we tripped our way back to the tardis mobile. The drive back to the cottage was like a roller coaster from hell. The driver got lost and was convinced he was in a Formula 1 race. He sped round the lanes on full throttle with his foot firmly planted to the floor.

We were all along for the ride and everyone was screaming, not really through fear but because in our distorted world it just seemed the appropriate thing to do. I suppose I should have been terrified up on the roof but I wasn't, I was flying. I lay there spread-eagled, hanging on like a limpet in a storm. The car careened all over the place and the sides were taking a real battering, as were my legs when they got too close to the hedges. The road leading up to the cottage was straight and about half a mile long. The driver could see the chequered flag in his mind and floored it.

I remember that stretch of road well and spying the cottage in the distance with wind blown watering eyes I urged the driver on with screams of, "faster, faster." The car overshot the entrance and then the anchors were applied. I didn't stand a chance.

I don't remember flying through the air but I do remember seeing the tarmac coming up to meet me in slow motion and the noise of the thud as I came back to earth. The next thing I remember is being in a front room and staring up at the old WW2 parachute hanging from the ceiling. There were people all around me asking if I was all right, I said I was and reached for a can. I pulled the ring back and the cracking noise was all I heard, I never even took a sip, just passed out again.

I woke up the next morning feeling as if I'd been run over by a train. I was grazed, bruised and covered in blood, again. I levered myself up, with every muscle screaming at me to stay still. I wasn't having any of it, I wasn't about to lie down and die. I got up via a series of small painful jerks and finally stood. I only had one thought in my mind; I had to reach the bottle of vodka in the cupboard next to the sink. Nothing else mattered. If I could just reach that bottle then everything would be all right. I limped slowly towards the kitchen, the bottle imprinted on the inside of my head. I found it and drank it like water. Soon after, my spirits recovered enough to stand up straight. By the end of the bottle I was ready to administer some first aid. There was nothing too serious and everything was still in the right place. In fact without the aches I felt reasonably fit. As the vodka was working its magic I spent the rest of the day drinking either at the cottage or down at the pub The lady of the house was called Alison and she was going out with a mate of mine who was the official house holder. Alison was only fifteen or sixteen and was wise beyond her years. She was kind, funny and beautiful and I was in love with her the first time I ever saw her, although I couldn't let her know that as that would have been dishonourable, so all the time I lived at the cottage I was forever thinking of what could be, might be, hoped would be with Alison but always kept my mouth firmly shut.

The following day it was back to hod carrying. We were building a huge wall around a car park and it was good pay, so body trashed or not I wasn't going to miss out. I felt like I'd had the worst hiding of my life and by lunchtime admitted defeat and decided to get some medical help. The cement dust had gathered in all the cuts and grazes and was mixing with the weeping liquids turning parts of my body into grey mud. I had to be back in an hour to continue working so the hospital was too far away and there were no doctors surgeries around. The only place that was local was a vet, which I thought would do the trick. I cleaned up a bit and set off.

I stood in line behind a golden retriever waiting for its shots. When my turn came I tried to explain my situation and eventually caused enough of a fuss for the vet to usher me into his room. He patched me up and told me to go to the hospital, I agreed with him knowing full well I wouldn't go. I had to go back to work, plus we had a party to arrange.

The morning of the party I joined a motley crew on a trip down to the local off-licence to stock up on supplies. We must have looked like quite a sight; we were all bikers or crusty and weren't too bothered about our appearance.

Once the supplies were collected we went to our second home. This particular pub was similar to all the others I felt comfortable in. It was rough and ready to serve us. There weren't too many niceties, a wooden floor that doubled as an ashtray, 'The Ace of Spades' on the jukebox and a pool table with a surface like the dark side of the moon. We spent the rest of the day whiling away the hours, drinking and playing pool and discussing how good the party was going to be. The mood in the pub had been getting increasingly tense. We left at sundown and ambled back to the cottage.

When we arrived we were met with quite a sight. A pea-soup fog from all the spliffs going round and there were massive pots of mushroom tea bubbling away on the Rae burn. Everyone had a mug of tea in his or her hands and there was a lot to get through. I grabbed my mug and took a great gulp. I looked around and for the first time took in the scene properly. There were many strangers, nothing new there, except they were all dressed like witches or wizards.

A few people were playing with an ouijiboard and a group sat huddled in a corner sipping tea and calling on the hidden spirits to reveal themselves. All in all a bit spooky and very strange, even for me. I walked around feeling out of place and on edge, for some reason I felt everything was too full on. I grabbed a beer, and went for some more tea. One of the pots had been finished and the bottom of the pan was full of mushrooms. I reached into it and pulled out a handful, munching them slowly to release as much 'magic' as possible.

After a short while I felt like I'd entered a time warp and found myself sitting next to the fire holding an iron bar with every muscle tensed in my body. I've no idea how I got there but I guess the paranoia and fear set in and I retreated to a place where I could feel some sort of safety. However I hardly felt safe. My senses were all on full alert and my fight or flight system was tuned into full fight mode as I sat there and waited. I was petrified, terrified and frozen. I was twitching at every noise, my mind turning each sound into a threat. I could hear the music inside and the shouting, it seemed that everyone was shouting. There were crashes and bangs as crockery went flying, glass was breaking and there were intermittent cracks of furniture being broken. I couldn't move. I sat there, nailed by fear to the spot, rigid, holding the bar with all my strength, my one slim piece of security in a wild world spinning out of control.

I must have been sitting there for hours as my hands had started to blister from the conducting heat of the fire, I could see the injury as it was happening but couldn't feel any pain. There was a sense of impending doom, like the earth was about to end. I was aware of the grim reaper standing by my shoulder and if I so much as blinked, his scythe would slash down and cut me in two. This sure was a bad trip.

The door to the kitchen led onto the garden opposite from where I was hiding behind the fire. There was suddenly an almighty crash and a figure came flying through the air, out of the door and hit the ground with a thud. Instinctively it rolled into the foetal position. Two menacing figures followed, one with a pickaxe handle and the other a huge iron bar. The guy lying on the floor sensed them coming and uncurled, his arms stretching out in front of him, desperately clawing at the ground to pull his body out of danger.

The first of the blows were unseen but I heard them and jumped with each sound. The noise of a body being hit is disgusting and I felt like *I* was being hit with each blow, jumping with every strike. They pummelled his legs; over and over they hit him laughing like maniacs. His shinbones were being destroyed and his legs slowly turned into jelly. Then they moved up the body, the ferocity of blows consistent. There was a mad pleasure written on their faces. This was fun to them. The poor victim was still scrabbling away with his hands, screaming in pain, but over the noise of the party his screams were not heard.

They let him move slightly, and then rained down blows with their weapons, each strike driven with a bizarre lust. They hit him all over his body and arms and moved towards his head. I sat there watching in sheer horror. I'd had my fair share of fights but this was something different. If I'd been frozen to my spot before then I was now growing roots. I just stared with unblinking incomprehension.

They paused; laughing and faking blows towards the guy's head and looking at each other with uncontrolled glee. When the final blow came, I shut my eyes but heard the bar connect. It sounded like a huge wet fish being slapped on a counter. Then there were no more sounds from the body, now limp and lifeless. The noise was just laughter like a pack of hyenas.

An old Morris Minor van was parked nearby and they gathered the body, still laughing and carried him to the back. One of the attackers dropped the head end and let it fall to the ground like they were carrying a log. He opened the door and they chucked the limp person inside. They then got in and drove off down the lane.

I must have passed out because I woke up with the light of a new day, the fire smouldering and the bar still clutched in my hands, moulded to my skin. The pieces from the night before started to filter through my shattered mind and I looked across to the spot where it had happened. I still couldn't believe what I'd seen and told myself it was just a horrific hallucination and maybe it was. I peeled the bar from my hands and watched a few layers of skin go with it. I winced and levered myself up not looking opposite me.

I finally convinced myself to look and from where I was could see no physical signs of from the attack. I felt relieved that it hadn't happened. As I walked towards the door I glanced at the ground and it was covered in blood. 'Shit', I said out loud then told myself I was still tripping and started to push the memories deep into the back of my mind. I tried to forget what had happened but the memories still come back to me even today.

I stumbled into the living room, looking for some booze. It looked like a tornado had ripped through the place. I found a couple of leftover special brews and sat down swigging on them like they were oxygen. I gagged and heaved but got control of myself and drank the cans dry. I looked down at my hands; they were in tatters with skin hanging off them. I was sweating but cold and my chest was red and sore from the fire.

I looked around searching for my next move and decided to go back outside and go for a swim in the reservoir. I needed waking up and wanted something to shake me out of the memories from the night before, a freezing plunge made sense to me. Just as I stood up, a dog ran in and threw up right in the middle of the room; a whole baby rabbit appeared, covered in mucus and stomach juices. I heaved and felt my body quiver. I wanted to be sick and throw myself inside out to make all the madness disappear. This is it, I though I have finally gone mad, I wasn't scared but confused and panicky.

I lurched towards the door dry retching and made it outside in time to be sick. I wiped my mouth and took a deep breath and trudged towards the water. It was the first day in November and there was a frost on the ground. I waded into the water and mud and soaked myself in the freezing liquid like someone only half conscious. I'm not sure how much it helped me as I staggered out and collapsed on the bank shivering. I woke up a bit later still shivering, probably in the first stage of hypothermia and focused my mind on reaching the cottage. I made it and collapsed on the sofa pulling a rug from the floor around me.

I was completely fucked. Not like a hangover from a heavy Friday night but mentally and physically wrecked. The next time I woke I was in a world of pain, everything hurt, ached or throbbed. This time I wasn't getting up. I was sick for a week; I was throwing up and had a burning fever. I passed in and out of consciousness and the guys, force-fed me Lemsips, porridge and vitamin tablets. It must have worked because at the start of the following week I was back on my feet albeit a little shaky.

In amongst all of this I was still fighting my depression and always had the thought of ending it all just as I had had when I was a kid. Although the happy things that happened helped to keep me going, like the occasion when Alison announced to everyone in the cottage that no more joints were to be skinned up in the front room. She whirled round the house collecting empty beer cans and bottles in a bin liner, that was her way of cleaning the place up. Her sister Tracy was visiting with the quarterly food parcel. As food was not high on the agenda all donations were gratefully received, as was the time when Dave's sister visited with one of the said food parcels, Dave was another left over seventies hippy who lodged at the cottage with us. Dave ran to greet his sister and as he jumped the barbed wire fence his 1970's flares got their revenge and snagged on the barbed wire, Dave was spun into a somersault in mid air and landed head first looking up at his toes with his flares still snagged on the fence, no matter how Dave tried to convince his sister that he had not taken any drugs she wouldn't believe him.

Life at the cottage was one of the best experiences of my life, living there really was like having a family for the first time ever, albeit a happy dysfunctional one, on the work front though, things had dried up a bit due to the fact that everybody's building work had been done on insurance after the '87 hurricane, this meant I was on the look-out again. I needed some cash and started asking people where there might be some work going. I was boozing one night and met this bloke who offered me a job of steel erecting. I had a real fear of heights but being in alcoholic mode and with a full tank said I'd be fine, after all, like most addicts with a belly full of booze I could do anything.

When I woke at six the next morning things were a bit different. We turned up at the sight and I could already feel the panic begin to grow inside as I looked at the steel frame of the building I was supposed to climb. I didn't have a clue what was involved but as usual bluffed and bullshitted my way through. I managed to pick it up as we went along and cleverly dodged any of the high work. I just couldn't face walking along a beam, fifty-foot up with no safety net. I managed to avoid the work up top for the whole three weeks contract, quite an achievement I thought.

The guy I was working for was a typical hard geeza. Tattoos, broken nose, hard as nails but with a heart of gold. His name fitted him well, Butch. I was earning good money considering I wasn't doing any of the dangerous stuff. However, things were about to change.

The new job was working away and we were to be put up in digs. I couldn't believe my luck, as the digs were above a pub, my perfect residing place. We arrived and after throwing my bags into the room I went downstairs and settled behind the bar. Butch came and joined me but didn't drink too heavily, mainly because he didn't stop talking. He could talk for England.

The new job was erecting a giant warehouse and there would be nowhere to hide, it was definitely up top for me. I ended up in the usual state that night and took half a gallon of Scrumpy to bed with me for some morning courage. I woke with the thought of climbing the beams and my stomach started to churn. I needed a drink but every time I swallowed a mouthful it would come back up. It was a battle; wait for it to return to my mouth, and then try not to let it spill out and swallow it back down. I struggled like this many times, I knew that if I persevered I would win. I persevered and held my nose. After successfully completing a few mouthfuls I swigged the rest down. I was once told that a good 'hair of the dog' was a port and brandy but to me anything sufficed as long as it stayed down.

With the alcohol successfully flowing through me I was ready to tackle the day. The fear evaporated and we set off for the site. The first thing to do was get to the top and that meant a cherry picker ride. Basically it's a metal bucket suspended from a crane and holds four guys. We stepped in and off we flew. When we got up top everything was still looking good; I was pissed and ready for work.

I wouldn't recommend my method of overcoming vertigo to anyone else; it does the trick but doesn't really decrease the risk. Several times whilst trying to balance 50ft up in the air on a 5-inch beam of steel I almost fell. It wouldn't have been a pretty sight if I had. There was a lot of groundwork going on underneath and tonnes of steel reinforcing had been set in place for the concrete. This meant that if I had taken a fall I could have landed on any number of 3ft steel spikes hungrily waiting to skewer me.

I should have been terrified but instead of fear I felt elated, I guess if I'd been sober I'd have been back to terra firma in a blink. Each near fall sent a new rush of adrenaline through me and mixed with the booze created an exhilarating effect. It got to the point where I would purposefully engineer situations where I came close to a fatal fall. I look back and think how little I must have cared for my own life.

7
Time Gentlemen please!

Butch and I were developing quite a friendship, we talked a lot and laughed a lot, I think he took me under his wing a bit. He told me that there was a lovely girl living with his girlfriend and I might like to take her out for a drink at the weekend. To be honest I wasn't that bothered as I was married to the bottle at the time and didn't give much thought to the opposite sex. Still, he insisted it would be good for me so I agreed. I was pissed when he told me the name of the pub I was supposed to meet her in, so when the weekend came round, all I knew was that it was definitely situated in one of two villages. I had no idea of the time he set for us either.

I had a plan, I'd start early and work my way from one end of the first village to the opposite end of the second, naturally it would be rude to simply walk in and out of a pub so I stopped at each one for some refreshment. After twelve pubs, a pint and a chaser in each one, I reached the thirteenth. Some would say unlucky but as I walked in a girl looked up from the bar that matched the description I'd been given.

I walked up and introduced myself. I was right, she was my date for the night, and her name was Criss. I sat down and ordered a pint. I was pretty pissed already and had a taste for it, so with defences down and my focus on obliteration I told her my route to our meeting. I then thought that I might as well put all my cards on the table and if she didn't like it and buggered off then fair enough. I told her of my drinking habits and preference for drugs. She was totally unfazed and shrugged her shoulders. We stayed in the pub till closing time drinking steadily and chatting.

I don't remember how the night ended but I awoke to unusual surroundings and it took me a while to get my bearings, replay what memory I did have from the night before and slowly work out that I was at her house, passed out on the floor. I felt pretty rough as usual and needed my powdered breakfast of speed to get me going. I sat up and felt for the familiar plastic in my back pocket. It always amazed me that no matter how wrecked I got I was always prepared for the next day so I could continue from where I'd left off. I couldn't be arsed to cut the white powder into lines and simply emptied the bag into my mouth. For those of you who have never tasted speed, it's a purely chemical taste and totally foul, it covers all your taste buds with what must be similar to little crystals of a caustic-cleaning product. There were some cans of Special Brew left over from the night before, unfamiliar surroundings, but I kept the same routine wherever I was.

You might think that I lacked will power because I could never say 'no' to my morning routine, but will power I had in droves, it was just directed down the wrong path. To wake up each morning with stomach cramps and a throbbing head but still manage to force a pint or two down your neck certainly takes some kind of power.

Criss came down and we chatted amicably for a while. She watched in amazement but without judgement or comment, as I drank down can after can of Special Brew, waiting for the pubs to open. By five to eleven we were standing side by side at the nearest pub door. We went in, sat down and started drinking; our drinking relationship had begun.

I had quite a bit of money at the time and paid for her drinks. It was a simple deal, I kept her in drinks and she kept me company whilst I drank, a perfect alcoholic arrangement. Criss was renting a house from her sister about a mile from where I was staying and I had moved in within a week. It was no big deal and seemed totally natural. I had become bored of the comings and goings at the cottage and needed a change. I don't think Butch's girlfriend was too happy but we ignored any disgruntled looks and I had a new home.

On my first night, we returned from the pub as usual and as soon as the door was closed Criss launched into a violent verbal assault. I was totally unprepared and although had noticed that she had been in a scratchy mood all night was not expecting this. She paced the room like a caged beast talking nonsense and babbling to herself, occasionally looking at me and yelling, swearing her head off. I stood there not knowing quite what to do. Unfortunately she took this badly and focused on me screaming insults and asking me why I thought *I* was so fucking perfect. I didn't know what to do and calmly tried to quieten her down and make her see sense but it was useless. She kept going on and on and then started threatening to cut her wrists.

She ran to the kitchen and brandishing a knife, put it to her wrists screaming at me to push her just a little more. I knew this had to stop and managed to get the knife away from her. She ran into the adjoining living room and with a final scream like a dying animal passed out or fainted on the couch in a drunken stupor. I sat down opposite her and thought hard. What the fuck had just happened. I wasn't angry, I was just confused and worried for her, quite clearly something was terribly wrong. She was what would be called in the medical profession a P. D. [personality disorder]; in my mind at the time she was just a fucking nutter, who for some reason I felt sorry for.

That night I slept in the chair and tried to keep an eye on her. I woke up just after dawn and she was still lying on the couch looking peaceful. I didn't really think about what had happened the night before and just put it down to the drink. I did feel sorry for her though and knew that she needed my help. I don't know why but I really thought I could help.

She woke up a bit later and turned to say, 'good morning' to me. She stretched and yawned and got up as if nothing had happened. This really pissed me off and I was very short with her throughout the morning. She asked me what was wrong so I told her about the night before; I needed some sort of explanation or recollection. She looked confused and embarrassed and claimed to have no memory of it. I had to swallow this but knew she was lying through her teeth. The mix of morning alcohol and profuse apologies made me forgive her. I knew I had to stay to help her get better, I knew I had to make a difference.

That afternoon, unprompted, she told me all about her past, at least the bits she wanted me to know. She showed me the cuts all up her arms and I sat there listening like a big open-mouthed fish as she cast the hook and slowly wound me in. By the end of the day I was totally convinced that she was a woman in distress and I would be her shining knight and rescue her.

The next morning I was relieved to be going to work. Without the pressure of her presence, I stopped thinking about her and soon became blasé about the whole thing. I set off searching out my locals and started to make good use of them. When I got back on Friday evening from the week away on site, you'd have thought I'd been at sea for six months. I got a hero's welcome and couldn't put a foot wrong. Criss was lovely to me and seemed in great form. I hugged her and knew I'd made the right decision, she really needed me and I had the power to help her.

The following Saturday, we had been invited to a party, someone's 21st I think. We were both looking forward to it; a lot of my local drinking buddies would be there so it would be a really good piss-up. We got there and split up, she went to her friends and me to mine. I spent a good night drinking and laughing with the lads and we were having a great time. A fight broke out and I wasn't in the mood for it so, as it was late anyway, decided to go home. I started to look for Criss but couldn't find her anywhere. I went through all the rooms and out to the barn but there was no sign of her. After asking her friends, who hadn't seen her for ages, I came to the conclusion that she must have gone home in a sulk.

I went home and my mind started creating all the nasty images of what might have happened. I was really worried about her and started to run I hoped that she hadn't done anything stupid. I got to the house and breathlessly shouted for her but there was no reply, she wasn't there. I went round the house and checked all over it but no sign. By now my mind was racing, where was she and what had happened?

I went back to the party, half-angry and half-worried. Why couldn't she just have come home? When I got back to the party everyone had gone, there were only the passed out and a few people starting the clearing up. No one had seen her. I went back to the house, hoping that she would be back by the time I got there. I didn't run this time. I was pissed, tired, confused and becoming increasingly angry. I didn't need this kind of shit every weekend. I started an argument in my head between the side that wanted to stay and help and the other that wanted to piss off. I decided to wait and see what had happened.

I sat in the house waiting for her thinking things over. The 'leave her' side was gaining strength and by the time the phone rang I had made up my mind. I didn't need to play hero to a mad bitch and was going to tell her I was leaving whenever she made it home. I picked up the phone and heard Criss's voice on the other end. It was 8am and I'd been up most of the night getting increasingly frustrated but I couldn't help but dissolve when I heard her speak. She sounded so fragile and weak. She told me she had climbed into a cupboard with a broken bottle and slit both her wrists. It was hardly the right moment to tell her we were over. I told her to come home and we'd talk about it.

I searched for some resolve deep inside and while I was waiting I had stern words with myself. My life wasn't in any sort of state to be able to support a crazy woman. I knew I couldn't put up with constant death threats, threats of suicide and general schizophrenic behaviour. I would calm her down, put her to bed then pack my bags and leave.

She arrived soon after I had made my decision and looked like death warmed up. She said she was OK but felt weak, as she had lost quite a bit of blood. Apparently she had passed out in the cupboard and had only been found when one of the people cleaning up opened it. They must have had quite a shock, as it's not a usual post party situation. I made her a cup of tea and sat her down, then tentatively asked her why she had done it. She told me that she thought I had gone off with someone else and that she couldn't stand the thought of me being with another woman. I listened, and told her I had been with the lads all night, I hadn't even looked at another woman. She looked down into her tea and started to cry.

Something inside me melted and I thought that if I'd paid her more attention then she would have been OK. My plans to leave disintegrated. I felt guilty but important. The woman I was sitting beside had tried to kill herself because of me. I wasn't going to let it happen again. I knew I had to stay and try to help her but I'd have to be seriously vigilant and watch her like a hawk. At the time I felt important and loved, as mad as she was she seemed to need me and love me, no one had ever done that before and I felt valued.

I was supposed to be working away, down in Somerset but Criss had other plans. She begged me not to go using her entire supply of feminine powers of manipulation. I was powerless so agreed. She was impossible to say 'no' to when she was like that in such a fragile state. I telephoned the boss and needless to say he was none too pleased. He offered me an increase, up to £100 a day, which under normal circumstances I'd have jumped at but not this time. Reluctantly I turned him down and put the phone back in its cradle. I was always a stubborn arsehole and once I'd told myself I was doing something I'd stick with it no matter what. That twisted sense of honour that mum and dad drilled into me was still there ready to mess me up all over again.

Getting local work didn't prove too difficult. Although I was a renowned drinker, I was always on time and always worked hard so was respected as a grafter, albeit a pissed one. I might have drunk like a fish but I worked like a mule. Monday morning I turned up at one of the most ramshackle pubs you could imagine. It was under new management and the owner was determined to make a go of it. The place was a total dive and he had his work cut out. Jim, the landlord, met me at the backdoor at 9am sharp. He was dressed in a white T-shirt, well I say white; it had white patches, the rest of it looked like a pint of Guinness had been liberally applied.

Jim was an ex-naval man and had a passion for two things in life, tradition and rum. His first words were to commend me for my timekeeping and his second were to invite me for a morning 'tipple'. Never one to refuse a drink I eagerly accepted. The morning tipple turned into a mid-morning session and before you could say, 'mine's a Pussers rum', it was lunchtime.

I'm not sure how I ever got my work done but the mess slowly disappeared. Jim and I would spend a large portion of the day chatting away and supping on pints of rum, or 'grog' as he called it.

Jim's wife, Queenie, was as bad as he was on the drinking front, so we formed a great little trio.

Criss was as chaotic as ever and I had got into a routine with her. It's amazing what you'll put up with once you've got used to it. At first all her madness seemed horrific and an impossible situation but after it had happened a number of times it becomes the norm and you just deal with it. At first I thought it was me that set her off but after watching her closely I soon realised that she was a dry mass of tinder and the spark was booze. She'd drink a bit and the fire would start. When she kicked off I got used to just being calm and quiet, made sure there were no sharp objects within reach and then it was a case of riding out the storm.

The first half a dozen times I found her passed out with pills scattered all about her, I flew into panic mode, called an ambulance and spent the night waiting for the inevitable news in the waiting room. The 'worst case' scenario never came and the nurse would inform me, with a sigh, that she had passed out drunk with very few pills actually inside her. It became a regular pattern, I'd find her, take her to the hospital, sit and wait, take her home and look after her while she whimpered on about never doing it again. I became totally blasé about it. I became a carer to her and after the umpteenth trip to the hospital I knew that maybe we needed to get some outside help.

She was great in the counselling sessions, all 'pity me' and 'poor me', telling tales of her traumatic childhood. She could have won Oscars for her performance. To start with I was hopeful but I soon realised it was just a front. Once out of the sessions she'd return to her old ways. She was a sweet tortured little girl in front of the counsellor and away from him would turn into her bitch from hell mode. It was quite a thing to behold. I guess I thought that if she could be nice for someone else then maybe one day she'd be all right with me.

Sometimes if I had been out by myself I'd return from the pub to find her pissed and coiled, tense and ready for a fight. I became a punch bag both verbally and physically. She blamed me for leaving her and blamed me that she was drinking. She'd drink and dwell on all her anger, guilt and frustration and wait until I walked through the door before unleashing it in giant verbal assaults. As usual I just stood there and soaked it all up like a human sponge. After all, in her eyes, it *was* my fault. The reason she was unhappy was me, her childhood was my fault, the Iran war was my fault, BUT NOTHING WAS EVER, EVER HER FAULT.

The irony was that I had stopped taking drugs, had controlled my drinking and was caring about someone for a change. In return I got a constant stream of verbal and physical abuse, not a great trade. The one time I clean myself up a bit I become a target for someone else's destructive behaviour.

I was becoming a well-known figure in the local police cells as well. If she had been on a bit of a bender then the violence level would increase. She had become increasingly violent but as it was gradual I guess I didn't really notice it. The once unacceptable had slowly become acceptable. She would find anything that was breakable and throw it at me, or the wall. She would whip herself into a one-woman destructive whirlwind and smash me with any objects she could get hold of, or find a sharp implement and slash herself. At the peak of her madness she'd scream at me to stop, and although I was a passive witness, she'd call the police and tell them she was being abused. Looking back I must have had my own screws loose to put up with it but I did. I was very patient with her, hoping for the lovely side to emerge and take control.

At the back of my mind I knew what she was doing. What she was really after was for me to give her a fucking good hiding, and then she'd have something real to hold on to. It was totally fucked up logic. She spent the whole time lying about me and giving out amazing levels of abuse and deluding herself that I was totally to blame and in her mind I was the abusive one. On my side I had to remain totally passive because if I ever did anything then she'd no longer be lying and she'd have won. In my mind I was in control because I was innocent, but if I lashed out then she'd be right and I would lose all my moral high ground. I would become the person she said I was and I never wanted to be that person. Looking back I can see just how screwed up the situation was and how sick I was for staying with her, the fact of the matter is, it was abuse and I had been used to being abused all my life, it felt normal, natural, I knew where I was with abuse, it was the only playing field where I knew all of the rules, thanks to my mum and dad.

This thought kept me calm and stopped me from ever hitting her no matter how bad the provocation got and at times it was severe. I remember being repeatedly hit with a lamp over and over, while she screamed all sorts of disgusting abuse at me and I had to retreat into my head where I replayed my twisted moral code whilst being battered. I remembered my Grandfather saying to my Mum," I only ever hit your mother with the flat of my hand", although I knew that not to be true. My code was never hit a woman ever, I stuck to it.

The other thing that kept me from going off at her was the knowledge that if I ever did go for her then that would be it. I had soaked up so much abuse that if the tables ever turned it would come out of me in an absolute torrent and I'd probably kill her.

Down at the local nick, I became quite friendly with the local desk sergeant, as I must have been arrested twenty to thirty times, for one thing or another, mainly Criss's lies. Each time I'd be picked up and then put in a cell overnight but I didn't mind too much. In my head I knew I was in the right and she'd never press charges, plus I got a good night's sleep in peace. The police presumed that Criss was telling the truth and it was only after a good few times of her phoning up the following day and dropping charges and me telling them my version that they finally came round and believed me. It sounds as if life was all doom and gloom and to be fair most of it was. The problem with these sorts of situations is that once you're in them, it's almost impossible to see a way out so you drift through life simply accepting what you're given. I couldn't leave her because she'd kill herself and I'd never hit her so things wouldn't reach a head that way. We just went round and round in circles, repeating cycles of destruction and I became more and more immune to it.

There were a few laughs outside the house though. I'll never forget Jim's face, the first time he opened the pub for lunch. In the local village, there was a young lady called Monica who lived for horses. They were her total passion and every Sunday she'd walk down to the field where her horse, Ginger stayed. She'd tack him up and exercise him for a few hours round the lanes and over the local fields. After galloping around for while she'd make her way back to the field via the pub. She'd been doing this for a while and couldn't stand to leave Ginger outside. The previous owner was a fellow horse lover and having no pride in his pub had been happy for Ginger to become a Sunday regular.

He'd squeeze through the door and stand at the bar drinking a pint or two of bitter from an ashtray before heading back to his field for a nap. As far as Ginger was concerned it was a perfect way to spend a Sunday afternoon. He was well known in the local as a novel regular and to my knowledge never once made a mess on the floor. He was no good at darts though and was a tight git, I never saw him buying a round. It was a very funny experience to sit at the bar drinking your afternoon pint with a horse.

The Sunday Jim re-opened the pub; Ginger walked in and took his usual position. To say Jim was shocked was an understatement. He just stood there open mouthed being told what to do by a couple of experienced regulars. It is still one of the funniest things I've ever seen.

I was living, for me, quite a clean life. I had cut right back on the drinking and had stopped taking drugs, so I needed something to fill the gap and decided to get back on a bike. I missed the adrenaline rush so shopped about and finally bought a Kawasaki 1000 custom. It was a serious bike and would do 75mph in second gear and still pull a wheelie. I got totally immersed in riding again and because I was riding all the time actually managed to stop drinking For the first time in as long as I can remember I was clean completely.

My bike was a beautiful burgundy colour, with loads of chrome; I used to hang out with an ex-professional rider, who raced at Brands Hatch and lots of other racetracks I can't remember the name of. He was shit hot and asked if he could have a ride. Being a new bike and the most precious thing I had I was hesitant but agreed as long as I sat on the back. He took off like the proverbial bat out of hell and didn't stop. Every gear was redlined and the front wheel was hardly on the ground apart from in the corners when the foot pegs would shower sparks behind us. I'd never experienced speed like that before and afterwards vowed I never would again, it was terrifying. I was convinced we were going to end up as a red pulp on the tarmac but we made it home, just, with both the bike and us in one piece.

The pub was finished and I wasn't working very often and Criss and I were spending more time together. It was actually quite good for a while and we got on well. We even managed to make it down to Cornwall for a camping trip on the bike; it was the best time we ever had together. I remember riding back to our home thinking that maybe things were finally going to be OK. We arrived back home in good spirits all ready to make a good go of it; then we opened the post.

In amongst the mountain of junk mail was a letter from Criss's sister, our landlady. The letter informed us that the rent hadn't been paid for ages and we owed her a couple of grand. I was totally taken aback as I had been giving Criss the rent money each month presuming that she had been paying it. I showed her the letter and she swore that she had given her sister the money. Criss put on quite a show and I believed her when she said the money had been paid. I phoned her sister and had a blazing row, accusing her of trying to con more money out of us.

The whole thing got completely blown out of proportion and solicitors became involved with threats of eviction and so on. I stood by Criss even though she was quite clearly lying through her teeth. She had a way of twisting me round her little finger by telling me how sorry she was and putting on a puppy-dog face. I got totally sucked in by the endless promises of 'it'll be alright soon'. The mythical perfect 'soon' never came.

Criss's father got involved as well and as he could never find fault with her took her side. So with Criss, her father and me all against the sister, she was outnumbered. I didn't enjoy lying but I was stuck, as I didn't have the two grand to pay off the arrears. However I did have my cherished bike. I reached a 'back against the wall' point and had to sell the bike. It went for half the price I paid for it and I was gutted. But, it got the courts off our back, smoothed out the family problems and meant things quietened down at home.

It was a huge loss having no bike, no job and living in a hamlet surrounded by pubs and two off-licences. I was also pissed off severely and depressed at the bike going. It was time to get back to familiar ground and before long we were in the pubs pretty much constantly.

My birthday was looming, now I was twenty it was another justification for a piss up. I knew I wanted a massive blowout, even though most Friday, Saturday and Sunday nights were big drinking sessions, this one was to be really big. The word went out and before I knew it thirty or so people was crammed into our little front room drinking heavily and generally partying. Things were going well and I even knew a few of the people there. Still, it wouldn't be a party if Criss didn't have a fight with someone for no apparent reason and tonight was going to be no exception.

A couple of guys had skinned up in the garden which, although didn't bother me, had for some reason sent Criss into her usual whirling dervish routine. Like Mount St Helens, she blew her stack. It was the same old pattern, language that would make a docker flinch, followed by pushing, shoving, slapping then kicking in that order. I never really understood how she managed it, as she looked like a strong wind would blow her over but once the fury was unleashed she was hard to stop.

Things escalated and it wasn't long before the back garden was in a state of bedlam. The whole place was turning into a massive bar room brawl when suddenly the door burst open and in charged two local policemen. The main copper lived up to his name and was a real nasty bastard. He stood there surveying the carnage. He had a reputation for being a bit over zealous with his fists and sure enough started to wade in. Now I'm being totally honest when I say that I was trying to calm things down and attempting to restore some sort of peace at this point but he singled me out, due to previous form I guess and back handed me. Cop or no cop I wasn't having it and thrashed out with my right fist. I caught him right on the jaw and he went flying. His younger stooge held him back and a couple of my mates grabbed my arms. We stood there struggling and spitting vile insults into each other's faces. As usual, there were a lot of people at the party that I didn't know and it turned out that one of these was the copper's daughter, who looked twenty but apparently was only fourteen. She was pissed out of her face, smoking a spliff and yelling at her Dad to 'fuck off and leave!' He grabbed her and stormed off, strange how I never got booked for hitting him.

In the morning, opening the living room door was a job in its self, what with the glass and other debris covering the floor. I started to hoover and came across a shiny metal object. Bending down to pick it up I realised it was the cap badge belonging to the policeman from the night before. I chuckled to myself as I slipped it into a pocket. That badge stayed with me for ages as a kind of talisman although it didn't seem to work much as I needed a lot more than a talisman to help me with my life at that time.

It was around this time that Criss announced she was pregnant. I remember having no fear at all and we were both delighted at the news, the relationship wasn't wanted but this child certainly was. We started making plans to buy our own home and begin the process of nest building. I knew that there was only one thing that would make a difference and enable us to realise our dreams, cash. I was going to be a good father and that meant nothing dodgy going on, I wanted a clean life, and house.

I started roofing and went at it full steam. I worked evenings, weekends, Bank Holidays, whatever it took to keep a steady stream of money rolling in. The only time I went to the pub was for a Friday evening drink and even then I took it easy. The parties stopped, Criss was doing her bit, she stopped getting drunk and cut right back on her cigarettes. We had finally got our act together. With the upcoming creation of our own little family, I think Criss really wanted to get in touch with hers. The row over the rent had caused quite a rift and her sister had cut all ties. Criss tried over and over to get in touch, phone calls, letters and desperate pleas to her father to intervene. They were all to no avail and Criss became very upset about it, she really wanted her sister to share in her good news and be part of her life again.

I arrived home one evening to find her slumped beside the sofa, the empty remains of half an off-licence wall scattered around her and a bottle of pills sitting on a table in front of her. Luckily she had drunk too much and passed out before she could take too many of the pills but it still gave me quite a fright. I had resigned myself to the fact that if she wanted to fuck herself up there was little I could do, but now there was another life to consider.

I wanted to yell and shake sense into her but I couldn't. I felt totally helpless, powerless to prevent her from her destructive actions. My baby was inside her and I could do nothing to protect it. I tried talking to her but she was on a giant guilt-trip and no one could shake her out of that. I tried using the baby as a reason to quit but she turned on the melodrama and wailed on about how the world would be a better place without her and everyone would be much better off. I'd been down this road too many times to bother holding her hand on the walk, so I shrugged and walked away frustrated, that night and went back to the cottage in the country where I had spent some of my good times. I had memories of Alison flooding back to me, although she wasn't at the cottage that night a couple of the boys were and for a little while I was back in the past amongst friends telling myself that everything would work out. Early the next day I returned to Criss, She told me she had lost the baby, at that moment I hated her, she had no emotion on her face, and said it as if she wanted to spite me. I simply walked out of the door, went to the pub and drank until I passed out there was nothing else I thought I could do. During the session I convinced myself that I would finally leave her but in the morning whilst hung over I gave up again, hoping for the change that never came.

With my head buried in the sand, my thoughts and feelings numbed I settled down to a routine of work. I was doing a lot of scaffolding around this time and a large percentage of the gang was travellers. We got on quite well and as always I was looking for ways to make money and was soon embroiled in my first money-spinner. I had befriended a guy called Jinx and he had a horse to sell but needed some help. The pony involved was called Ginger and at this point I thought that maybe all horses were called Ginger for some unexplained reason.

Ginger and I weren't the best of friends. I have to admit that animals didn't come too high on my list of priorities and I was pretty ignorant about what to do around them. One day shortly after our introduction, Ginger and I were in his field when he turned round to show me his flank. He kept going, till I was pretty much staring down a horse's arse. It didn't occur to me that anything was amiss as I presumed that this was another of the 'things' that horses did. I was just about to crack a joke when I was lifted off the ground and catapulted 10ft into air. Ginger had decided that I needed a good kick.

Now this wasn't the first time I'd been laid into, but there was usually a good reason. I jumped up and my initial reaction was to run up and smack the horse in the mouth. By the time I'd gone two steps I'd mentally weighed up the two sides of the impending fight and deciding that discretion being the better part of valour, Ginger could win this one. I walked away my pride in tatters, I'd been beaten-up by a fucking horse. Needless to say, my relationship with Ginger was on a downward spiral from that point on.

Not long after the decision was taken to sell Ginger and we made a couple of hundred quid on the deal so I let bygones be bygones. The peace I had made with Ginger was about to be shattered though, as part of the deal included delivery. The buyer's field was about five miles away via a busy shopping centre.

We were selling a snazzy looking two-wheeled trotting cart with the horse and they looked pretty cool together. Jinx needed to take the car so we could get back so I had no choice. I'd never driven a cart and horse before but not having tried something didn't usually put me off and after all I could drive a car, how difficult could it be? I got a quick crash-course on the main pointers and off we went. Armed with my new vocabulary, trot-on, walk and so on I climbed aboard and took the reins. I shouted at Ginger to walk-on but he just stood there. I tried again, nothing. I looked down at my hands and had a flash of inspiration, of course the reins. I'd seen plenty of Westerns and so knew what was missing. I whipped the reins the same way I'd seen John Wayne do it but was unprepared for the reaction it created. Ginger took off as if someone had lit a rocket in his arse. I nearly flew off the back of the cart but just managed to hold on.

I started yelling, 'whoa, whoa' at the top of my voice but Ginger didn't respond and was thoroughly enjoying himself galloping at full speed down a pretty small road with cars parked all the way down on either side, he was in seventh heaven charging straight onto the main road. The cars screeched to a halt and eyes bulged out of terrified driver's sockets. It must have been quite a sight.

Having started off with a professional demeanour, I now lapsed into full panic mode shouting again and again 'stop, stop, whoa you fucking stupid horse'. This didn't work. We hurtled through a red light, pedestrians running for cover with my apologies getting lost in our slipstream. We headed for the roundabout and using all my strength I pulled on the right rein, Ginger responded, just, and we hurtled round, the cart on one wheel. We were now out of the town and heading for the field. Somehow we had made it without causing injury. Eventually Ginger ran out of steam and slowed to a trot. However it was hardly an enjoyable country jaunt.

We arrived at the field, my cursing still strong and loud. I jumped down and hobbled out of kicking range. Jinx sauntered over, smiling. 'Everything all right?' he asked innocently." All fucking right?, I'll give you all right". From the tone in my voice Jinx knew not to ask any more questions. He even gave me trouble getting him into the field, I slammed the gate with an almighty crash and vowed that the paths of horses and myself would never again be crossed.

When I got home, all I was good for was collapsing in a heap on the sofa. Criss was in an unusually good mood and made a fuss of me making my tea and generally being lovely. I was too tired to be suspicious so just sat there smiling and accepting. Once my appetite had been satisfied I felt in better spirits. She sat down beside me and took my hand. She looked directly at me and beamed. 'I'm pregnant!' she said. I was happy but wished that I could carry the child as I didn't trust her as far as I could throw her, I resented her so much for loosing my first baby. We just sat there and hugged each other for ages. I knew that everything was going to work out this time round. The self-abuse that had killed our last baby wasn't going to be repeated. I didn't know what I would have to do to stop her from losing this baby but what ever it was I was prepared to do it.

Criss was ecstatic about being pregnant again. This time we were going to do everything right from the word go and that's what we did. We had early nights, ate properly, knocked the booze on the head and kept all the appointments at the doctors, so other than feeling ill because of the withdrawals from not having any booze, for a while everything actually did fall into place and we lived happy contented lives. Criss was blooming and her radiance was matched by her mood. I had my head down working hard and making a nice little home for the soon to be three of us. I had decided after a look at our finances that I needed to get some stability in my life. If I was to provide a secure home for a baby then consistency was the key. I wanted to buy a house so I went looking for a 'proper' job. It wasn't long before I became a postman. I hated it, every minute. Struggling out of bed every morning was hard enough at 4am, but the trudge round in all weathers would leave me totally knackered and despondent on some days. Still it did the trick and meant I could get a foot on the housing ladder.

Criss was still phoning her sister, unable to bear her rejection. One night after I had collapsed into bed exhausted after my days work, Criss decided in her own twisted way to burn the house down to get back at her sister, I didn't find out that Criss started the fire till four years later, at the time Criss set fire to the house using the rubbish bin as the fire set, it looked like it had been started by an electrical socket that was above the bin and I just took the fireman's word for it. Criss woke me after starting the fire and once the house was full of smoke, her selfish, mad, stupid actions left us with nothing except her in her nightly and me in a pair of jeans and a pair of Dr Martins. As I stood fifty yards away from the burning house I knew we weren't insured and so did Criss, so there we were outside the burning house with me comforting poor little Criss. If only I knew then what I know now. Over the next few days we stayed at her dads whilst I went hell for leather earning money to start over from scratch, having nothing never bothered me but it wasn't just me now was it?. After a couple of weeks I had earned enough money to get us into a small flat, looking back it was a shabby shit hole, but it was the best I could get at the time and it got us out of her Dads house. As far as I am aware Criss never did rebuild a relationship with her sister. The day the contractions started I was sitting in the sorting office blissfully unaware. Criss didn't call me; she sat in the house suffering the pain until I got home. For ages I had been planning the 'special' moment but it still hits you like a bolt from the blue when it arrives. In a panicked state I rushed round the flat getting all the carefully laid out necessities and we bundled everything into the car including ourselves. I stayed throughout the birth, which isn't meant as a grandiose statement, My reckoning was that if the woman had to be there, then so should the man. That night my daughter was born, Laura.

The first time I held her in my arms I felt I had witnessed a miracle, my miracle. I was besotted with her and couldn't get enough. I was a doting father and did every feed and changed her. Her big brown eyes could melt anybody's heart at fifty paces and I stood by as people stopped and commented on how beautiful she was. Shortly after Laura was born, Criss and me decided to marry, it was a small affair at a registry office and we had a monumental piss up before during and after.

I wanted our home to be secure for Laura but it didn't take long for Criss to return to her old ways. Looking back I now know how ill she must have been and that she needed serious help but at the time it was down to me and I went into sponge mode. I lost count of the times I would find her collapsed on the floor with pills scattered round her with me wondering how many she'd taken. Another favourite trick was to cut her wrists then call the police to tell them her husband had attacked her with a knife. The routine would play out the same way every time. The police would come round, arrest me, throw me in the station cells and I'd wait for her to sober up and call them to get me released. The time spent in jail was terrifying because I would sit in the cell panicking over Laura and what might have happened to her. It was such a relief every time I got home and found her safe.

The stupidity of some of the police never failed to amaze me. How anyone, let alone a member of the 'protection' force, could leave a clearly drunk and unbalanced woman, who had supposedly just been attacked, to look after a baby was beyond me. She used 999 as her personal chat line but the police always took her side and were somehow blinded to the facts. Many a time they'd turn up, after she'd been in a manic state on the phone telling them all sorts of stories about me beating her up and worse, to find a woman without any fresh cuts or bruises, just the self harm scars across her arms and wrists and a calm husband trying to tell the truth. In all cases, whom do you think they believed? It must have taken dozens of visits and arrests before they finally believed *me* and started to understand she was a lying nutter.

If I sound bitter about all that happened, it's because I am. It seemed like I never got a break from it. But what did I do? Like a fucking idiot I stayed with her. After every episode I forgave her and as I stood there listening to her apologies flood out through rivers of tears I thought to myself that maybe this time she would act on her words. Deep down I knew the truth; it would never stop. It was like being on a roller coaster, up and down the whole time but hoping that the ride would eventually stop. I was convinced that if I tried my hardest and never gave up I'd eventually make a difference and would bring her out of her troubles.

You may be thinking it was some kind of post-natal depression but it wasn't. She was like this before the birth and my experience of her had never been different. The truth is she was very ill and I didn't know how to help her. All I could do was provide a rough blanket of support and basically let her do what she wanted. I would stand by watching as she behaved in a myriad of destructive ways and tread on eggshells when around her hoping that she didn't get upset. I was fighting a losing battle but couldn't swallow my pride enough to allow myself to admit defeat.

In the middle of the bedlam, we managed to buy a beautiful little house in my hometown. During the moving process I had created all sorts of images of how this was going to be the big break, a new house, a new life. What a load of bollocks that was. Within the first week we had met the local police. I was still working as a 'postie' from 5am to 10am. Although this sounds like half a day I was actually running my round so I could get back in time to take Laura to work with me on the farm. And so it went on like this, working from 5am to 5pm holding down two jobs, looking after Laura during the day and changing her or feeding her at night. Sleep was a rarity and I didn't mind as long as Criss stayed pressure free.

Taking away all of her responsibility might seem like a bad idea but I'd tried everything else and nothing had worked. I was determined that Laura would be cared for properly and Criss was in no fit state to do it so I shouldered the responsibility.

One evening Criss announced to me that she thought it would be a good idea to have another baby. I was shell-shocked. I sat there trying to understand how she could even consider how she could have another baby when she couldn't look after the one we already had. In the silence created by my incapacity to talk she reeled off a list of reasons. By the time she'd finished I could simply manage a smile and as usual she started to nag me on a daily basis to get her own way, which eventually wore me down into saying yes. At night, as I reflected, I knew this wasn't a good idea. Me coping with a mad woman, two babies and two jobs, but even so I could see some positive points. Laura did need a brother or sister and selfishly, I thought that if Criss was pregnant then at least she wouldn't be going out, getting drunk, coming home and forcing me to go out and pummel some new bloke who had made a pass at her. That might sound callous but she calmed down when she was pregnant and I could really do with a break from her destructiveness.

It wasn't long before she fell pregnant and true to form she changed completely during the pregnancy. She was happy, calm and for most of the time actually OK to be around. The release of pressure on my responsibilities was fantastic; we were a family and I relaxed and enjoyed life again. She even suggested that I go out every now and again. This was great and I threw myself into the booze, guilt free if only for one night a week. I didn't lose it though as I still had my two jobs and a house to run, albeit a slightly easier one now that Criss was helping out.

Adie, my son, was born and again my heart melted. He was so beautiful and I remember thinking how he'd grow into a heartbreaker because he was so gorgeous. I loved my kids and still do more than words on a page can ever describe. I approached our first Christmas together with gathering joy, tempered with some trepidation, as I thought it would be a perfect time for all of us. I was so looking forward to it and hoped that Criss would be all right.

The day itself went well, the kids loved all the excitement and the presents were given and received with broad smiles and lots of giggles. In the evening a couple of friends came round and I remember sitting there thinking about what a lovely day it had been, I walked out of the kitchen and turned to face the stairs going up and there was Criss hanging from the banisters, a dressing gown cord tied round her neck and her legs kicking. I got her down and as usual she was half cut and a nasty bitch. As I was getting her down I cursed the Doctors who had failed to section her, and the police who left her time and again with the children even though I had told them what was going on.

Criss was getting increasingly difficult to manage. Now Adie had been born her old behaviour returned and this time it was more frequent and more destructive. Looking back I should have left but I couldn't leave the kids and she would cry and beg me not to go. I didn't want people to think that I couldn't make it as a husband and father. The same behaviour happened time and time again, the stories of other men and me charging out to defend her honour was common. In fact, I went out looking forward to the fights as they gave me an opportunity to release my anger. We were travelling in ever decreasing circles. Each time I reached a new level I was amazed at how far down a path so painful, human beings can travel.

I just felt numb or in pain all of the time but at least the painful parts proved to me that I was still alive, the rest just happened in a strange fog. If you can't understand then I pray that you never do and if you do understand then you have my deepest sympathy straight from the heart.

It amazes me how people can get so used to physical and emotional pain but when that's all they live with they become so used to it, it becomes normal. On the odd occasion that we did go out together Criss would more often than not cause trouble. One such situation happened one evening in our local. We were both in the pub, drinking with two different groups of friends at opposite ends of the bar. The evening was going along OK and I was enjoying myself. I ordered a scotch and as I was bringing the glass to my lips Criss suddenly stormed across the bar, grabbed the drink from my hands and threw it into my face.

If this had been a bloke, he'd have been smeared across the nearest wall within the following five seconds, but with Criss I had learned how to remove the initial rush of temper and hold it somewhere in my mind whilst externally I stayed calm. The pub had gone silent and the atmosphere became charged like the air before a storm. I looked at her and with a level voice said, 'Can I have some more water with that next time, please.' I didn't want to give her the satisfaction of me reacting at all so she could launch into accusations about how I was always like this and then reel off a list of stories detailing my violent behaviour towards her to get the pub's support and sympathy although most people knew what she was like by now.

I walked out of the pub hating her and wishing this mad horrible bitch wasn't the mother of my children. The walk home was about half a mile and I knew that the walk would help calm me down, as it usually did. Then I heard the click clacking of Criss's high heels behind me and the abuse started. She was yelling uncontrollably at my back doing the usual thing of vomiting out her usual foul, vile words. When she got within range I would receive the obligatory punches in the back of the head and lower back. Normally I would go to a part of my mind that allowed me to ignore her attacks but tonight I couldn't seem to calm down.

Somehow Criss managed to avoid death that night. I say this because it was the closest I had ever come to giving back to her the abuse she gave out. I was ready to bloody kill her. She just wouldn't stop and I had no escape. Eventually I exploded. I turned on her and with full force and three and a half years of accumulated rage grabbed her coat lapel and thrust her up against the nearest car. I let fly a right punch with all the strength I had that would have taken her head clean off. Instead, it went straight through the window of the car shattering the glass into hundreds of little pieces, even after every thing she had done I still couldn't hit a woman not even that horrible bitch. With my face an inch from hers I screamed with my throat burning, 'Shut the fuck up, just shut the fuck up!'

She was visibly shocked and did go quiet. I turned and carried on walking home. I was trembling as the adrenaline coursed through my veins and I didn't feel any pain. I could feel the blood dripping but didn't know how bad it was. When I got in I examined my hand under the light and only then did I see the scale of the damage. In the movies, some action star will quite happily punch through a window and then arrest some guy without a scratch. In reality it doesn't quite happen like that.

My hand looked like it had been through a blender. My right little finger was almost severed and was hanging on by a small amount of skin and a few stringy bits of tendon. The knuckles were all bleeding and my bone was clearly visible. This was not good. I didn't panic, as I never did; this was hardly the first time something like this had happened to me but I knew I'd have to act immediately. I found the tin of needles we had and took out the cleanest one I could find. I held it under my lighter flame and then poured a capful of disinfectant over my hand. As I looked properly I realised that there were bits of glass embedded in various bits of my hand and went to get my toolbox. After locating my long nose pliers I began the process of removing all the glass. I knew I had to be really careful so I didn't do any more damage to my little finger. After all I didn't want to lose it.

After removing all the glass I could see, I sat down at the table to begin the sewing. It was difficult, as there was so much blood. I took off my belt and tying it in a tourniquet round my arm stemmed the flow of blood a bit. I put together the various flaps of skin, like placing the last pieces of a jigsaw, and began to sew. It was a really difficult job. Pushing a needle through human skin is much harder than you'd think; it's like old shoe leather.

I sat there struggling with every stitch, sweat pouring off me and had nearly finished when the door suddenly flew off its hinges and five policemen rushed through in full riot gear. There was nothing I could do really and after the initial shock, it just seemed par for the course. Criss, bless her, had called the cops and told them I had lost it with her and beaten her severely, smashed up a car and was going home to kill the children. No wonder they sent the riot squad. However, the picture they'd been given was far from the truth. I calmly went with them to the hospital and had my hand dealt with properly, which I'm still grateful for.

I spent the next twenty-four hours in the cell, periodically chatting to the desk sergeant. Our conversations focused on one topic, me leaving Criss. Despite his best efforts he couldn't convince me although I wish he had. I was actually looking forward to going home, as I knew I'd get a week of grovelling. It wasn't long before the expected call came in, which totally exonerated me. The sergeant wished me good luck with a wry smile; he knew I'd be back. Looking back I can see how they must have thought that I was one of 'those poor bastards', who couldn't see the wood for the trees and they were right, for some reason I allowed my madness to go on, always feeling like I deserved to be punished just for being me.

Although I lived in this chaos I managed to keep some semblance of normality, in terms of external appearances. My family knew nothing about what was really going on, although I'm sure that hardly talking to them helped. Criss's family was kept more or less at arms length as well but then her father became ill. He had always been a fit man for his age but recently he had become very poorly. He was seventy-two and it had started with a bout of pneumonia and then he had put his back out. Once the problems started, he went down hill pretty rapidly. He didn't seem to be able to recover and had been for a load of tests. The results came back and he was diagnosed with cancer.

It was a quick demise and before long he was dead. If that sounds callous then it shouldn't. I didn't really know him well and my thoughts were quite selfish. I knew that once he was gone the burden of looking after Criss would fall squarely on my shoulders, a task I didn't really relish. I did feel sorry that he was gone but my reaction was nothing compared to Criss's.

Up until the time of the funeral she had more or less held it together or at least was grieving in a semi-healthy way. She was able to talk through her feelings and describe how she felt although she struggled when she wanted to cry, as the tears never seemed to flow fully. She also had the problem of her stepmother. The woman was straight out of Cinderella. She was a vicious and vindictive bitch, so screwed up herself that she took it out on the rest of the world.

On the day of the funeral she asked if we wouldn't mind not going to the farm for a few days as she said she needed a few days alone to get over things. Naturally, during her time of need, we agreed. We left a week for all concerned to get over their initial grief and then made our way down to the farm. When we arrived we were totally blown away by what we found. The house had been completely cleared. There wasn't anything; the place had been gutted. There were no furnishings in the house and anything of value had been stripped. It was like no one had lived there for a long time and the stepmother was nowhere to be found.

To say we were gob smacked doesn't quite do our feelings justice. We both stood there trying to figure out exactly what had happened. The cherry on the cake appeared in the form of a skip, conveniently parked behind one of the sheds. Piled up inside were all the sentimental things associated with Criss's life. All the pictures she had drawn as a child, pictures our kids had drawn, and basically anything you could think of that would have pulled the old man's heartstrings. Criss was devastated. She stood in front of the skip looking at it with a blank expression on her face unable to comprehend what she was seeing, her life in a skip. All I could do was try to console her knowing that this was going to be the calm before the storm.

We went back to the car in silence and drove home without saying a word. I tried to concentrate on the driving and attempted to block out her pain but couldn't. As I sat beside her I could feel her anguish and desperately wanted to help her but there was nothing I could do. It hurt me so much knowing I couldn't take her pain away. I knew then that despite everything I must have loved her, despite the abuse she dealt out.

Back home it was like a black cloud had settled over our house. The grieving continued and Criss was in a rough state. She smoked almost non-stop and one night, after the shops had shut she ran out of fags. I told her I'd nip down the pub for some and whilst there bumped into Butch. He launched into a rant about the 'bitch' I was with and that I should leave her. Now, as with most people, it's fine for *you* to slag off your wife but if anyone else had a pop then that was out of order. So, I stood there and gave him two options, either apologise or step outside; I'd fallen for the oldest one in the book.

Butch opened the pub door for me and as I naively walked through it he punched me on the back of the neck. He smacked me a right goodun' and I stumbled forwards as he went for more of the same. As I regained my feet I managed to fend off two haymakers. Once I had regained my balance I reined a series of blows and got him with half of them, one a good juicy right hook. The fight descended into mayhem with fists, feet and head butts flying about all over the place. It finally reached a point with Butch on the ground and me straddling him in control. I was about to hit him with all my might when a bottle came out of nowhere and for a moment I passed out. I woke up to see one of Butch's mates standing over me with a grin on his face and a broken bottle in his hand, People came running out of the pub to see what the hell was going on, Butch was lifted to his feet and his mate was slagged off as being a coward, which he was, leaving me on the floor rubbing my head. I hated losing fights, especially if they were unfair.

I started the walk home knowing that Butch was right, she was a bitch and a nutter but again that misplaced sense of loyalty that mum and dad drove into me had worked.

Criss was none too impressed with my gallantry and after some calming down finally realised that maybe it wasn't totally my fault. She had taken to long walks around the farm trying to come to terms with her father's death but I couldn't see how it was really helping as she seemed to be wallowing in pain rather than trying to find a positive way through it. She had settled into a nightly rhythm of drinking slowly till about twelve and watching telly or videos. For me there was some respite as at least she was quiet. One night I was woken from sleep about 3am by noises downstairs. As Criss wasn't in bed I presumed it was her and went down to see if she was OK. As I entered the kitchen I saw her fully clothed and distraught. I couldn't work out what was wrong but went over to comfort her. She fell into a hug and sobbing into my shoulder told me that she had been for a walk to the farm and in a fit of anger she had set alight the farmhouse.

One of the good things about living in a mad world is that very little shocks you, and so I just hugged her saying, 'there, there, don't worry'. In my mind I wasn't that bothered, as there was no one in the house so there was no danger. My immediate concern was for the old bill as they were sure to be round any minute, as it wouldn't take a rocket scientist to work out who the main suspects in the fire would be.

And sure enough at 5am we got a knock on the door and it was time to answer a few questions. I was quite taken aback by their thoroughness and speed. By the time they had got to us they had already worked out that it was a break and entry and the fire was definite arson.

We were told what had happened and informed that we were the only probable suspects and therefore were being arrested for questioning. Without thinking it through fully, I admitted full responsibility. It was a protective knee jerk reaction, as I knew that Criss wouldn't be able to take a full questioning at the cop shop. I didn't really worry about me, my only concern was for Criss and so I stepped up and took it on the chin.

I sat in the questioning room and calmly told the officers how Criss's dad had died and then elaborated the story about the evil stepmother and then confessed to entering the house and burning it down. I claimed that my motive was revenge against the stepmother. They questioned me substantially and I thought I had done a good job. At one point the copper asked me about my relationship with my father-in-law and I said straight faced that I had got on with him like a house on fire; I think he realised I was being sarcastic at that point.

After the interview I was bailed and left to go home. As I was leaving I saw Criss go in for her turn and looked across knowing that our stories were going to be completely different. The copper asking the questions was as sharp as a razor and from the look on his face I knew that he had already worked out the truth but there was nothing I could do.

As it turned out, Criss made a huge mistake in her planning. The silly cow had booked a taxi to take her to the barn and then asked him to wait. The taxi had driven right into the yard and waited whilst she broke in and set fire to the place, then she asked him to take her home! For the cops it was pretty much an open and shut case. The outcome was that I got threatened with wasting police time and Criss was charged with arson.

When she got home she was in a real state and stayed like that for days. When she was awake she was always scared about what was going to happen to her and she hid from this in booze and anger. Naturally when she needed someone to yell at, it was me. Hiding what was going on from the kids was really tough. I hated lying to them and they knew something was wrong. It certainly didn't help that Criss was going out on drinking binges and coming home in the early hours with a drunken entourage who thought it was OK to put on loud music whilst the kids were sleeping in bed, criss couldn't have given a toss about anyone or anybody but herself.

Time and time again I'd wait up for her, get too tired, fall into bed and then have to get up a few hours later to come downstairs, turn the music off and kick everyone out. Once the house was empty of drunks the fighting would start. I'd have to stand there soaking up all her abuse and then she'd switch from me onto herself and start with the threats and attempted action of wrist cutting. After this would be the passing out stage and in the morning she'd be in full self-loathing mode and I'd turn from punch-bag to ashtray as she kept trying to stub her cigarettes out on me and then into her comforter. This merry-go-round of madness never seemed to stop and I'm not quite sure how or why I kept going, but I did.

It became so normal, like watching the telly; part of my mind shut down, it was like I was there but not there. To an outsider it would have looked like an intensely emotional row but from the inside I just went through the motions with no feelings, I had run out. All I felt was shame and despair and over whelming love for my children.

I didn't really share my problems with anyone. The people I hung out with weren't what you'd call real friends and I had hardly any contact with my family. The only people I really spent any time with were connected to the only true friend I knew, alcohol. Whenever I had the chance I'd be straight on the booze and with the alcoholic blanket wrapped round me the problems faded away and for a short while I was free. However, as the sobering-up began they floated back to me as if on elastic until reality finally found me again, ready to slap me in the face.

8
Off to the seaside

As the court case loomed in front of us the tension became intolerable. Criss was permanently on edge, ready to kick off anytime and my nerves were totally shot. I knew she wouldn't cope with the court and the thought of prison didn't even bare thinking about. One night we sat there talking it through and I had a flash of genius. I knew that there was only one thing we could do and like any self-respecting alcoholics with a serious problem we moved. In the world we lived in it was called a geographical. All we had to do was decide where and after discussion we agreed the coast, so the decision was made. It was a real turning point in my journey and when I look back I can see that if I was on a rocky path to begin with, this turn took me well and truly out of the frying pan and into the fire. Without doubt, it was the worst decision in my life, except for getting together with Criss that is. At the time it was exciting and seemed to be the chance of a new start. I didn't see the pattern then but now it's as clear as day. Trying to move from your problems is like trying to run away from your own legs.

After a few scouting trips I found a place that I knew would be right for us, St. Leonards. I knew it was right, as St. Leonard was the patron saint of nutters and vagabonds, perfect. It was easy to find a flat and we were ready to go. I posted the keys to our house through the letterbox of the building society that held the mortgage, loaded up the van and we drove off to begin our new life. The weather was clear and sunny and as we drove into town we saw the sun gleaming on the sea and breathed in the fresh new air. It was fantastic being in a new place where no one knew our mad existence and us. To everyone we saw we were just a nice little family, rather than the dysfunctional, destructive hopeless cases we actually were. I can say hand on heart that even with all this bedlam going on I tried my best to look after my children and despite Criss`s attempts to sabotage our lives at every opportunity I was doing a good job, looking back I can see that I should have given myself a pat on the back for the effort I put in, I had been on the edge of a break down since being with Criss but had kept going because I loved my children so much.

Our first exploration on arrival was down to the beach. I took the kids with me and we played around for hours, it was a great day and I really thought that this time was the time it was all going to change. The trip to the beach turned into a daily routine at least for the kids and me. Criss would either stay at home drinking or be down the pub. Although I enjoyed the trips to the beach there was a big part of me, the addict that wanted to be in the pub as well. I would come home and act all self-righteous because I wasn't drinking and was fulfilling my parental duties whilst she was getting trashed. Inside it was jealousy that created my anger because that's what I wanted to do as well at times.

I remember one morning I was walking along the beachfront and came to the part where the drunks and layabouts hung out. I looked at them with contempt in my eyes and heart. I thought how disgusting they were, strewn along the front like human litter. I regarded them as scum and mentally compared myself to them as I caught my reflection in a shop front.

Criss's drinking had sunk to a new level and it was pretty much all she did. This meant finding companions with the same habit and it wasn't long before some of the 'scum' started coming round to the flat to take her out to drinking places. I was furious and completely disapproving we had row after row about it, she started staying out overnight and only coming home to get changed. I didn't mind at first, it was good to have a break from her and I liked being able to relax with the kids.

After a month of living like this, basically on my own, Criss returned from one of her jaunts, smelling like she'd slept in a brewery, and announced that she had her own flat and the kids and her were moving out.

My emotions were at breaking point and we had the row from hell, I wasn't about to let her go off with my children but I didn't have anything left. Inside I knew that all I wanted was a rest, a rest from everything, I felt powerless as she pointed out spitefully how the law wouldn't give me the time of day, she was such a good liar and I knew she would get her own way somehow. I caved in hoping she would let me see my children and knowing she wouldn't manage, and that I would be there to pick up the pieces. The addict in me was thrilled and was already looking forward to the self-annihilation before the door had shut on their leaving. The relief from being permanently worried about where she was and whom she was with was immense and I felt like a lead cloak had been taken off me. The fear for the children's health stayed with me though and got worse. Although Criss had said I could visit and have them as often as I wanted, the reality was very different. I found it almost impossible to contact her and when I did finally get hold of her she had the Mr Hyde-side turned on. I just left them alone hoping that if I didn't make her angry then she couldn't take it out on the kids, a weird logic but it worked for me.

The need to drink and escape my reality was strong within me and soon the pub at the end of my road became my second home. It was quiet, which was perfect for me, as all I wanted was to drink in peace. An added bonus was that Criss's cohorts never went in it, which was important. She had by now told anyone who'd listen, what a bastard I was and how much of a bully I had been to her and the children, beating them all. She was whipping up great clouds of sympathy wherever she went and everyone soaked it up just as they always had.

Naturally this made my life a bit interesting, as in certain circles I was public enemy number one. There was nothing I could do about it other than run round telling everyone the truth but if it was a 'who's telling the truth competition'; I think I knew who'd win. I knew there were a few characters that were out to get me to administer some street justice so I was always ready for it. It was just tiring keeping on your guard the whole time. This was another justification I gave myself for staying in the pub. Criss had made my life hell whilst I was with her and now she was making it hell for me now that I wasn't with her.

I'd made a friend in the pub, well, more like drinking partner. His name was Phil and he was a real character, always dressed in a blazer with a military motif on the pocket. He was ex-army and proud of it and he was loaded and loved to talk. If you got him into conversation you were quid's in on the drinking front as he bought all the rounds. This became a habit, as it was easy listening and free booze.

One night we'd been chatting away, I was drunk and happy. I said my good-byes at the pub door and began my cold walk home. It was a crisp night and the air smelled fresh, it was at times like this I would think to myself that maybe life wasn't to bad after all and the constant weight of depression that was always in my head would start to become a little lighter. About a hundred yards up the road two guys suddenly jumped out on me from a dirty allyway. One guy held me from behind and had hold of my arms so I couldn't strike out; the other stood in front of me, a vicious grin on his face and a baseball bat in his hand. He took a back swing and aimed for my head. I reacted instinctively, knowing that a blow with the bat would be serious trouble for me, and tossed my head back with all my force. I heard a crunch and the guy behind let go immediately. I knew I'd broken something, either his nose or teeth, hopefully both.

Just as I got free the guy with the bat swung out wildly and caught me a glancing blow on the left shoulder. Although it was better than getting a knock in the head it still fucking hurt and this spurred me on. I kicked him full in the stomach. Combined with the motion of his swing it doubled him over and spun him round. He shouted something and started a stumbling run down the road zigzagging in pain. I was still filled with the bloodlust that a fight brings on and turned round looking for the other guy. He was sitting on the pavement in shock, holding his face with blood dripping through his fingers. I looked down at him and going against my honour to not kick a man when he's down, laid into him with all my anger.

The punk got a right thrashing. I kicked him in the head and stomach and as he rolled up into the foetal position to protect himself I went in to give him another dose of kicking. I stood there laying into him, kicking him over and over. I was getting out of control and then someone grabbed my arms and presuming it was the other guy returned, I spun round, ready for the next onslaught. With my arm cocked and fist clenched I sighted my prey but stopped mid punch as it turned out to be Phil. He had heard the shouting as he was walking home and had turned round and seen the whole fight. I'm glad he stopped me as the red mist had taken over and I didn't feel in control of what I was doing and might have killed someone. As usual I was unable to allow anyone see the pain I was in, I was aching like I had been run over by a truck but Phil asked me if I was OK and I assured him that I was, he asked me if he could trust me "course you can fuckin trust me, what you talking about?". I replied. Myself and Phil made arrangements to meet at the pub the next day. Phil had some work for me that I knew was dodgy I just didn't know how dodgy. I met Phil the next day at the pub at the time we agreed, as it turned out Phil was on the brink of bankruptcy and had a car lot, the plan was I brought the cars off of Phil for next to nothing, then we sold them on still cheap and split the cash, of course money never changed hands when I bought the cars from Phil all that did was to change the owner of the car from Phil to me, just so the bankruptcy receiver couldn't take it off of Phil. Phil and I didn't discuss the amount I would get but he said he would sort me out and I did trust him on that score. Over the next couple of weeks I worked on Phil's car lot and I was a good sales man. I lost count of the cars we sold but we got rid of all of them, at the end of this Phil gave me an envelope with a lot of money in it, eight grand. I couldn't believe my luck I knew what Phil was doing was a little dodgy but as far as I was concerned I was just working as a car sales man for a couple of weeks, when the receivers moved in on the car lot me and Phil planned to go on a monumental piss up, the only fly in the ointment was a previous customer that owed Phil a couple of grand, Phil had asked him for the cash several times and had been given the run around and told to fuck off. Phil was a nice fella and could have done with the cash going bankrupt. We decided on a last ditch attempt at trying to get his cash and paid the gezza a visit, we drove to the address, it was a nice house in a middle class area, the house must have been a three or four bedroom with its own drive and garage, we parked up and knocked on the door, the bloke who answered it was stocky dripping in gold was bald and had an attitude like was trying to be an east end gangster, his first and only words to Phil were "You can fuck off too or I'll set the fucking dogs on ya". He then tried to slam the door on us, his attempt at this failed as I was already half way through it, he was all mouth and I had met his type a hundred times befor, he tried to punch me, then tried to kick me both of which I dodged, I had to defend myself and landed a right hook on his jaw making him fall backwards. Before he hit the ground I was standing over him ready to smack him again, needless to say it wasn't warranted and he verbally pleaded with me to back off, the geezer was a pussy. Phil was paid in full out of his wallet no less, all the loose ends had been tied up and Phil took me on the monumental piss up he promised. I remember going to the pub but that's about it.

I woke up to find the ceiling three feet above my head and it took me a while to work out I had passed out under the pool table. My throat was closed and my body was completely fucked. I rolled over twice and got to my knees. I looked around at the other bodies strewn across the floor and shuddered; it must have been one hell of a night.

After checking my inside pocket to make sure the cash was still there I crawled over to the bar. I climbed up the nearest barstool like a ladder and croaked a request for port and brandy. My hands were shaking so much that I had to hold the glass with both of them and make my mouth meet the glass rather than the other way around. The landlord who was bottling up asked for the money and with a trembling fist I emptied the contents on the bar, as I was shaking to much to count it. Phill was gone, I never saw him again.

I struggled for fifteen minutes trying to force the booze down. It was a battle between my mind knowing it would help my body and my body refusing any more poison. As I sat heaving and swallowing, my mind wandered to the money and what I was going to do with it. The thoughts didn't take long to reach the images of my children's faces and I smiled through the pain at the thought of spoiling them. Deeper inside my addict smiled too.

I stumbled through the door of the pub and into the next chapter of my life knowing I had an uphill struggle ahead of me. In my absence I knew that Criss would have been spreading all sorts of rumours about me and I might as well have bought a T-shirt saying 'Wife and child beater' on the front. I laid low for the rest of the day recovering as I thought I might need my strength in case one of the many gullibles Criss had convinced might want to 'jib me up', which means to stab as Criss so delightfully put it.

The unfathomable amount of hate she had engendered in me was boiling away as I tried to think of my next moves. Now I'd had time away from her and gained perspective, albeit warped, I knew with a rock-solid certainty that I wanted no part in her life. I also knew I needed to be apart from her. I weighed up all my feelings and knew that I had to face her for the sake of my children; I desperately wanted to see them. Once my mind was made up I felt pretty confident about it. I had a big wedge of cash in my pocket and was ready for anything including the dangerous crowd she now hung about with. As my Granddad always told me, 'don't worry about the one in the gang, look out for the one on his own'.

After getting some supplies I lay on the bed and began preparing to call Criss. This preparation mainly involved drinking a bottle of vodka. I picked up the phone and waiting for the worst, dialled the number. She answered and was perfectly reasonable, considering she hadn't heard from me in nearly two weeks, she even said she was worried. I didn't believe a word of it but played along and made arrangements to meet the following day. That night I slept deeply as I was exhausted and drunk, as I was virtually every night. I woke up and finished off the vodka, just topping up my system to the point of working. I had my plan, formulated the night before. I was going to get

the kids loads of presents and as soon as Criss saw me
plant a load of cash in her hand, that should shut her up,
simple but effective I thought.

After trawling all the toyshops I made my way down to the
sea front for the arranged meeting. I saw the kids first and
shouted to them. They came running down the front and
threw themselves into my arms shouting 'Daddy, Daddy',
the sweetest sound in the world. After the beauty I looked
up for the beast and sure enough, Criss was heading
towards me with thunder in her eyes. I strode out to meet
her and as she opened her mouth to speak thrust a few
hundred quid into her hand. It had the desired effect, at
least for the time being, and she said 'thanks' and walked
back to her bench diffused.

That afternoon was the best time I'd spent with the kids
since Criss had left. We played on the beach for hours just
like we used to and then went through the bags of presents
with shrieks of delight. It was a wonderful time, only
spoiled by the daggers constantly in my back from the eyes
of Criss's cohorts. She was sat on the bench with a ring of
drunks around her in varying stages of decay. I kept
glancing at them throughout the afternoon and despised
them. In my eyes they were scum, although exactly what
the difference is between drunk on the street or a drunk in
a pub escapes me, but it kept me feeling superior.

I knew that one of them would want a pop at me at some
point but carried on playing with the children. With my
money in her pocket, Criss was able to splash out on
bottles of cheap cider and cans of Tennant's Super. She
liberally passed them round to her support team and the
lot of them got increasingly drunk as the day wore on. It
was like being watched by a pack of hungry wolfs waiting
to move in for the kill.

At mid-afternoon the kids and I walked back towards the
bench and Criss got up to confront me, the guy she was
with got up with her. With booze running through her it
was back to the good old days and I got myself ready for
the onslaught. As I got within hearing distance she started
up. A stream of half-understandable abuse was levelled at

me with the guy next to her trying to back it up with a variety of threatening looks.

She had gone into her mental mode and was trying all her old tricks to provoke me. As ever I just stood there and took it. I sighed in the middle of a tirade and told her that she wasn't worth me wasting any time on her and turned round to the kids. It was a mistake. The guy stepped forwards and the next thing I knew I'd been punched in the back of the head. Then it went off. I turned and swept away his legs and once he was on the deck repeatedly smashed into his face with my fists. He cowered and tried to protect himself as I waded in with my feet as well. The crowd around Criss had turned from cheering him on to yelling at me. They advanced on mass and surrounded me. For me, this was just a small increase in the challenge as I lashed out at anything within range. They were pulling and ripping my clothes and yelling all sorts of obscenities. The guy I'd pummelled was going mad, his face pouring with blood.

The gang had backed off as most of them had received some sort of slap by this point. I marched through them pushing two onto the beach. Criss had got her own way and the kids had seen their dad going mental. They were standing there, silent, with a look of total shock on their faces. I was completely frustrated, as I knew there was no way to get them to understand what had just happened. In their eyes I had gone mad and beat up a load of people, fulfilling all the lies that they'd been told. I felt helpless and angry.

Walking away from Criss was my only solution as I'd learnt a long time ago that trying to be rational with her was impossible. As I walked away I began playing one of the many scenarios I used to calm myself down. I knew that one day she'd trip herself up and the truth would come out. I had to hold on to that hope as my only solace. I had built up such a store of hate that if the remarkable ever did happen I had a long list of quips and remarks to rub salt in her wounds. As I walked away listening to her still spitting out obscenities I was glad I was removing her target. Phase two usually involved her attacking me and I'd had enough of those to last me a lifetime.

Over the next few months a pattern emerged of me receiving abuse every time I went to see the kids. I hated it but it was the price I had to pay for being with my children. I only hoped that the price I was paying wasn't a down payment for the abuse they might have been receiving from Criss. I pray that the pain they suffered was less than mine and hoped against hope that it wouldn't mess them up for life. Whenever I would pick them up I would ask subtle questions about mummy and if they were OK. They never said a word against her but that didn't prove anything.

9
Blood guilt

The combination of a destructive addict and a pocket full of cash proved to be a successful one for the addict in me. I was fast drinking, smoking and snorting my way through the money I had. I'd wake up every morning ready for an instant hit and that would be the first of many. My days were spent getting progressively drunk with a variety of different characters, their only similarity being the ability to drink more than their bodyweight in alcohol. I woke up one morning to find that the wedge had turned into a pocket full of coins and I'd have to flee the flat without paying. I knew I'd have a number of offers to kip on floors so resigned myself to that eventuality and sipped on the last of my vodka bottles for comfort.

It would have been nice to speak to Phil at that time, he knew where I was coming from and would have helped me out with some cash.

I had been knocking about with a woman called Carol for a while and when I left the flat I moved in with her. She lived in a particularly notorious part of town. A mixture of drunks, druggies and dealers, which suited me down to the ground, inhabited her road. She had heard all the stories about my violent behaviour towards Criss but after getting to know me was convinced they weren't true. That didn't mean that we had a trouble- free ride. We rowed passionately and neither of us was easy to live with. She matched me for addictions and destructive capability but we preferred to be together rather than apart and that kept us going. For me, it was a walk in the park compared to Criss. I loved having a relationship with a woman that didn't involve me getting beaten or needing to go to the hospital every other week.

The most voracious rows occurred at night after we'd been drinking all day. They'd get to the point where nothing was being resolved so I'd do my usual trick of removing myself from the line of fire and head off to the park or the beachfront. I'd take a bottle of cheap cider and sit on the beach listening to the waves trying to block out my existence. My descent into this world hadn't happened all of a sudden, it was quite slow, I was twenty- six years old now and had endured a whole mess of pain in that short time, my acceptance of pain evolved gradually, like watching the hands on a clock I couldn't see any difference at the time, it was always in hindsight that I saw the corners I was turning.

The morning after the rows I'd be in one of the drinking haunts with the rest of the drunks enjoying my Tennant's Super breakfast and we'd usually meet up. I had got used to hanging out in the places I used to walk past with a look of disgust on my face. It was quite a turnaround for me but as the money ran out I was forced to find the cheapest solutions to my needs. I had slowly got to know most of the drunks and druggies about town and along with Carol's confirmation had convinced them that Criss was a horrible lying bitch. Sitting in groups, drunkenly laughing or fighting became my daily routine and I had long ago got used to the looks from passers by. As much as anyone walking past might hate you, it's nothing compared to how much you hate yourself.

As you walk through any town you will always see a drunk or two, or a beggar with a dog on a piece of string and ninety-nine percent of the time you will avoid eye contact or might even cross the road. You hear people saying to the person next to them, 'why don't they get a job?' or 'how could they let themselves get so low'. Having been there I'd like to point out that almost everyone I ever met who was a drunk, street-beggar or undesirable, was not born into that life. They were not completely stupid or incapable but were born into a world where if you lose everything or are born with nothing then that's exactly the help you are given, nothing, unless you get some lucky breaks which not many people do get.

Many of the people I came to know were not mindless morons, in fact I would like to bet that if you took a group of drunks from anywhere in the country, you would find amongst them individuals with professional training and wealthy types who had lost the plot due to some tragedy or another. The younger ones, some of whom were brimming with talent, had never had a fair chance in life and for them, reaching the bottom is a much faster road, a lot of these kids came from inflicted abuse from there care givers at home to abusing themselves using abuse as a crude coping mechanism. One of our 'fellows' was a professor whose wife had left him. He couldn't handle it so had resorted to finding refuge in a bottle of cider. Unfortunately many so-called 'normal' people don't try to find sympathy or even empathy with the problems behind the booze; they only look at the surface symptoms of what they see as a filthy social disease. Like any social disease it's an ugly sight and it's on that sight that the judgements are made.

Meanwhile, from within my little socially problematic world, I was about to see Criss finally get caught in the web of her lies. I relished the time black Alex told me about her down fall, she was a parasitic woman at the best of times and giro day bought out the worst in her. She would hang around the pubs waiting for guys she knew had a pocket of cash and flirt with them for a few drinks. One evening she was with her prey for the day and as they were leaving the pub a gust of wind from a nasty storm got the better of her and she tumbled onto the pavement. Never being one to miss the opportunity of acting the drama queen she persuaded the guy to take her to hospital where she was fitted with a neck brace.

The following morning she was sitting in the park telling a story involving her flat, a beating, and me, she even managed a few tears apparently. Criss had overestimated her hold on the group around her and as she unfurled her tale, the guy that had been with her the night before took the wind from her sails and told the truth. He told the stunned crowd what had really happened. Criss's credibility was shattered and she left the party embarrassed, shouting accusatory comments about how they had betrayed her and that no one understood her.

You might think that I would have enjoyed hearing what had happened and be happy that she had been caught out. I did feel some sense of satisfaction as anyone would who had been attacked, abused, arrested and defamed and was glad that maybe now I wouldn't be looked at like the worst type of scum. However although I hated her for all that she'd done to me I also pitied her. Underneath the relief of being validated I had a strong feeling of regret that she had taken things so far. I knew that she would be in a worse state, as the attention that she needed to survive would fade now that people would question everything she said. You can't have two children with someone and not have some feeling for them even if that feeling is only sympathy, I felt that I was the only one who really understood her but she had gone way beyond the 'too far' point for me to try and help her. With the kids at school she was free to do what she wanted during the day, maybe now she would have to do what was right because her credibility was totally gone.

In my heart I knew she was mentally ill but also knew she couldn't be reached so resigned myself to blocking her out of my life, I just hoped that she looked after the children OK. Her search for attention led her to live a highly promiscuous life and although it used to drive me mad I now hoped that she might find someone and settle down. Still as the saying goes, 'Hope springs eternal' and it may well be an eternal search for her.

Myself, Criss, Carol and the rest of our degenerative posse were part of an infrastructure that exists in every town. It was a society within a society cut off from the main one and with its own rules and laws. It was a very dangerous world to live in. There was a pecking order and if you were at the bottom you were preyed upon so you tried to work your way to the top, although if you went too high you spent the whole time defending your position and that meant violence and lots of it. As I spent more time in this world I became a part of its systems including the pecking order. Before long it was my only world and so I had to survive in it. My addictions were running high and there was no way a giro every two weeks could keep up. To get ahead in a society of drunks, druggies, dealers and psychopaths you didn't have to be worst than the worst, you had to be smarter and more calculated and that was my mission.

There were probably over a hundred various street folk where we lived and many others who came in contact with us. They all had one thing in common, substance abuse. I didn't meet a single one without an addiction of some kind. One of the ways I kept up my high level of abuse was to keep a mental record of people's paydays. These were the days they got their state benefits. If you were with someone who'd just got their cash then it wasn't long before you could cadge their substance. Whatever they were having you'd join in. Because of my size and reputation I wasn't refused. When your body is constantly processing a cocktail of drink and drugs it needs regular top-ups and you don't care how you achieve this you just do.

As you can imagine, this world within a world was about as violent as you could get, at least in a supposed civilised world. There was always a drama of some sort or another, be it a fight, overdose or murder. It was an insane environment where extreme behaviour became the norm. The world was split into clans who spent their time high or trying to get high and in the process, committing a staggering array of atrocious acts of barbarity. The longer you lived in it the more numb you became. What starts as shocking quickly descended to normality.

I moved about the clans like a scavenger. I didn't affiliate myself to any one group, meaning I could make the best of all situations. If there was someone being ripped off or beaten or both I'd always take the victim's side. This was for two reasons, the first was I felt sorry for the underdog and the second was when I had won the fight I knew I'd be recompensed. If someone's being beaten you know they've got something to take. I'd step in, thrash the assailant and take some of the spoils with a smile. Once this side had been milked I'd move on to the assailant, apologising to them for stepping in and making up with a drink, smoke or snort, whatever they had. It was a handy system and worked well. I carried on like this conniving various ways to feed my addict and doing a reasonable job. However when you place yourself in harms way on a daily basis it doesn't take long before harm starts looking for you.

People come and go in the street folk life regularly. The ones who stay are usually physically and emotionally wrecked and in this world I excelled. Over the years, along with my unhealthy addictions, I had been addicted to exercise and had learnt to box. Because of this I managed to become a big fish in a small stagnant pond.

The problem with being the one who stands tallest is you become the target for all the punks who think they should be top. I'd seen some pretty tough blokes come a cropper on more than one occasion like this and was determined it wouldn't happen to me. One such bloke, a guy called Gary, had been dealing puff and speed for about a year and had always given short measures, to feed his own habit. He was a hard fucker though and no one would mess with him. The few people who tried were given a kicking that would sicken them for a week. In this climate of fear he could do what he liked.

One day, two drifters from London appeared. They were just passing through and kipped down on the beach for a couple of nights. Whilst there they decided to sample the local delicacies and scored a load of puff from Gary. Being new to the area and getting his usual crap deal, they went to see him to sort it out. They found him in the park where all the street folk hung out during the day. They approached him and amicably asked him to give them the deal they'd paid for. Gary looked them up and down and then told them to 'fuck off!' and then turned back to his conversation.

The two guys stood there without expression. Then, suddenly, the one on the right pulled a blade from his coat sleeve and plunged it straight into Gary's neck straight for the jugular. Gary's neck turned into a red fountain as the blood spurted everywhere. He collapsed to the ground clutching his throat, his eyes displaying total shock. While he was writhing on the ground the guys rifled through his pockets and cleaned him out. The crowd in the park disappeared like smoke on the wind and I went with them. When the shit hits the fan you want to be well out of it.

When you live in this world your life becomes worth less than a fix and that was the same for everyone. Life means nothing and kindness is seen as a weakness to be exploited. You find this out very quickly and hope that your lesson isn't a painful or lethal one. Reading people becomes a survival skill and arrogance can kill you. Gary's death was an example of this and I was going to make sure it never happened to me.

The death and crime rate in our world is so high that the police don't bother with it. The only time they get involved is when we stepped out of our filth and interfered with the 'normal' world through a mugging or robbery. When an addict or dealer is found dead, it's just another one out of the way as far as the police are concerned. For them it's a result. This isn't just the opinion of the people who live with it; I've heard it from a policeman's mouth.

The arguments between drunks and druggies can be over the simplest of things and have deathly consequences. The playground mentality is rife although the results are a lot harsher. I was involved in one such incident on a lovely summer's day one year. We were sitting in the park, as usual, drinking, smoking and taking the piss out of each other. The mood was quite happy for us lot, although there was always an underlying tension that never disappeared. Before long the laughing took a serious turn and an argument broke out that was so pathetic it would have been laughable if the results weren't so serious.

A row had developed between a female and male drunk. The guy had accused the girl of drinking from his stash, a common cause of argument. The girl denied it and the guy waded in. I watched for a few seconds, like everyone else. The guy started slapping the girl around and it was getting a bit heavy for my liking so like a dishevelled and certainly not white knight I waded in. Not all drunks are emaciated wasters; some are lean, mean and evil. When their substance is threatened they become savage like animals protecting their young. This guy was turning that way so I knew I had to steam in.

The guy I was about to do battle with was like a deranged animal. He had obviously been through a few wars in his time. His clothing was ripped and his face was decorated with the scars of conflict. He had no front teeth and looked like a serious thug. We squared up and he looked into my eyes with a piercing glare, I knew this was going to be a bad one.

He was coiled like a cobra and his lean body was tense and ready for action. Like usual I was ready to finish it quickly and as he pounced was going to punch him in the face aiming for the back of his head to try and take him down in one. He leaped at me and I took aim and released my hardest punch. He took it straight on the nose and his face exploded in a red mist. He fell back with blood pouring off his chin but seemed to bounce on the ground and come back at me with more force than the punch I'd landed. His fury was immense and he laid into me with everything he had. My punch hadn't stopped him at all it had just inflamed his anger, like trying to put out a fire with petrol. We started exchanging blows at a terrifying pace. Arms, elbows, legs and heads lashed out and landed with great thumps and cracks. We both landed good, heavy blows that should have stopped the fight but this one was different, neither of us was going down. The crowd were baying for blood and getting it. In a previous fight I had dislocated two knuckles on my right hand that were now glowing with a pain like white heat. He had got in a piercing punch to the side of my head and my left ear was humming and blood was running down the side of my face. I was in real pain and running out of energy. It didn't seem like anything I did hurt him in any way, it was like he was on P.C.P.

The crowd had swelled and was shouting encouragement but to me it was just muffled screams of delight. I put all my energy into a giant kick that sent him sprawling and earned a couple of second's respite. I looked about and thought I could run for it but if I did my standing in the community would have been shattered. This one would have to go the whole mile. I knew I had to end it but didn't know how, I had given him all my best punches, and kicks and butts and he just came back for more. He jumped off the ground and rushed at me with arms whirling. He landed a heavy punch into my right eye and it swelled up almost immediately and started to bleed. He was all over me like a rash and I was losing ground. I put my hands up for defence as he waded in but this was no ring fight with Queensbury rules and his knees and elbows peppered my body.

I got in close, like I'd been taught so he couldn't get any leverage and pummelled away at his body. I was loosing the fight and knew if I couldn't put him down soon it would be all over. If I went down he wouldn't stop, such was his fury and I knew it. With this thought I got a rush of adrenaline and with a great primeval scream threw both arms around his neck. Once I had him in a headlock I squeezed as hard as I could. It was like trying to hold onto an eel and he was wriggling and trying to punch me with great strength. I looked around for inspiration wondering how I could stop this and noticed the railings round some roses about ten feet away.

I ran at the railings half carrying, half dragging him and still at some speed ran his head into them. He collapsed under me with blood spurting from a cut on his crown. I took a giant breath and thought it was finished but nothing could put him down. He climbed up my body with one hand and tried to hit me with the other. I was at my end and started to panic. If that couldn't stop him, what would? We spun round each other trading blows and leaning against the railings for support. He got me with an uppercut that jarred my entire head. The pain was excruciating and my legs were beginning to give way. With one desperate and final effort I got him in a headlock again so tight I thought it was going to break his neck. He was squirming so much I couldn't get a proper hold. It was now or never and with all the energy left in me I lifted his head over the railings and plunged it down onto the spikes. One of them entered his mouth, went through his cheek and came out near his ear. He screamed like an animal and I sank to my knees, safe. I looked up at him impaled on the railings and knew it was over. My only thought was relief; it had been the hardest fight of my life.

I sat there panting and dazed and looked around the park. The crowd had vanished. There were only two drunks left who were shouting at me to clear off before the police arrived. I could hardly hear them as my head was ringing. The guy on the railing was stuck and was emitting noises I'd never heard before. I looked at him and knew I couldn't leave him. With a superhuman effort I got to my feet and started to pull him off of the spikes. The two drunks ran over and helped me. We pulled his face off the spike trying to keep his head straight and he slumped to the floor wailing. It was only once the spike was out that the blood began to flow.

The two drunks helped me walk and I hobbled out of the park as the 'normal' people were gathering. I was taken back to a squat where the three of us downed a bottle of scotch in five minutes; I drank the lion's share. I sat on a filthy chair and started to examine my wounds. My right hand had ballooned to twice its natural size and the knuckles were a few inches higher than they should have been. Experience had taught me to bathe it in cold water, wrap it tightly and wait a month for it to die down. After cleaning up all the blood, the only other lasting problems were my eye and ear. The eye would be fine but my ear worried me. It was weeping a clear fluid. I wiped away the fluid tensing with the pain. I managed to put a wedge of cotton wool into it even though a draft felt like a six-inch nail was being inserted. I was pretty sure it was ruptured but there wasn't anything I could do, it would just have to stay that way. The rest of the cuts all but cleared up within a month but I still have a slight ringing and deafness to this day that reminds me of the fight of my life.

Needless to say, I laid low for the next few days. I didn't go to the usual haunts and didn't want to be anywhere where I might have to answer unwanted questions. I knew no one would talk to the old bill, as the 'law' was never brought into these matters. It was our world and our laws. Justice was dished out with fists, knives or guns and nothing else mattered.

During this time I didn't really think of the spiked guy. I had no guilt or remorse; it was just what happened. It might seem an incredible thing to impale I guy on a spiked railing but it was kill or be killed and luckily it hadn't come to that. It was accepted that the loser would be looked after and receive a few pats on the back for a valiant effort. Meanwhile, the victor would be ensured an elevation in the pecking order of a society plagued by madness. I look back now and see the dehumanising effect the micro world has. The unacceptable becomes acceptable, immoral behaviour becomes the norm and any sanity left gets pushed down beneath an emotional slagheap of pain.

My addictions were fast becoming who I was and my days had long ago become a ritual of consumption. The mornings were the worst. I'd always leave some booze beside me wherever I slept. On waking my first activity would be to spend twenty minutes or so trying to down enough alcohol to get my system working. It was hard as the battle was between swallowing and heaving. The worst booze to use was cider. It would be the cheapest brand that could strip paint and all I wanted to do was throw it up but if I did I couldn't move so I had to force it down. This morning ritual was vital as without it I couldn't stand properly or my head would spin so much I'd be sure to take a tumble.

Without fail, no matter how out of it I was the night before, there'd always be booze next to me when I woke up. It was hardwired into my brain. Once up, I'd fish out my speed bag and set up a few lines. Carol and I would snort our breakfast and this would usually be enough for me to get down to the nearest off-license for our day's supplies. The offie would open at eight in the morning and a few even opened at six. You might think, who in their right minds would be drinking at that time and you'd be right, no one in their right mind would but our minds were far from being right. The offie we went to was well versed in the ways of our world and every morning there'd be a queue of drunks waiting for their morning fix, gagging for the relief from withdrawal. More often than not Carol and I were in the queue.

During this time Criss seemed to have calmed down quite a bit and was behaving herself. I had become a kind of older brother to her and spent time listening to her woes but thankfully not getting involved in them. This made my life a whole lot easier and meant that spending time with the children became a complete joy, without a cloud hanging over it. She had shacked up with a guy called Bob, which was good news for me as she had another poor sucker to focus on. It went well for a while but as with all things Criss touched, the rot soon set in. She settled into her old ways and went round telling everyone, including me, a veteran of her bullshit, that he had been beating her; she never had a mark on her though. I listened and didn't say anything. It was tragic that she thought the only way she could feed her craving for attention was through pity.

On the sea front there's a two-mile stretch of promenade that made for a good morning walk. I'd regularly wake-up with the shakes, down a few mouthfuls and head off at six am. Along the walk there would be dotted at various points the early drinkers whose bodies needed a fix. One of these was Bob and we would meet and chat. I would sit and listen to his problems with Criss and I might as well have been listening to a tape recording of me from a few years before. Poor Bob was in my old boat and would ask me for advice. There was nothing I could offer him except to tell him to get out which I wasn't going to do because I knew that his presence meant the kids had a better life. It was twisted but then everything was. I would walk back wondering why he stayed with her and then why I did, I never found any answers. I felt sorry for the poor sod and was glad it was him and not me.

Back at the flat Carol and I were getting on well, there was always the odd argument but we had settled into a gentle rhythm and things were good. In the evenings we would settle down together and indulge in substances. Our drugs of choice most nights were methadone or heroin, puff and the ever-present booze. Many mornings we'd wake where we'd passed out. The telly would still be on and our morning booze would be waiting for us. One of us would lean forward and grab the cans, usually Tennant's Super or on special mornings some spirits would be left. When we'd forced it down a few lines of speed would be laid out to get us going. One morning in the middle of snorting my first line there was an almighty banging on the front door. In our world, someone banging on the door meant trouble.

I got up and looked about for a weapon and seeing nothing usable decided fists would have to do. I went to the door and pulled it open hard ready to surprise whoever was there. My pent up anxiety drained into the floor when I saw it was Criss. She was in a terrible state and had the kids with her. I was shocked at first and then delighted to see them. I gathered up both kids in a giant bear hug. It felt so good to hold them. My next thought was trouble, Carol had always said that she'd take Criss's head off if she ever came round and now she was here I was stuck. Luckily Carol must have called a truce in her head as she was all smiles and invited Criss in.

We packed the kids off to a bedroom with some pens and paper and made a cup of tea. Criss broke down before the first sip and told us she couldn't cope, as her home life was impossible. She went into a long story about all sorts, which I can't remember because as soon as she started I switched off through force of habit. I pounced on one sentence though; she had asked me to take Laura, my daughter, off her hands for a while so she could straighten her life out.

I didn't need to think, I jumped at the chance of having her. I looked at Carol who smiled a 'yes' and the decision was made. We called the kids in and explained to both of them what was happening. Adie, my son wanted to stay with his mother which was fine with me. He had always gotten on better with his mum and Laura had always been a Daddy's girl. As much as I loved Adie I knew he would spend the whole time wanting to go home so it was best he stayed with Criss. We said our goodbyes after listening to a million apologies, none made sincerely, and shut the door. You couldn't wipe the grin from my face, I had my little girl and I didn't care how long it was for I was just thrilled to have her with me.

Having my little girl back meant some changes to my lifestyle; the booze and drugs would have to go. I focused all my energies into looking after Laura, the school run and cooking her tea became my priorities instead of stealing to fuel my self-abuse. I loved it, every minute, I had a purpose again and it felt great, which is more than I can say for my system. Instantly cutting off a body's supply of narcotic is no picnic and I went into severe withdrawal. I ached all over, had sweats constantly, the pain was terrible but it was worth it. There was no way I was going to be the drunk and druggie I *was* in front of my little girl.

I went to the doctors and got prescribed Heminevrin, which is a drug that counteracts the effects of booze withdrawal and began discussions about a proper methadone programme. I felt new and invigorated, I wanted to stop permanently and become a real father to Laura. I adored her as much as I adored Adie and adored being a father. For the first time in a long while I felt my life had meaning. Carol found it harder to adapt but she put in a lot of effort and laid off the hard drugs. She also gave a lot of love to Laura and was becoming a pretty good surrogate mum. Laura was happier than I'd ever seen her and she loved all the attention.

Everyday I woke with a smile and once the pain of withdrawal had passed bounded out of bed; I even started thinking about getting work again. My days had a positive structure, I would pick up Laura from school, bring her back for her tea and then the three of us would have playtime. Laura loved it and I was in heaven. As with all periods like this in my life, it was about to come to a catastrophic end.

10
Rock Bottom

The flat where we lived was in a five-storey converted Victorian house. We lived on the top floor and there were five other flats that were occupied by some of the addicts that knocked about town. The flat below us housed a Scottish guy who had not long been out of prison for murder. He was a chronic heroin user and completely unbalanced. In the flat below him, three blokes shared the rooms and were a riotous bunch. I had never seen them sober and they'd take anything they could get their hands on. The final two flats had a heavy drinker in one and a junkie in the other.

I didn't know any of them well but had spent some time talking to the drinker on the seafront. In one of life's bizarre coincidences he had actually been at the same school as me but we had never spoken. He was a quiet kid and it was common knowledge that he had been adopted. What we hadn't known was that his stepfather had been a right horrible bastard and had sexually abused him from an early age. When he was old enough he had tried to stop him and had been beaten almost to death with an iron bar. Whilst in hospital recovering, the truth had come out and he was taken away and given new parents. He had a son somewhere but his girlfriend had left him when she reached the end of her tether trying to deal with his depression and drinking. So here he was, another victim of the holes in the safety net. It's surprising how many slip through.

So the block wasn't the perfect place to bring up children and looking back I can't believe we even thought we could do it but then I wasn't exactly thinking straight. When Laura arrived I went round the flats telling everyone to try and keep the noise down, especially the flat with the three guys, as they would play music at full blast all through the night. Every other night they'd have a fight of some sorts and it would sound like they'd invited a heard of elephants round for a tea party. Laura would be terrified by the noise and cling to me for comfort. I wasn't surprised as on some nights it sounded as if they were killing each other and even Carol got frightened.

I had been down on numerous occasions to tell them to keep quiet but yelling at someone who's out of it is like talking to a brick wall. One night I had put Laura to bed and Carol had read a story to her and we were sitting on the sofa snuggled up. We had dozed off in front of the telly when we were suddenly woken up by a commotion downstairs. It sounded like a pub full of people had come back and started fighting. I went to see if Laura was OK and when I opened the door I was greeted by a sight that is still etched in my memory. She was sitting on her bed with her back to the wall her arms wrapped round her knees, clutching her teddy. She was crying silently and had a look of complete fear in her eyes. I had reached my breaking point.

With Laura reaching the point of full terror I reached full fury and after telling Carol to look after her stormed off to make whatever was making the noise stop, permanently. I crashed downstairs and with each step the noise grew. I didn't care how many there were, I was absolutely livid. I had one good thing in my life and they were destroying it. As I turned round the last corner of the stairs I was faced with the problem. The three guys from the flat and the Scottish bloke were all standing round a tree that they'd bought in from the garden and it had got stuck in the doorway. On another occasion I'd have laughed out loud but tonight the only thing on my mind was violence. They were all totally plastered and yelling at each other at the top of their voices.

When they heard me, they all looked up and the Scottish bloke broke into a tirade of obscenities that I could just about make out, apparently I wasn't welcome. He was waving a machete about and slamming it into the tree at various exclamatory points. I stared at him and yelled, 'shut the fuck up, I've got a child upstairs!' They had obviously worked themselves into a bit of a frenzy trying to move the tree and when I opened my mouth they switched that frustration to me. The eldest of the three lads started up the stairs without a word but hadn't really thought it through. When he was a few steps away his head was level with my foot and I kicked him as hard as I could. He almost back flipped and was sent smashing down the stairs onto the tree, I don't think he touched any of the stairs on his downwards journey.

He was out cold and the others stared at him. The two lads tried to make a getaway through the door but it was stuck because the tree was against it. They stood there scared and quiet. The Scottish guy however was just getting going. He started up his yelling again and was thrashing about with the machete. He was certainly dangerous but with his back against the hall wall and surrounded by branches was pretty much pinned down. I stepped towards him and let him swing the machete. I dodged and then grabbed his arm, he wasn't that big and certainly was not clever. By this point I was ready to unleash weeks of pent up anger and frustration at all the noise and with the machete in my hand now I could have easily killed him.

He quickly changed tack and cowered pleading with me not to kill him. The other two were screaming at each other and I turned round, ready to pop. I yelled at them to shut up but they carried on and turning the machete in my hand so the blade was vertical swung it with all my might with the flat of the blade into the face of the nearest one. His nose flattened against his face in a red explosion and blood poured down the front of his shirt. They went quiet immediately and a silence descended on the hall. The only noise was a whimpering sound coming from the guy I'd clouted.

The only one still standing erupted into fits of apologies and tried to tell me he had nothing to do with it. I raised the machete and told him to shut it, which he did. The Scottish guy returned to the fray and suddenly jumped on my back trying to strangle me. I couldn't believe it and ran backwards, with him holding onto me and with all my strength shoved him into the doorframe. He let go and I turned round and with all the hate I could muster I laid into him kicking him over and over. When I had used up all my rage I stood there heaving, taking great lungfulls of air. It was then that I heard crying and turned round to see Laura standing at the top of the stairs looking at me, holding Carol's hand. I can't describe the emotions I felt. The hall looked like a war zone. I leaned in, putting my head close to the guy who hadn't had a beating and said quietly but with venom, 'if I come down here in the morning and see you I swear I'll kill ya'. I turned round to go upstairs and looked up at Laura, she was frozen with fear and was looking at *me*. We went back into the flat and after cleaning myself up I went to try and calm her down. She wouldn't let me touch her and kept crying and saying over and over, 'I want mummy, I want to go home.' She was five.

When she had finally gone to sleep I sat on the sofa with Carol and felt lost. I knew Laura had to go home and I knew that the flat was no place for a child. I wondered how I had got myself into a position where I couldn't even have my own kid stay with me. As the truth of losing Laura turned into a reality I had to face, the sorrow that welled up inside consumed me. The one normal and decent thing in my life was going and as self-pity turned into anger my sorrow began to harden into hate. Everything I touched turned to shit and I lay there blaming everything and everybody I could think of. All I really had to do was look in the mirror but it would be a few years before I did that.

In the morning I phoned Criss and explained everything that had happened. Criss knew the blokes in the flat and was aware of their reputations. She said there was no problem with having Laura back. In one way I was relieved, at least Criss lived in a reasonable area without drug crazed, machete-wielding nutcases running about. I took Laura home and she didn't say a word. When Criss came to the door Laura left my side and went indoors without turning round. My heart sank and I began to ache inside. I kept a straight face with Criss, as always, never showing my weakness.

I walked back towards the flat in a daze with lead in my boots. I wished I was dead. The last chance I had of happiness had just walked away from me, probably for the last time. I passed our local offie and looked at the door. I went in and bought three two-litre bottles of strong, disgusting cider and trudged home. As I packed the last of Laura's things I drank heavily from a bottle. The void in my heart that had been temporarily plugged by Laura's presence opened up again and threatened to swallow me whole. I took a giant gulp from the last of the bottles and felt like collapsing both physically and mentally. I remember feeling so low at that point, the thought of suicide was very strong in my mind.

The morning came and with it the pain. I drank the last of the cider to get me going and got up. I knew I had to kill any emotions I had and the only way to do that was to get obliterated. My money situation was bad so I had to go on a shoplifting spree to get the booze I needed. I'm sure that the staff knew I was stealing but with my appearance being somewhat frightening decided it was best to leave me to it. It would have taken a brave man to tackle me. I had filthy clothes, various cuts and bruises, a foot-long beard and missing front teeth; combined with my height and permanent scowl, I think I'd have avoided me if I'd seen me coming.

In twenty-four hours I had regressed from being a caring, clean and sober father to a hopeless angry drunk who felt at war with the world. On the way to the shops I saw the guy I'd kicked downstairs the night before. He was playing the big man in front of a small group of punks and had a bottle of methadone in one pocket and a roll of cash in his hand. I felt the rage start to grow inside me and was all ready to take him down and nick his stuff. Carol read my mind and gently linked arms with me quietly saying we should go somewhere and chill. I didn't argue but glared at him and we walked off.

Carol was on a prescription for methadone and I was scamming various drugs from my GP. I had developed quite a talent for manipulating and without much trouble acquired Valium and mogadon, exactly what my mother was on. Most of the gear we got legally we didn't use ourselves; we sold it at a local drop-in centre. It might as well as been called a dropout centre considering it was a melting pot for the vagabonds that hung around. Very few of them were genuinely attempting recovery and would eagerly purchase whatever we had. The only thing we sometimes kept was the methadone, which was a good chill out drug for the evening sessions.

After a long walk I had calmed down and we set off from the centre with our stash. As we entered the building I was shocked to see Mr Big Shot yelling at one of the centre's staff. He was out of it and making little sense. The guy behind the counter was trying to explain that he wasn't allowed into the building with any booze and Mr Big Shot was arguing the toss. I walked up quietly behind him and grabbed his arm with all my strength. He yelped and turned round. With a smile that could melt butter, aimed at the staff member, I asked if I could help. Mr Big shot had suddenly gone very quiet and when I suggested he give me his bag of booze to look after there was no argument. Carol met her usual buyer for her stash and then we were out of there, we went back to Carol's flat with the same intention we had most days, to escape reality.

I was chuffed, as I hadn't expected such a result. Mr Big Shot had stocked up pretty well and I had a nice choice of poison. I opened a bottle of scotch and settled onto the sofa. As the joy of getting free booze waned, my thoughts drifted. I began to reflect on my life and how it was that I was sitting on a sofa in the most disgusting block of flats imaginable drinking booze stolen from a drunk; it wasn't exactly the life I wanted for myself. As I went through the course of events leading to my current predicament I listed all the people who had contributed to my downfall. As each new character came to mind I visually blew them away with a saw-off shotgun. The list ended with Mr Big Shot downstairs and as I gulped away I fantasized about how to kill him for fucking up my life. As far as I was concerned I'd reached rock bottom and it was the fault of a lot of people who'd fucked me over in one after the other.

As usual, when stores were high in the house, the night was long and Carol and I got totally smashed. My plans for Mr big Shot were scuppered by my own addictions as I passed out before I could do him any damage. My body woke me at five- thirty. It hadn't had any alcohol for five hours and was screaming for supplies. The phrase drunks use to describe the problem is 'clucking' and it means the point when you physically shake and rattle. My Tenants Super was an arm's length away and I opened it and sat up, shivering but not cold. As I hugged myself and tried to focus I heard a strange sound. I was used to all sorts of noises in the flat but this one was new. It was like a kind of crying. I tried to ignore it but as the booze flowed through my system and I came back to life the noise became more intrusive. Eventually curiosity got the better of me.

I went to the front door and opening it strained my ears, or at the least the one good one I had left. It was definitely crying and I went down the stairs to investigate. Before leaving the flat I went to find a weapon. Investigating a noise where we lived usually meant trouble and I didn't want to be unprepared. With my axe handle at the ready I crept downwards. On the stairs sat one of the three stooges with his head in his hands, he was weeping. I nudged him with the end of the handle and asked what was wrong. He looked up at me his face red and blotched and said, 'Dave's dead, he's fucking dead!' My reaction was flat, 'who the fuck's Dave?' As it turned out Dave was the real name of Mr Big Shot.

As I walked into the flat my nose was assaulted with the stench of booze, piss and I guess death. It was rancid. There were cans everywhere, needles on the floor and broken bits of furniture dotted about the place. If someone had kept animals there half the country would have gone out on a protest march. As it was, these poor fuckers lived there. The lights were broken and the room was dark, which added to the seediness. A filthy sheet was hanging from the curtain rail over the window and I took the end and yanked it off. The whole lot came crashing down and the room was bathed in glorious morning sunlight. In this place however it was hardly glorious. I followed the fingers of light shining through the dust and turned to look at Dave; I almost choked. He was lying on a ripped mattress staring into space. He had turned a nasty colour and his face looked like blue marble. The flies that had been attracted by the filth in the room buzzed around his mouth.

I took the sheet and bent down to lay it across him and gagged as the smell hit me. I turned round and put my sleeve over my mouth and took a deep breath to steady myself. As I was controlling my urge to vomit I saw a large, almost untouched bottle of methadone next to the mattress. With my shirt still covering my face I leant down and swiped it. I also rifled through Dave's pockets, I'm sure he would have done the same for me, he had a couple of dozen lumps of cannabis all wrapped up separately, it looked like he was going to start doing a bit of dealing. I heard a car outside and looked out of the filthy window, it was the police, shit what do I do now, I did the only sensible thing to do at the time. As quick as I could I swallowed all the puff and hoped that the cling film it was in was good, as I was doing this I remembered being a kid again about five or six and swallowing old coins in a bid to get some attention from my Mum or Dad that wasn't violent or aggressive, I remembered wanting sympathy from them. In an instant my mind's attention had turned to getting back to the flat with my find. I was mentally calculating how much I could get for it on the street as I made my way back to the door.

As I walked past the guy on the stairs I asked him if the old bill were coming and he said that they were on their way, I knew that they were already here. I went back upstairs and woke Carol. I quickly explained what had happened and that the police were coming. We both instinctively looked round the room at the detritus of drug paraphernalia and then back at each other. 'Where are the bin bags?' I asked and we managed to find one. I went round the rooms collecting all the empty cans, spliff-ends, speed wrappers and pieces of burnt foil. We hadn't tidied for a while and the bag was soon full. I remember thinking that Dave's death had some positive effects, we got a cleanish flat and some drugs, looking back now I can see how inhuman I had become, I can't believe I was so cold and callous.

Once the flat was drug free, we decided the best thing to do was get out so we didn't have to answer any questions. I hardly wanted to be asked about the fight. We walked down the stairs, past the guy sitting who hadn't moved from where he was sitting and had gained some composure, I handed him a can of Tenants as a way of saying we were sorry. We weren't sorry we didn't give a fuck.

We spent the rest of the day gossiping and drinking in the regular haunts, using our fake grief as an excuse to dive deeply into any substance we came across. The day was funded with the cash from Dave's methadone, sold to a desperate heroin junkie. I knew it was wicked and mercenary but in our world we all did it. The gradual chipping of morals happens slowly.

After a few days, the official verdict that Dave had died from respiratory failure brought on by substance abuse, passed through the street grapevine. Carol and I discussed whether my fight with him contributed to his death. I knew I'd given him a good kicking but in my mind he didn't die at the time so it had nothing to do with me.

In most people's life death is a horrific incident and causes great shock and sadness. In mine it was an almost a daily occurrence. In the world of addiction, the substances make no judgement on your character. You could be the nicest guy sitting on the beach laughing away but if you take dodgy gear or argue with the wrong person then that night could be your last night on earth. After the first few times someone you know from your circle dies, you develop an emotional lead barrier around your heart. If you didn't, you'd be distraught the whole time.

I lost count of the faces we would see about for a while only to be told by another 'face' that they had died a few days earlier from drink, drugs, suicide or murder. Murder happens a lot and the ones that die in our world don't go on the statistics book. It was a well-known fact that the police couldn't be bothered with scum like us; the more of us that died the better; it didn't matter what the circumstances were.

There were some people who genuinely tried to help. They were usually religious or just out of college, those with ideals beyond the reality that faced them. Although they meant well they were more often than not told to 'fuck off!' and any help offered was rejected with contempt. Any help that had been offered to us usually got bled dry if it would help feed our habit in any way. In their eyes we were individuals to be redeemed and brought back to a society that really *did* care but we had left that world a long time ago and didn't want to return. All we wanted was a chunk of cash so we could get wrecked and most weren't offering that.

As I've just mentioned the murder rate was higher than you'd think, as life was so disposable. It isn't as uncommon an act as ninety-nine percent of people believe because 99% of the deaths happen in a separate world at the bottom end of the social scale. It's brutal and frightening and you block your mind to it but occasionally even then something happened which would affect you.

One such event happened to a guy called Zack. He was an older fella who had come to our world late on in life. He lived on the street and sometimes in squats when he could. He looked about seventy although I knew he was only forty-six because I had queued up with him at the dole office. He hung around with a needle gang and had slowly wasted away. At five feet three he was little anyway and with the abuse had lost all but a vital amount of weight, he can't have been more than six stone. Whenever I met him we would take a walk together. I would link his arm through mine as we walked as he was nearly blind and was almost always out of it, a combination that led to a fair amount of accidents.

He always talked about his past, often repeating the same stories. He had been employed in some big bank in the city and had been a man of importance. He had also been married and would show me the pictures of his wife that he carried in a worn out leather wallet. They were taken on his wedding day and they looked happy and healthy, a far cry from the man that stood beside me now. As I said he was part of a needle gang, a group of avid heroin users. He paid for the privilege by sharing his smack regularly. On giro day he would exchange all the money for smack and spend the best part of the following week holed up in a notorious squat. The gang that lived in the squat were friends to him only as long as he supplied them with gear, when that ran out so did their friendship.

He had been waiting for his incapacity benefit to kick in and when it arrived it was quite an amount because of all the back pay. It was a big enough sum to warrant opening a bank account, which was a big deal to Zack and would have been for any of us. It was a rare chance to reach out from the void and touch the real world. When you had a connection with the fabric of 'normal' society, however fleeting or small it might be, you felt great. It was a different kind of high, like a breath of clean air after walking through thick smoke. Zack was no different and made a fuss of his new bankcard and account, proudly showing it off.

The next day Zack was found in the garden of the squat, a needle sticking out of his neck and his wallet gone. The verdict was accidental death and as usual no one knew anything about it. It would have been some accident to fall onto a syringe with your neck. His eyes were so bad that often someone else would inject him so perhaps it was they who had the accident. We were all responsible in some way because we never let the knowledge of who had done what out of our world, we covered-up the truth all the time. We had all been witnesses to a variety of dodgy deaths but we never came forward.

Carol and I were drifting along as usual, week after week, blending into one long line of abuse. Everything was much the same as it had been for a while; our days spent finding ways to feed the habits of addiction to a variety of substances. The round of shoplifting, stealing, scamming and using became as familiar as a nine-to-five job is to others. We never considered ourselves to be junkies though, as we never injected. We would take our heroin by smoking it, in our eyes the junkies were a level below us. The sum of our addictions was costing us over two hundred quid a day and there was never enough cash to fill the gap between our demand and the supply we could get hold of. The truth is that our demand could go as high as we could get and the amount we took was only capped by our inability to score.

Carol's flat had turned into a right state since Laura had left. It was a complete pit of squalor, our external world mirroring our internal. We hated living in it but could never be bothered to clean up. We had got to a point where leaving became possible only if we were high or had cravings so strong our bodies forced us. We were on a downward spiral that never seemed to bottom out, like a child's slide at a funfair with no end.

One morning after breakfast drinks we went to our dealers to score our week's heroin. It was a sunny day so we went to the front for a walk first as he might have been down there, we said our hellos to the various drunks and druggies we knew and on the walk met a woman we knew was a chronic addict. We asked if she knew whether our dealer was in and she told us not to bother going as she was now dealing and had acquired a better source of gear. We weren't fussed if this was true or not but knew that she lived closer which meant a quicker route to getting our hands on some gear.

The three of us went back to her flat, which was one of the worst hovels I'd ever been in. We weren't exactly expecting the Ritz but this was something else, it was like a breeding ground for bugs and rats. The infestation was a pest controller's dreams come true. She wasn't the full ticket and had encouraged the rats by feeding them and they were everywhere. As we went in you had to kick them from around your feet and the place stank of rat's piss. It had to be seen to be believed. It was like being in a scene from an Indiana Jones movie.

All we wanted to do was get the gear and leave and as she took us through to the 'lounge' that was my only thought. However, when we entered the front room we were surprised to see that it was relatively rat free; I guess even rats have their limits. There were eight people sat in a circle in a variety of states. Some were drinking, others smoking puff or smack and two guys injecting. We recognised a few of the people and said our 'hellos'. The other strangers made acknowledging noises and then settled back to their work. There was a kid in the corner who looked about fourteen his eyes glazed over.

We opened a can and were offered a free smoke so our intentions to go evaporated, as you never refused a free 'joint'. It was generally agreed that we'd all keep an eye on the kid in the corner, propping him up so he was sitting against the wall and checking his breathing every so often. We found some floor space and joined the circle settling in to the group and starting our drinks. We made our deal and smoked the free sample and within a short time of arriving we were pretty much out of it, conscious but not with much of a handle on reality.

As we got more wrecked, the concern for our fellow man had disappeared, our memory of responsibility shutting down. The guy propped against the wall had slumped to the side and lay in what would have been a very uncomfortable position if conscious. We had propped him up once more and then laughed as he slid down again into what we presumed was sleep. We were all too high to work out what was really happening, our reality functions put on pause. As the heroin periodically wore off and we came back to what served as some semblance of reality, someone tentatively suggested we check his breathing again although by that stage we all knew what had happened.

I walked over and bent down to look at him. I didn't need to get as far as his mouth, I only had to get into his line of sight, or lack of it. I had seen those eyes before, the eyes of the dead. I looked at the expectant crowd and confirmed their fears, 'He's fucking dead', and added, 'fuck, fuck, fuck!' because he looked so young a wave of despair swept over me.

'So who the hell is he?' I asked and looked round the room for someone to take responsibility. There was no reply, nobody knew who he was, and they didn't even know his name. A stranger from the street just passing through and then passing on. He had turned up in the morning and asked about on the seafront for somewhere to get his fix. One of the guys in the room had brought him along but had hardly spoken to him. We were stuck, we couldn't call the old bill because then we'd all be in shit and we couldn't just leave him where he was, even the lady in the disgusting house drew a line at having a dead body in the front room. The first thing we did was go through his pockets to look for some identification. All we found was some drug paraphernalia and £25. Carol slipped the money into her pocket and there was some brief discussion as to why she became the recipient of his estate, which I silenced with a hard stare and carried on. The day had crept by outside, evening was approaching and darkness with it. We knew what we had to do but no one wanted to be the one to say it out loud. The dealer who looked panicked by now exclaimed' right we're going to have to get rid of the body.' Murmurs reverberated round the room but there was no disagreement, we were all in this together and we knew it.

I remembered seeing a carpet in the hallway on the way in and told the guy who'd brought the dead bloke to the house to get it. He sloped off and returned with the brown, tattered and stinking rug. Countless numbers of rats had pissed on it and God knows what had been trodden into it over the years. The smell and filth was registered on the bloke's face. 'It's fucking disgusting!' the guy said and threw it on the floor, glad that his part of the 'job' was over. They spread it out on the floor next to the body and stood back. Everyone gathered themselves for the next part.

It took three of them to lift him onto the carpet and we were all holding our breath as they took his weight, laid him out on the carpet, and stood back and wretched. By this time I was trying to persuade the dealer that the best thing to do was just call the police, hide all the gear, say we didn't know he was a user, if she stuck to her story the chances were she would get out of it without being held responsible in any way. I was probably keen to do things the right way as it wasn't me in the frame. No one actually threw up but we were all pretty close. A combination of the carpet's smell and the guy's face was a good enough combination for anyone. I guess the numerous times we'd all forced booze into a repulsing body and learnt to control the urge to vomit finally paid off.

They rolled him up and I asked the lady of the house for some string. After a brief search she came back empty handed. She was crouching by the rolled up corpse and swore, as they had to have at least two ties to ensure it held together, you could nearly see the cogs in their brains working searching for ideas and suddenly a flash came to one of them. They partially unrolled the carpet and I looked down at his shoes. He had thick army-type boots on done up with long black laces, perfect"Are you gonna fucking help?." one of them asked me panicking. The fact of the matter was, I was not going to help, I just wanted to score what I needed and to get out of there and that meant not deserting the dealer completely. Even if I was there only for moral support it was something.

When that job was done we sat around pondering the next stage. We all needed some Dutch courage and cans were passed round. A few of us downed the first in one and then immediately started another. Someone else was skinning a joint and as it was passed round we contemplated the site for the burial ground. Someone suggested a small coppice on the edge of town and it was agreed. Only one of the assembled throng had a car and it was brought round to the front. By this time we were all a bit wasted and with the body rolled away from view, the immediacy of what we were doing had been removed.

The body was gathered up awkwardly and after checking there was no one looking, they took it to the boot and tried to get it inside. It's not like it is in the movies, where they simply chuck the body in and it fits perfectly. It takes some manoeuvring to get it all in. We couldn't all go and I had had enough, plus if the old bill stopped the car there was no way I wanted to be there to answer the questions. The poor guy with the car was obviously vital and it was agreed that the guy who'd brought the now dead bloke with him was the most responsible, so he went too.

After the car had left we all wanted to go our separate ways very quickly and get as out of it as we could, it had been one hell of a day. Carol and I sat in our flat drinking Tenants super on top of methadone and chain-smoking spliffs. We didn't talk, we just abused and there was no stopping till we passed out. All we wanted to do was block the day out and escape. I tried very hard not to take a good look at what I was like now and when I did get a pang of guilt or moral judgement I would change my train of thought immediately as I hated what I had become.

The following day curiosity got the better of us. It had been agreed that the lady of the house would anonymously call the old Bill and say she had seen something strange in the woods. We got tanked up and walked up to the road by the coppice. There were cop cars all over the place and yellow tape round the trees. We had seen enough and walked home ready for another session. After that day it was never mentioned again.

Criss was still on the scene but not as often as she had been. That meant seeing the kids became increasingly difficult. Her relationship with Bob seemed to have improved and I think they saw me as an intrusion on their lives. I guess that was fair enough, I'd have felt the same way. When I did have the kids for a day it meant that I had to be sober. I was strict about that and was determined that they would never see me in a right state.

Now that might not sound too difficult, having one day off, but when your body is used to a daily dose of abuse it misses it like crazy and reminds you with a variety of pains. I'd struggle through the day, the kids distracting me from the withdrawal and five minutes after they'd left I'd be pouring back the booze and sucking on a spliff with all my might trying to make up for the lost hours. It was also to obliterate the sober reality of my life, as that was the scariest thing for me.

11
Psycho

The relationships I had in the world I lived in were mainly fleeting but occasionally you do come across someone who becomes more than a passing acquaintance. Around this time I was developing such a relationship. I won't use the word friend, as they didn't exist. The people that became more permanent always had an agenda but it was usually a mutually beneficial one, and such was the case with Psycho. He was the kind of guy that you'd never take to meet your mother for fear of her having a heart attack. He had tattoos everywhere, including his ears and face. Across his forehead were the words, 'Made in Britain', and adorning the rest of his face was a spider's web.

Our relationship started because we found that we were a pretty good combination when it came to shoplifting. Together we made quite a pair and terrified all but the bravest shop-workers. Anyone that did approach us, and it was a rare occurrence, was treated to a Psycho outburst and he threw such a fit that no one noticed I had walked out of the shop with our booty. We would then meet up at a designated spot and share the spoils. We also became drinking partners and in that we excelled.

Hanging around with Psycho had brought me to a new level. Having abandoned any moral attitudes and become completely immersed in the filth of street life, my human side had faded till there was very little left. I had become a walking sponge for substances and that was my only need to exist. To feel anything beyond this was to stretch beyond where I could reach. I had no respect for anything, including life, especially my own. A year before I'd have looked at Psycho and stayed well clear. Now he was my 'mate'. I had fallen to the lowest point yet surely it couldn't get any worse.

I was skint. My habits had swollen and I needed more gear each week to keep up with the tolerance building in my system. Carol and I were arguing more than usual and it was always about money. It was driving me mad and I had to find a solution. At the end of a particularly nasty row, I stormed out of the flat and fuelled with anger and frustration stomped down towards the beachfront. I was determined to find a solution to our problems. Sitting on a bench looking out at the sea I wracked my brains, or what was left of them, for a way to make money. I needed money to take drugs to blot out all the reality of my situation. Then the answer hit me, it was so simple, become a dealer again but this time try not to use my entire stock myself. I knew I had to do something, as I was sick of sleeping rough every time Carol and me rowed, that seemed like every other night and winter coming, I needed cash.

The problem was one of capital. I didn't have any money to start the process and buy my initial stash, however, I knew a man who might be able to help and set off in search of Psycho. Psycho had been in the area for a long time, on and off, and knew just about everyone and where to find them, those that were still alive anyway. He knew all the dealers and where they lived. I found him on the front, drinking with one of the gangs. I suggested we go for a walk, putting emphasis on the word 'walk'. He looked at me and instantly twigged something was afoot. We walked away from the others and I laid out my plan. It was simple, we would go through the list of dealers Psycho knew and pick the least vicious one, beat the shit out of him, rob him of his stash and replace him in the chain.

Psycho loved the idea and started reeling off names of dealers he knew. All dealers are pretty nasty pieces of work and have a group of henchmen they know to protect them. If we chose the wrong one, we could be getting ourselves into serious trouble. As Psycho went through his list, thinking out loud, he suddenly stopped and with a glint in his eye and a cruel twist to his lips said, 'I know just the fucker we need'. The 'fucker' Psycho was referring to, was a small-time dealer who was at the weaker end of the vicious bastard scale.

After picking our victim we came up with a plan. We would ask around, posing as potential customers and find out what day his delivery arrived. Then it was a case of simply turning up and robbing him. As it turned out we only had to wait three days. He lived in a normal street by our standards, badly lit by the one remaining streetlight in good working order. There was rubbish lining the pavements, abandoned shopping trolleys and a smashed-up old car. We walked up the road pumped up on booze and adrenaline. We were both looking forward to the night as the rewards were going to be great. Psycho took pleasure in violence and that had always worried me, I didn't take pleasure in it but was very good at it.

We reached the address and Psycho pounded on the front door. There was the noise of shuffling and a mumbled shout. The door opened but only a few inches as there were three sets of chains attaching it to the frame. In a slurred voice the dealer asked who it was. 'It's me' growled Psycho. 'I haven't seen you for a while, what do you want?' asked the dealer. 'What do you fucking think!' The chains came off and as the door opened, the light from the hallway illuminated the small path we were standing on. As previously arranged, this was my cue to burst in and take care of any henchmen. I needn't have worried. I ran into the house smashing the door against the wall and sending the dealer flying backwards. He landed, sprawling across the hall floor. It was clear he was on his own and I jumped onto his chest, knee first. This winded him and once I was in position I moved my knee up to his neck.

The door to the right of his head thundered in its frame and a hell of a noise boomed from the other side. It sounded like the Hounds of the Baskervilles. The doorframe continued to rattle as the huge dog behind it put all its efforts into coming through to join us. The dog behind the door didn't want to lick us to death.

I leant forwards and when our faces were an inch apart spat out, 'we want all your fucking drugs, where are they?' His face was very red by now and he could hardly speak but managed to squeak, 'fuck you!' I put more pressure on his neck and asked him again, he repeated his answer, although by now could only manage a whisper. At this point I looked round at Psycho standing in the hallway. This wasn't in the plan, we presumed that the location of the drugs would be given up pretty sharpish after some simple persuasion techniques. Psycho looked down at the two of us and told me to let him go. With a look of evil in his eyes he said, with menace, 'I know how to make him talk, bring him into the kitchen.'

I took my knee off the dealer's throat and he gasped great lungfuls of air. Taking hold of his lapels I dragged him along the hall, with the dog still barking at us. After manhandling him into a metal chair I stood back and looked at Psycho. The dealer was still recovering and was silent. I had no idea what Psycho was planning and the look on his face scared *me* let alone the dealer. Psycho picked up the toaster and unplugged it. Tearing out the flex he threw the toaster across the room. With the wires hanging from one end he replaced the plug and turned the switch on. At that moment I realised what he had in mind and was frozen to the spot. With a crooked smile, he looked at me and said, 'hold him down.' I moved, in what felt like slow motion, and stood behind the dealer my arms around his chest.

Psycho took the flex and pushed it into the dealer's throat. I let go immediately. He convulsed and his eyes seemed to bulge in their sockets. He pissed himself and when Psycho took the flex away screamed, 'Tumble dryer, it's in the tumble dryer,' He slid off the chair and fell to the kitchen floor as if he were made of water. I was stunned but kept my cool. Psycho already had his hand in the tumble dryer. His whole arm disappeared and as he withdrew, produced a large bag full of gear from behind a secret panel. He threw it to me and I pocketed it quickly. He turned to the crumpled figure on the floor and kicked him hard in the stomach. 'Cash!' he yelled, simply. The dealer whimpered and pointed to a ceramic coffee jar on the worktop, his power of speech long gone. Psycho picked up the jar and smashed it on the counter. In the pieces lay a bundle of notes that Psycho put in his pocket.

He picked up the flex again and the dealer flinched and curled up into a tight ball. 'If you know what's good for you mush, you'll be leaving town!' Psycho said calmly and with cold malice. I stood there in silence trying to take in what had happened. This was now my world and I had to accept it. I must have had something decent left in me, as I knew I didn't like any of this. We walked out and strolled down the street. Putting on a posh accent, Psycho smiled at me and said, 'I thought that went rather well, didn't you?' Relieved it was over, I just nodded "yes.' And with that sank another few feet towards complete despair.

Whenever I was sober enough to reflect on where I'd got to I'd amaze myself with the depths to which I'd sunk. I never seemed to stop increasing the danger I put myself in. On top of everything I now had to worry about an enraged dealer after me. I hoped we'd scared him too much to bother but I knew I was just kidding myself. In the state I was usually in it was just another element to add to the paranoia. I now believed all the stories I had heard about Psycho. He was worse than his infamous street legend and now *I* was his partner in crime; what did that make me?

We spent the night at another drinker's house, partying and celebrating. Any thoughts of regret quickly washed away. We shared out our day's work, which was better than we'd hoped for. We had four and a half grand in cash and a couple of grand's worth of puff and heroin. I'd been thinking of packing in the heroin as it was slowly killing me and I knew it. I felt awful afterwards and more importantly weak. The last thing you wanted to be on the street was weak. I wasn't eating as it was difficult to keep anything down and I didn't want to end up a walking skeleton. I stayed in the house for the next few days coming off the smack. The owner didn't mind as long as I paid him in booze. I lay on the floor during the day, shivering and sweating and trying to force booze down. Regular trips to the toilet to deal with the diarrhoea were made excruciatingly painful by the cramps in my legs but I was determined to become a strictly booze addict.

I struggled through the week to find myself at the end feeling better and stronger than I had in quite a while. I went out for the first time in over a week to buy myself a slap up breakfast in a local café, I wolfed the lot down feeling dead proud of myself for battling and winning the smack addiction. In the course of events I shouldn't have been so smug as I simply upped my intake of booze and puff to compensate. After a week away from Carol I found myself actually missing her and after my breakfast returned to the flat.

My giro day was coming up so I knew that even if she didn't want to see me for me she would want my cash. The relationship I had with Carol was painfully transparent. We both knew we were using each other and pretending it was love when it was actually convenience. What I might have thought was her missing me, while I was away, was actually her fretting at the diminishing contents of her purse.

The main reason we stuck together was that when you live with a constant sense of impending doom it's nicer to do it with company. We both needed to have another human being around just to remind us that we were still alive. When it came to Carol and I, we were stuck with each other, no one would put up with us other than us; a perfect partnership of co-dependence and convenience.

When I walked back into the flat I was met with a fierce woman. She was yelling at me, 'Where the fuck have you been!' and 'What the fuck have you been doing?' I stood there, a bit stuck but made up some bullshit. This became a familiar pattern, as I hadn't told her I'd become a dealer and I was out and about at all hours tending to my customer's needs. She was getting sick of me going out for hours on end with no real explanation. I had places to be. I kept her quiet by giving her some of my supplies but it couldn't go on forever and in the middle of a blazing row one night told her the truth.

I was selective with the truth and swapped the reality of the situation with the dealer for a concocted story about back pay from the DSS paying for a load of puff. I lied and told her I was only selling puff and neglected to tell her about the smack I was supplying to the needle gangs we so despised. As dealers go, I was a pretty bad one. I was drinking and smoking too much of the profit and was over generous, handing out sympathy deals to desperate punters who couldn't pay the full price. I felt sorry for some of them and knew how they felt and that the only thing to keep the pain away was the gear in my pocket. I felt good about helping them, but in fact was only enabling them to continue their slow deaths.

The money and drugs slipped through my fingers like sand so when it was time to replenish my stocks I was forever dipping into my float to keep going. This was not good economics and before long my float was sunk and so was my dealing. I had debts owed to me all round town but wasn't a hundred percent sure who they were, each day melting into the next with little memory of events. I tried to call them in but miraculously people faded into thin air and I was soon left with nothing again.

The money and free drugs had come to an end, again, and that signalled the re-emergence of the rows. When I wasn't keeping Carol in the state of oblivion she had become accustomed to, I would be subjected to all manner of foul abuse and anger. I did my usual trick and picked up a blanket and set off into the night to find some doorway that was free from dog shit or piss and settle in for the night. All I had to do was make sure I kept warm which is easier said than done. When you're in withdrawal the shakes become permanent and I wouldn't have been the last drunk to die from hypothermia thinking it was merely withdrawal. I don't think Carol realised how ill I felt. When the waves of withdrawal come over you the paranoia and fear that go with it are terrifying. Your brain seems to short circuit and permanently floods your mind with thoughts of attack and other dangers. You exist on tenterhooks waiting for the inevitable knife or bat to come swinging in from the darkness.

As I curled up in the doorways the only thought that gave me comfort was suicide. It sounds strange but imagining the relief and escape from all the pain calmed me and made me feel safe. How twisted was the world I lived in where the thought death was the only thing that comforted me. I wasn't enjoying a single part of my life. All I felt were feelings of pain, doom, guilt, shame, despair and confusion, the perfect recipe for a descent into madness. The only place that had become tolerable was one of complete denial, when I was cloaked in drunken or drug-addled abandon. To this end my world revolved around getting into that state and trying to stay there.

I was curled up one evening in a doorway praying I wouldn't wake up when a familiar voice cut through my thoughts. 'Oy, what the fuck are you doing out here?' It was Psycho. He had two dogs with him, one of which was trying to revive me from my slumbered state with constant licks to the face. I gently pushed the dog away hoping he didn't get offended and find my nose the perfect fit for his mouth. I leant up on my elbows and looked up into the spider-web face. 'I'm off to military Mick's, you want to come along?' I had no idea who military Mick was but knew there'd be booze and it'd be warm so I said, 'Sure.'

I gathered my blanket and walked along the road with Psycho. We made our way through an array of darkened back streets and alleyways till we reached a door that hung half off its hinges. It was another of the many squats that existed in this part of town. Four flights of stairs later, I found myself with a roof over my head and began to feel warmth seeping into my body again. The heat came from a two-bar electric heater wired up, through a window, to a street lamp outside. It meant it only worked from six in the evening to seven the following morning but it was a lot better than being outside. The room was filthy and smelt funny but at least I wasn't lying on concrete anymore.

Psycho called through to the adjoining room,' Mike, I've brought someone with me, but don't worry they're all right.'

'Yeah, OK, whatever.' Came the response. I was shaking badly and feeling like shit, I hadn't had a drink in six hours. Psycho looked down at me, sitting on the floor and tutted.

' Looks like you need a drink fella.' He said, with a voice that was as close as he got to concern. He picked up a black bag from the corner of the room and I heard the familiar chinking that was music to my ears. My spirits soared at the thought of what would come out. I had had a result, a roof *and* free booze. The chinking meant bottles and that meant proper booze, no nasty cider or cans.

Psycho pulled out a bottle of dark rum and I smiled inside. He handed it over and I opened it savouring the crack of the seal. I gulped it down my throat as if I was drinking water. I had the familiar retching to contend with at first but soon was filling my damaged stomach with the liquid I so desperately needed. I lay back and relaxed, feeling warmer as the alcohol flooded my system.

Mike walked into the room, kicking aside the various bottles on the floor. He walked over to Psycho and took a bottle from the bag scratching his matted hair as he went. It was clear he didn't wash very often and dirt rained down on his shoulders as he itched.

'Haven't I seen you around before?' he asked, 'don't you deal puff?' I glanced sideways at Psycho and smiled ruefully. 'Well I used to but the old Bill were onto me so I'm laying off for a while' I mumbled. 'Well if you ever need somewhere to crash out then you're welcome here.'

'Cheers' I said, trying to sound tough and grateful at the same time. With the open invitation declared, Mike sauntered off again, one hand in his hair and the other clutching his bottle.

I looked up at Psycho, my feelings of dread and fear seeping into the carpet with every gulp. 'So what's the deal with Mike then?' I asked. He then went into a long story about how Mike was a professional dog breeder and that they were going into business together. 'There's loads of money in it.' Psycho said enthusiastically, 'I'll show you.' With that he disappeared and was gone for a while. I kept drinking, thinking that I'd get as much of the bottle down my neck before he asked for it back. He returned with his dogs and I'm pretty sure they weren't from the Kennel Club.

The two beasts stood in the middle of the room panting. The larger of the two was covered in scars and its right ear was half missing. It had a lost look in its one eye and the other was glazed over, presumably blind. 'He's a right hard bastard.' I said, trying to sound convincing, the last thing I wanted was to offend Psycho. 'He looks as if he can handle himself.' I said, although internally thought he might have had one fight too many.

'Oh yeh, he's a right champion, his name's Bond' beamed Psycho like a proud parent. His face changed and became serious as he leaned down to my level. 'You know what, it's a good job I met you today, do you think you could do me a favour?' Considering the position I was in I was hardly likely to refuse, I didn't like the idea of finding out what a refusal meant to Psycho. 'I'm going up to town to find a bitch for breeding and need someone to look after my two dogs.' Brilliant, I thought, the responsibility of two dogs, and two dogs that belonged to a violent nutcase, just what I needed. I smiled, 'sure, no problem, leave them with me' I said, knowing there was no other possible response.

Mike had re-entered the room and settled down on the floor. The three of us sat there drinking from our individual bottles and I asked how Mike had come to get the squat. He began a tale of woe that left me feeling sorry for him even though he was in the wrong. He had an ex-girlfriend and two kids in London who'd kicked him out due to his drinking and now had pissed off a single mum he'd been knocking about with because he'd nicked her DSS book, cashed what he could and drunk the profits. Apparently her two brothers were after his blood so he'd found somewhere to lay low for a while.

Before long the booze had flowed to its end and the sun had come up. Psycho got to his feet and said his good-byes. At the door he turned and with a look that could kill said, 'Now you two make sure to take care of my dogs.' And then he was gone. Mike and I looked at each other and then the dogs. Bond was lying down looking as sweet as an ugly beaten-up half-breed could and the pit-bull puppy stared at us as if to back up his master's words. The puppy wasn't so sweet and would bite its own shadow out of spite. Mike went to the booze bag and fished out another couple of bottles and we proceeded to swap stories and drink for the rest of the day. As sundown arrived we took the dogs to the back of the squat where they could have the run of an overgrown garden.

We went back to the main room and carried on drinking till we passed out. This was all we did for the next two days, increasingly wondering where Psycho had got to, neither of us were sure exactly how long it took to find a suitable bitch. On the third day we drained the last of the bottles and without booze were stuck for what to do. 'Let's go down the front and look for him.' Mike suggested. With nothing better to do I agreed and off we went.

As it turned out it was to be a solo trip as Mike was still too scared to go out in case the 'brothers' were waiting for him. I gathered the leads and chased the dogs round the garden till I got hold of them. As I left the squat being pulled in two directions I scolded myself for the 'good' idea to take the dogs with me for a bit of a walk. Bond was fine, although neither were trained, but the puppy was hell bent on taking out whatever came within biting distance, be it car, human or other dog. The only thing the puppy seemed to like was Bond and I thanked my lucky stars for that.

I made my way down to the front apologising as I went. The three of us must have looked some sight. I managed to reach a group of drinkers that I knew were known to Psycho and asked them whether they had seen him. I wasn't expecting the reply but was hardly shocked. An old lady, infamous along the front spoke up. She had taken to boozing in later life and always wore a dead fox stole round her neck. She said, in a plummy voice, 'You haven't a chance of finding our friend psychopath, he's on the run from the boys in blue.'

Apparently Psycho had robbed a garage on his way to town and the police were hunting for him. With his spider's web face, he hardly blended into the background and so was presumably laying low. So that was that, Psycho was on the run and I was stuck with his dogs. It wasn't the best position I'd been in but it wasn't the worst. I made my way back to the squat to tell Mike.

As I stood in the room relaying the story to Mike I could see him getting increasingly uptight. Mike was a nervous chap at the best of times but this uncertainty left him in a state. With the combined pressure of 'the brothers' constant threat and the unknown whereabouts of Psycho he snapped and stuttered out, 'F-f-fuck this, I can't handle being around here any longer, I'm off to London.' He walked round the room periodically taking giant gulps of booze, his hands shaking. 'I'm not staying round here to have the shit kicked out of me and I know people in London, I'm sure they'll take the dogs and find them a good home.

I stood there and thought about it, weighing up the two options I had. They were, stay where I was with the dogs and wait for Psycho to return, possibly after a stretch in jail, or follow Mike to London and take my chances. I had just got my giro and didn't like the thought of sharing my cash with a mangy dog and a devil spawned puppy so decided to go. 'Right then mucker,' I said decisively to Mike, 'it's off to London then.' And with that the decision was made.

Mike assured me that there wouldn't be any trouble finding digs, he said one of the groups he knew would find us space. I was looking forward to the trip and felt glad to be getting rid of the dogs, as they had become a constant source of problems. I wasn't up to looking after myself properly, let alone a couple of animals. We packed what we needed, me with my one blanket, giro and the four bottles of booze we had and Mike with a couple of bags of clothes. We got to the station, boarded the train and made it all the way to London without paying which was a result. Once there we made a beeline for Mike's aunt where we could stash our stuff.

She was a nice old lady and pretty blind, which was a good thing for us considering how we looked. We dumped the stuff, all but the booze, which wasn't going more than a foot away from my reach and said our 'thank-yous'. I stashed the booze in various pockets and we set off for a pub that Mike said he knew and where we could find someone to give us a place to stay. After walking for over an hour we reached a rundown boozer in some part of London. I say 'some part' because I was being led by Mike and didn't know where the fuck I was. He scooped up the puppy and went through the door. It was a 'no-dogs' pub so I said I'd stay with Bond outside and wait for him. And wait I did. After twenty minutes it began to rain and the wind got up. After another five minutes of standing in the rain I decided enough was enough and tied Bond to the nearest lamp post. He didn't like it and began whimpering and barking as soon as I'd walked off.

I entered the pub and looked around for Mike but there was no sign of him. I walked up to the bar and gave the landlord a description but he said he hadn't seen him either. 'Fuck!' I said loudly to no one and turned round to leave the pub. I changed my mind and ordered a pint; at that point I didn't care about anything and had to work out what was going on. As I drank I played through the day in my mind. The same, obvious question kept popping up, 'Why had Mike done a runner?' Surely I hadn't been invited to protect him and carry his bags, then again in my world that would be the most likely answer. I cursed him inwardly and drained my glass.

I returned to Bond who was lying on the pavement soaked to the skin and looking very sorry for himself. I untied him had ruffled his head, I felt sorry for him. I looked up and down the street and tried to formulate a plan. My best bet was to retrace my steps back to Mike's auntie and take it from there. The problem was, I didn't know where Mike's auntie lived. So I was basically stuffed. I had no idea where I'd come from and no idea where I was, brilliant.

I decided to try and retrace my steps, so Bond and I set off into the cold wind and rain. I had been walking for hours and had got more and more lost. I hadn't seen anything I recognised and was completely knackered. I looked down at Bond who had started to limp badly and agreed with him, it was time to stop. There was nothing for it but to find a doorway and camp down for the night. That was easier said than done as I had made the decision whilst standing on a suburban street. I picked up Bond who could hardly walk and set off to look for shops.

By the time I found a small parade the night was upon us and the streets were pretty much empty, no one choosing to be out on such a night. I settled in to the little alcove of an electrical shop's doorway and wrapped the coat around both Bond and I. We were both soaked and rain drops dripped from my hair and beard as they took a small detour on their way to the ground. I was thoroughly miserable and lonely. I didn't know where I was and was miles away from anywhere I knew. Of all my nights on the street, this was one of the worst. I had no blanket and the wind and rain found me no matter how hard I tried to push myself into the doorway. I took out a bottle and without moving the spout from my lips downed half of it.

As the light began to filter through the clouds as the beginnings of dawn approached I gingerly got to my feet. I took a breakfast swig from the bottle and stretched as much as pain would allow. In the hours before light returned I had mulled over my predicament and decided to try and find the house of an uncle of mine who lived in Brixton. I didn't know the address but would recognise the road when I saw it. It was a thin possibility but it was all I had and I had to do something. I knew that by nine o'clock the post offices would be open so I'd be able to cash my Giro and with money in my pocket get back to the coast at least. So with the faintest glimmer of optimism Bond and I set out in what was very possibly the wrong direction.

We walked ten minutes before Bond lay down and refused to budge. A night in the wet and cold had frozen his legs and he wasn't having any of it. I gathered him up and carrying him under my coat carried on walking. Eventually we came to a stretch of road with a load of shops on it including a post office. I couldn't wait to cash my giro and get to a café for a feed and warm-up. It was forty minutes past eight and Bond and I stood outside waiting for the grand opening.

As the doors opened I walked in shocking a somewhat bemused Indian guy. I was first to the counter and put my Giro through the glass partition. He consulted it thoroughly, then looked up at me and with a dismissive gesture passed it back saying, 'not the same address mate, nothing I can do.' I was so pissed off I didn't even have the energy to argue. My luck had descended to an all time low. I gave up and asked for directions to the nearest train station. My only option was to get a train home, hide away and hope I made it to the other end without any trouble.

The way things were going, however, that seemed highly improbable. Just as I turned the corner at the end of the street my luck changed. In front of me was my uncle's road.

In the state I was in it was as close to a miracle as I'd been to in a very long time. The next problem I faced was whether he would be home and if he was what would he make of me. As I got closer to the house I thought about turning back, he might slam the door in my face, or worse, after all I didn't exactly look like the prodigal nephew returned. The last time he'd seen me was at a family wedding and I was clean, suited and booted; now I was dressed like a Romanian refugee, had a foot long beard and was filthy from the ground up. I can't imagine I smelled too good either. I decided that whatever happened it was worth the risk and apprehensively approached the front door. I gave the bell a push and awaited my fate.

There was noise from behind the door and a call, 'OK, I'm coming.' I braced myself and got ready as the door opened. The man in front of me looked me up and down, squinted and then said, 'Is that really you?' I smiled showing the gap in my front teeth, 'Hi uncle,' was all I could manage. 'Come in to the warmth son, you look like you could do with a drink.' Luckily for me he too was a piss head.

He was very patient with me and didn't appear to be shocked. I sat in a comfy armchair and the pain and fear of the last two days melted away from my body. My hands were shaking and he three-quarters filled a tumbler with scotch and handed it to me. I grasped it with both hands. The difference between lying on a wet pavement in the wind and sitting in a centrally heated house is almost immeasurable. He sat down with me and I noticed that he'd brought the bottle of scotch with him. He poured himself a healthy measure and topped me up. We began to talk and didn't stop for a good hour. He didn't lecture me on anything but made gentle persuasive comments, including a suggestion to get in touch with my parents.

I hadn't spoken to them for years and didn't really think now was the right time. I tried to explain how I had got to my current state but mumbled a lot of the words and tried to hide my embarrassment. Eventually the combination of booze and familiarity meant I felt comfortable enough to ask him for the favour I needed. After a pause in the conversation I asked, 'I was just wondering if.. .' and that was as far as I got. My uncle held his hand up and without expression walked into the kitchen.

I sat there thinking I'd blown my chance when he walked back in, handed me forty quid saying I didn't need to pay him back, he also offered a bag of food for both me and Bond. He didn't want any thanks and said he'd feed the dog before I went on my way. I was shocked and slightly dumbfounded. No one had shown me any unconditional kindness for a long, long time, it was difficult to accept and understand. But I was grateful 'Thank-you' I said and left, walking up the street and feeling refreshed and warm. I was humbled by his generosity and felt sad that I lived in a world where it didn't exist. How I longed for something more that what my life consisted of. I shook my head and put it out of my mind, my addict telling me that things were good and booze was on the way. I focused on the day ahead, things were looking up, I had money and food and the wind had blown the clouds away and a soft wintry sunshine was filtering through the branches of the tree-lined road.

I set off for Clapham Common, using the directions I'd been given. Poor old Bond was in a bad way and was only just about able to hobble along beside me. I thought the exercise might do him some good but the look on his face told me otherwise. We made it to the Common and sat on a bench. I had gone via the offie and was stocked up with cans. I looked into the bag for some dog food and got out a tin. I bent down to Bond and rubbed his legs to get some blood flowing, then opened the can and gave it to him. He seemed to perk-up and wagged his tail. I took a long gulp of booze, sighed and sat back. What was I going to do now?

I looked down at Bond and thought of Psycho, wondering where he was and if I'd see him again. I had become quite attached to Bond but knew he'd have to go, I couldn't afford to keep him and couldn't carry him around forever. At that point a small black terrier appeared and started the sniffing routine that dogs go through. Bond seemed to like him and they wagged at each other. An old gezza with a soft face approached and said, 'Oh he seems to have found a friend there.'

A sudden flash of inspiration shot through my mind, 'Yeh, they look like old mates.' I said and gave the old man my best smile. 'It's a real shame though,' I said trying to sound as choked as possible, 'What?' asked the old man. 'Well, I've got to take him down Battersea later,' I whispered, 'I can't have him any more.' The old man took the bait and stood studying Bond. My plan worked and the old fella jumped at the chance of taking Bond under his wing. I walked off towards the exit nearest the tube and looked back over my shoulder. Bond was being lovingly stroked by his new owner and was feverishly wagging his tail; I think he somehow knew his luck had changed.

I was glad that Bond wouldn't have to suffer in cold doorways anymore and smiled at the thought that I had done a good thing. It didn't last long as I pondered the possibility of telling Psycho that I had given away his dog. I didn't think he'd take it that well. 'Still,' I thought, he was on the run and was possibly in the nick so I should be all right.......

With alcohol infused enthusiasm I marched to the station ready for the journey home and whatever lay ahead of me. I managed to get the last train back to the coast and settled down in the luggage compartment behind some bikes. I tucked into another can and began to reflect.

The meeting with my uncle had brought back a flood of memories that I hadn't given headspace to for a long while. I remembered a time when I saw my family regularly and felt part of something even though that part of something was bad. How had I got to where I was? I had never imagined that life could descend to such a state of despair and chaos. It felt as if I wasn't leading my life anymore, it was being led and I was a mere spectator watching on from the sidelines in horror as it sank deeper into filth. It was like watching a particularly gritty TV programme with me as the lead. Dead bodies, bloody violence, hopeless relationships and chronic substance abuse; surely this wasn't me.

I looked down at my hands and knew that the scars that adorned my body were testament to the truth that it *was* me living through this, spending every day struggling to get through a thick bog of immoral insanity. Each minute was a constant battle to survive and I didn't even want to, hiding away from the truth of my reality in booze, drugs and destruction. I was losing ground in the battles, daily, and wondered how much longer I could last.

It was around midnight when I eventually got back to the coast, glad to have familiar surroundings again. I needed clothes, which meant returning to the flat and getting ready for the inevitable fight. I knocked on the door and was ready to turn and leave if the arguments started; I was in no mood to go through the tried and tested routine. Carol opened the door and smiled, she threw her arms round my neck and hugged me tight, slurring the words, 'Where have you been, I've missed you?' She was speaking softly, without malice and I knew that that meant she was out of it. As I peeled her off my body and looked at her face I knew why she was being so nice. Her eyes were half closed and unfocused, her cheeks flushed and her body limp. I recognised the effects of someone drifting through a cotton-wool world of heroin.

She was totally unconnected to the real world but just about able to function in it. She staggered back to the couch and collapsed, murmuring, 'Psycho's been round looking for you.' The words, quietly spoken, sent shivers running up and down my spine. I went cold and suddenly the bleak reality of losing the dogs and facing up to their owner became something I had to face. 'When, when was he here' the words rushed out of my mouth, fearing he was still around. 'Oh, not that long ago, he didn't seem very happy.' I wasn't surprised. I was in the shit again. I had to find him and deal with it, but the prospect of telling a lethal nutcase who electrocuted people for fun, that I'd lost his prize possessions, didn't fill me with glee.

I went through to the kitchen, got a couple of cans from the fridge and went back to the sofa and folding her up like a concertina, moved Carol to one end. She sighed and folded her legs under herself like a child. I longed to be drifting in her world rather than sitting in mine. I swigged on a can and started to play the various scenarios that might happen between Psycho and me. The most unrealistic of which was for him to accept the story I gave him and shrug it off. The more likely version ended with me being dragged off to a disused squat and tortured to death.

I remembered a story about a guy who had wandered off with Psycho's bottle of booze when he was asleep on the beach. He had found him and tied him to a chair, then slowly broken each of his knuckles with a hammer, waiting for an apology after each blow; he took his revenge seriously. I was winding myself into ever-tighter knots and started to look for a way out. As ever, substances came to the rescue and I spotted the end of the heroin that Carol had used to fly high and pass out. I set myself up and filled my lungs. Within a few minutes the problems of Psycho melted away. I lay back and drifted into a senseless bliss, ending in blackness filled sleep.

The morning came and with it the stark truth, the problem of Psycho was still there and so was I. I reached out for my morning can and pulled the ring back. The sound of it opening woke Carol. She rubbed her eyes, and without the blanket of heroin immediately began to lay into me. I calmed her down and told her about Psycho. This was not a good move. She got up and stormed round the room yelling at me for being so stupid, 'He's a completely mad fucker, and he's going to kill us.' I tried to calm her down, telling her the story about him being on the run and that therefore he would be lying low. 'He's not lying that fucking low if he can come round here,' she screamed. I knew she was right and I came to the only conclusion available to me, I'd have to find him and have it out.

The post office where I cashed my giro was a hive of activity for street folk. As some queued up to get their giro's and others who'd already spent theirs hung around for cash scraps. I knew that it would be the best place to get the low-down on Psycho's whereabouts. I shouted through to Carol, who had gone to bed and was starting to withdraw, 'I'm off to get some booze and puff, I'll be back as soon as I can.' I grabbed my coat and opened the door.

I was frozen to the spot, struggling to deal with the sight I was greeted with, in front of me stood hell on legs, Psycho. His nostrils were flaring and the veins in his head pumped with blood. He had a furious, hungry look in his eyes and his knuckles were white, emphasising the words 'love' and 'hate' on each clenched fist. I think I knew which one was in charge this morning.

'Gimme me fucking dogs,' he demanded. For a split second I thought of slamming the door in his face but the repercussions flashed through my already troubled mind and they weren't pretty. In the few seconds I had I couldn't come up with a single plausible story and ended up blurting out the truth taking as few breaths as possible. He stepped forwards one pace till I could feel his breath on my face and smell the booze.

'I want my dogs and you are going to get them. You have two days to sort it or you better be ready to kill me, cause that's what I'm going to do to you,' he said slowly, his voice shaking with anger. He backed away keeping eye contact for at least four steps. I was still frozen to the spot, relief flooding through me that he didn't want to rip me apart there and then.

I shut the door and went back inside, I paced the room and wished I had some booze. That became my only thought and I set off for the offie. On the way I quickened my pace as I thought Psycho might return and have a pop at Carol to get at me. Word had got round that the dogs were in London and I started the scenario playing again. I was fucked, I couldn't go back to London, as there was a less than slim chance I'd bump into the old man again and Mike was God knows where. I was stuck between a rock and a nutcase. I knew I'd have to face the nutcase. I gathered the provisions and hightailed it back to the flat. Carol was lying on the bed shaking and shivering. I tossed her some booze and started to explain the situation. Without planning to scare her witless I managed to achieve it in record time. The words 'Psycho' and 'better double lock the door' triggered her fear response and set it to maximum.

She forced the booze down gulping and gagging. When her system was working again she got up and joined me in pacing the room again. We walked round and round shouting at each other and drinking furiously. As we became increasingly desperate the solutions became more outlandish. She suddenly stopped and said, 'Call the old Bill, that'll work, tell them you've seen him around town.' I stood still, faced her and in as serious a tone as I could, said, 'no fucking way, that's a line you don't cross.' Not calling the police was the golden rule. If I did and was found out, it would have been the ultimate sell-out and my name would be mud forever. I'd also been brought up to face your own problems and deal with them yourself, even if that meant getting a good hiding and I was certain I'd get that in this case.

The rowing and drinking continued long into the day and by the time nightfall came we were both well and truly pissed. We were tired and worn out and didn't have the energy for any more rowing so collapsed on the sofa and went quiet. As the booze had increased so had my confidence and by the time we collapsed I was convinced that I could take Psycho in a fight. I spent the remaining hours, before passing out, convincing Carol that all would be well and not to worry, as I'd sort it out. Carol wasn't convinced. The more I talked the more I convinced myself and my last thoughts were focused on where and when I'd tackle him and various strategies for ending it quickly.

The morning light flooded through the windows, waking us up to the sober truth again, and I found that my previous night's courage had evaporated during the night. We both had chronic hangovers and tucked into the remaining cans immediately. They were finished by mid morning and another booze run was needed. The prospect of facing a proper psychopath who would gladly cut my throat and leave me for dead loomed in front of me. This was it, I'd have to go thorough with my plans and I started to build myself up. I replayed my best fights in my mind and gathered as much confidence from them as I could. I stood up and shadows boxed getting the blood pumping like I had done years before when I would box regularly or spar with my mad family. Carol sat on the sofa looking scared, whether it was for my health or hers I couldn't work out. She simply wanted the situation ended and I don't think she was bothered if that meant my features became slightly rearranged.

I knew the best form of defence was attack and set off, mentally convincing myself that I was going to slay him. I stomped down the street gaining belief with each step. The morning was sunny and warm and I stopped off at the offie and shop lifted a half bottle of whisky. I walked as I drank and took big gulps finishing the bottle in less than ten minutes. With the right fuel and right mental attitude I was as ready as I'd ever be. The drunks hanging round the offie had told me that Psycho was on the front with some bloke and his dog. I said out loud, 'more fucking dogs, that's exactly what I need'. I knew where he was and approached with complete confidence. I could see him in the distance and ten steps later yelled, 'Oy, Psycho, come on then, you know what this is about!'
He heard me and shouted something I couldn't hear. I noticed the guy with him and the pit bull he was throwing sticks for. I put them out of mind hoping the dog didn't go for me and focused all my energies on one thing, the tattooed figure twenty feet in front. I broke into a run and as I got nearer started to sprint as fast as I could, without breaking a stride I leapt into the air and giving it all I had went into a double-legged kick which flew into Psycho's chest. I heard a crack and we both went sprawling onto the ground. He wasn't prepared for such an assault. I certainly hadn't planned it and Psycho was so shocked that he had not taken any evasive action.

I scrambled to my feet expecting a fight and glared at the bloke holding back the pit bull by the collar. I prayed he didn't let it go. Psycho stared up at me winded, a look of incomprehension spread across his face. He made a move to sit up and as he did I kicked him full in the face. I made contact with a sickening 'thud' and his neck snapped backwards, his nose crunching under the force and filling his face with blood. His nose was split from the tip to the point between his eyes and blood was flowing down his face.

I stood there heaving with the effort and shock; I couldn't believe I'd got the better of him, especially as there wasn't even a scratch on me. The bloke holding the dog looked at me in disbelief, no one had ever taken out Psycho before. The crowd of drunks that had appeared from nowhere stood in silence and awe, awe of me.

I turned away, without saying a word, and strode off along the front. The adrenaline was still flowing round my system at a terrific pace and I tried to calm myself down. I heard a terrible screeching noise as Psycho, regaining his wits, screamed as loud as he could and with all the bile he could muster, 'This ain't fucking over, it ain't fucking over you hear me, I'm going to find you and fucking kill you!' At that time nothing could touch me. I felt ten feet tall and could have taken on the world. I ignored him and walked on, I couldn't wait to get home, tell Carol and celebrate. The consequences of what had happened were the last thing on my mind.

I went back to the flat, via the offie, and told Carol. She was chuffed to pieces, and asked where the booze was. We knocked back a load of booze and then, with the flourish of alcohol and success went for a walk. We ended up in the park with the usual drunks and sat around drinking. Word had got out from the morning and whizzed round the street grapevine. I got a few slaps on the back and some admiring nods but mostly people wanted to know what I thought Psycho would do next. 'Come back for more, if he's stupid enough,' I boasted. It wasn't as if I'd put him in hospital or anything He would be back, but I chose to push this thought away.

12
Death's door

As the evening drew in I wanted to test the waters and suggested that we go for a drink to a pub that was one of Psycho's favourite haunts. If things were OK in there, then I knew it'd be all right. Quite clearly I must have been very drunk to think this was a good idea. Carol agreed and off we went. The atmosphere was fine and we didn't get any hassle. Carol had gone home and was OK for me to stay for a while. I was chatting with a few blokes I knew and we ended up drinking till closing. I got a take-out from the pub and wandered into the night. My legs were a bit wobbly to say the least but the sea air and the hill climb soon sobered me up. I was half way up the hill reflecting on what had been an excellent day when a voice called out behind me, 'Hey, give us a beer chav.' I turned round and said, 'Fuck off and get your own.'

The footsteps behind me quickened and doubled and I knew immediately it wasn't the beer they were after. Whoever it was wanted to do me in big time and I knew just who had put them up to it. Within a minute there was no gap between us, and one of the guys moved in front of me and pushed me in the chest. I staggered but kept my feet. His mate had worked his way round behind me and I looked from one to the other. I was surrounded but in the state I was in wasn't scared. My main concern was that I didn't loose my booze and increased my grip on the bag. I swung my left fist at the frontal attacker and soon there were the usual legs and arms all over the place. Very little was connecting and I thought I might get away with it.

I suddenly felt pain shoot through my hip and my leg went numb. It was as if a red-hot poker had been pushed through me and I yelped. 'Come, come on, I've fucking done it,' said one of the attackers and they both scuttled off into the night. I was leaning against a fence and put my hand to the pain, it came away covered in blood. I knew I'd been stabbed but I'd been very lucky. The blade had gone in near my hip- bone and had struck it before penetrating anything vital. I'd heard it said that it doesn't hurt when you get stabbed but was quickly realising that not to be true, as my whole right side was in agony. I looked down at my right hand; at least I hadn't lost my booze.

I felt myself falling inwardly and knew that I was passing out. The feeling was enjoyable, like letting go of all responsibility and I slid down the fence to the pavement, giving in to it. I suddenly became aware of myself and snapped out of it. I knew that if I collapsed now I'd go under and might not come back, I knew I was bleeding badly but wasn't sure how badly. A strong desire to live emerged from within and a voice screamed in my head, 'GET UP NOW.' I obeyed and staggered to my feet. The voice continued, 'GET MOVING, WALK.' Again I complied, aware that I was urging myself to get back to the flat. I put one foot in front of the other and started moving, each step was a challenge and I had to constantly fight the urge to be sick and pass out.

I clambered up the hill using whatever my hands rested on to pull myself along. I could feel blood running down my leg and it was warm. It was bad and hurt and I tried to focus my mind on anything but the thought that my blood was flowing down the outside instead of the inside of my leg. The ten-minute journey back to the flat must have taken about thirty minutes and I finally reached the front door, the booze bag still firmly gripped in my right fist.

I put the booze down for the first time since leaving the pub, fished out my keys and opened the door. My hands were shaking and I felt completely done in. I picked up the bag and wrapped the plastic round my wrist. I stood at the bottom of the stairs, looked up, breathing slowly and painfully. I gathered my strength and put my right foot onto the first step. A pain shot up my leg and drilled into my hip, I bit my lip and brought my other leg to join it. I reached out and pushed the light switch. The hallways were lined with delay switches and you had a minute or so before the light went out, the idea being that you would have reached the next one by the time the first was finished. At my pace it meant a few steps of seeing then a plunge into darkness.

The pain steadily grew and although the blood flow had weakened, with each step the wound opened and I felt a new, faint trickle of liquid heat flow down my leg. I made it to the top using shear will power, struggling and stumbling along each landing and collapsed in front of Carol's door to regain some energy. As I lay there I went through the next stage in my head. I didn't think a stabbed man lurching through the door and passing out on the couch was a good move and knew I'd have to get to the shower, clean up and try and pass off the incident as a usual punch-up. The last thing I wanted was Carol turning into a gibbering wreck. Plus, if she knew the full tale I'd have weeks of grief to look forward to. I grabbed the doorknob with both hands and pulled myself up. I opened the door and after a deep breath and trying to sound as normal as possible called through to the front room, 'Hi Carol, been in a bit of fight, I'm just going to get cleaned up.'

It wasn't the first time she'd heard this and replied from the sofa in a disinterested tone, 'You OK?' 'Yeh fine, just a few scratches,' I said, still trying to sound calm. I walked through to the kitchen, taking baby steps and wincing with each movement. I put the bag of booze on the counter, chuffed that I'd not lost it. I took out two cans, opened one and drank it. Going through to the shower I began to mentally prepare myself for serious pain and started the process of blocking it out. I pictured Psycho in my mind and tried to transfer all my pain onto his image. It worked a bit and made me feel a little better. I syringed off the clear fluid from the top of a bottle of caline and morphine and drank the fluid from the syringe, I repeated this until there was none left, that was the best painkiller I had at the time.

I tried bending down to take my boots off and was sickened with pain. Any movement involving my hip tore at my right side. I bent down to undo my boots and tried to match the searing pain from my hip by clenching my teeth. I knew that it wasn't good. I wanted to scream my lungs inside out but kept the noise to a strained growl. I managed to get my boots off and stood up, the relief was glorious, I undid my jeans, the right leg of which was caked in a red and brown blood mixture, and slid them down. Once free of all clothing, bar my socks, I stood up straight and looked at the wound. It was about the size of a two pence piece and out of it gurgled a mixture of air and blood.

The cupboard above the sink was well stocked with necessary items for such an eventuality, as they happened on a regular basis, albeit not as serious as this. I took out some TCP, a tube of superglue and some sellotape. I placed the repair kit on the side of the sink and wobbled over to the shower. I stood in the small cubicle and turned on the water. I couldn't move out of the way fast enough as the first jet of water hit my back, freezing cold. I screamed, a lot louder than was necessary, using the opportunity to let out some of the pain.

I washed the blood from my legs and generally cleaned myself up, enjoying the heat and comfort the water brought. The beer and morphine were doing their job and the pain subsided momentarily. I examined the wound again and it was nasty, there was only a small trickle of blood being washed away by the constant water. I turned the shower off and stepped out, taking a towel. Drying off was OK, although I didn't bend down. The wound was still seeping but only slowly.

I picked up the bottle of TCP. This was going to sting a bit. I poured a third of it over the wound and bit down as hard as I could. Then to make sure the wound was as clean as possible cupped a handful and rubbed it in. The pain was excruciating and my eyes began to water. Once the TCP had done its job, I dried the area completely and pushing the two sides of the wound together so it looked like a pair of puckered lips squeezed a liberal line of superglue along the edges. I held on to the sides as the glue set. This was the last stage and I concentrated my mind on the reward I'd receive from the booze bag a few minutes later. When I was satisfied the wound was sealed, I wrapped the roll of sellotape round my waist a few times and pressed down on it firmly. That was that, I was fixed.

I walked through to the bedroom stiffly and got a dressing gown. I was just about to claim my reward when I realised that the bathroom had a pair of jeans and a towel, both covered in blood, lying on the floor. I gathered them up wincing with the effort and bundled them into a corner, covering them with other clothes. I went through to the kitchen, retrieved the booze and sat down slowly next to Carol. I had to clench my teeth as hard as I could sitting down and Carol asked what had happened. I told her I'd been in a scuffle, then fallen down drunk on the way home and landed on my hip. She seemed to accept the story and we both quietly settled in to some heavy drinking. It felt good to be home, clean and fixed with a can in my hand.

The table in front of me was filled with just what I needed. Carol had been out and bought a load of puff and smack. For the rest of the night the two of us laid in to the booze and drugs as usual. I had a lot to escape from and needed to get as lost as possible and Carol matched me, can for can, spliff for spliff and hit for hit. By the end of the night I was comatose and barely conscious. The last thing I remember was Carol getting up to go to bed taking a last hit with her and me trying and failing to follow.

I woke in the morning like I'd been woken from the dead. My whole body ached; there wasn't a single bit of me that didn't hurt. My hip had frozen up and my system was screaming for substance. My mouth felt like the bottom of a litter tray and every movement took a monumental and gruelling effort. I tried to get up but the pain beat me and I lay back down and drifted off to sleep again. The next time I woke the sun had been up for a while and my throat was dust dry. I looked over to the table and saw a can with an extinguished spliff butt on top. I leaned out and lifted it, it was at least half full. I flicked the butt off the top and took a couple of small swigs in swift succession; using my teeth as a filter. I breathed heavily through my nose trying not to taste what I was drinking. The urge to vomit was almost overpowering and I swallowed over and over forcing the booze into my system.

Once the can was empty I replaced it on the table and lay back waiting for the effects that would allow me to move again. I often thought at moments like this that when people say addicts have no will power they are completely wrong. Addicts will go to any length to fulfil their needs and push themselves towards extinction just to get a fix. We would never give up, and go through incredible pain if the ends justified the means. The problem isn't one of will power, as we have so much power we'll continue abusing till we're dead. The problem is that we don't direct that power towards stopping. Rather, we risk dying to achieve our twisted goals and unfortunately regularly achieve this.

After sitting up I needed more booze and knew Carol would have an emergency stash in the bedroom and this was an emergency. I hadn't felt this bad in a long time. I shuffled to the bedroom and started to quietly rummage around looking for liquid relief. A few times I banged something or knocked something over and peered over at Carol to make sure I hadn't disturbed her. When I opened the cupboard a load of stuff tumbled out and I was sure she'd wake up and start shouting at me and that was the last thing I needed considering the state I was in. I looked over at her and became puzzled. She was a fairly light sleeper and should have woken with the noise; I walked round to the side of the bed.

I don't know if you've ever stood over someone, a lover, baby or parent, looking for signs of breathing to confirm that they're still alive but that's what I did. I stooped down flinching at the stab of pain in my hip, and studied Carol's face intently. The curtains were drawn and there was less than half-light as I watched for movements of life. As hard as I looked I couldn't see any sign that she was still in the land of the living. I couldn't see or hear any movement. I looked down to her chest, it was still, I put my fingers to her lips, and they were cold. I expected her to stir but she didn't; she was dead.

I sat on the edge of the bed as gently as possible, the way you do when visiting someone in hospital, and stared at her. I wasn't just staring at her; I was staring into space, a black void that had suddenly become blacker. All thoughts of pain and booze left me. I sat motionless in a kind of trance, numb to all thought and all feeling. I sat like that for an hour, shut down in a vacuum of nothingness.

I was woken from my catatonic state by some shouting from the street, I had no idea what time it was, I had been there for hours. Forgetting the wound I stood up quickly and pain shot through my side reminding me of the madness from the night before. I walked through to the kitchen in a daze and put the kettle on. My mind had closed down and cut off all emotion like a robot. I could only feel physical pain. I didn't panic or worry; in fact I had almost no emotional reaction to Carol's death. It was like I'd read about it in the paper and it was happening to someone else. I made some coffee and stood in the kitchen calmly thinking through my next moves. I don't know why I drank coffee, when all my life consisted of was booze, booze, booze, and more horrible bloody booze. I hated the stuff for what it had done to me and countless others like me, or so I thought.

I decided I'd pack up all the possessions I could carry, phone the police and leave, and that's exactly what I did. I walked round the flat on autopilot; collecting anything I thought was important and dumped a bag by the door. I went back into the bedroom and tidied the bed sheets, pulling the quilt up to Carol's neck, as if to protect her from the cold, I ran my fingers through her hair and flattened it down so it looked nicer, there was no way Carol would let anyone see her without her hair looking O, K. I didn't think I was being callous, I *had* loved Carol in some way and making sure the police found her, instead of letting her rot, was the only thing I could think of, I knew what feelings were, logically, but was unable to attach any emotion to that knowledge, I didn't feel anything; I was completely barren.

I spent the rest of the day in the park nursing myself with Special Brew, woefully telling anyone who'd listen that Carol was dead. The news spread and people came and paid their respects. By the afternoon I'd drunk myself stupid. Starting from a point of all encompassing self-pity I was slowly drinking myself into a state of total despair.

In the evening the people around me disappeared, not that it mattered; it felt like I'd been on my own all day anyway. I had to go somewhere, somewhere quiet where I could be alone and away from everything.

In my addled state I headed towards the woods, the one place I knew I could sit in solitude. I had kipped in the woods on many occasions during the summer, and my favourite place had been a beautiful pond that teemed with life in the sunlight. I had sat on an old, worn out bench opposite, watching the dragonflies and birds and wondered how such beautiful creations could co-exist with such a destructive species. In the mornings the sun would wake me and the first thing I'd see on opening my eyes was a magical mist hovering above the water. But this wasn't summer it was winter and the pond didn't look beautiful, it was dead, stagnant and filthy. I sat down on the bench and began to drown in self-pity.

Everything I had ever held dear to me I'd either lost or destroyed. My family, my house, my children, my ability to make a living, my health and now the one thing that had kept me going in the darkest days had gone, Carol. The events of the morning had yet to fully sink in and I doubted they ever would as the booze and drugs kept everything at arm's length and beyond. The substances covered my world in a thick impenetrable fog that blocked out reality. I sat there becoming increasingly suicidal and the one thought that kept returning to me and began to take the place of all others was death. The sky was clear and I looked up at the stars and longed to join them. The thought that I had made a clear and final decision lifted my spirits. Sitting on the bench under a star filled sky was as perfect a place as any to end it all.

Ice was beginning to form on the pond and I hugged the old post office grey coat I had found in a charity shop, closer around my body. Before leaving the flat I had raided the various cupboards we kept the pills and potions in and had stuffed my pockets full. As I dug my hands deeply into them now, for warmth, I felt the edges and circular tops of the various containers holding my escape-route from existence. I began pulling them out, one by one, and lining them up on the bench. There were all sorts, from anti-fit tablets through to a medium sized bag of heroin, a mixture of the legal and illegal.

I had heard of people committing suicide before and presumed that a person must be in a mad and frenzied state in order to make such a decision. I found that quite the opposite was true. I was relieved and felt relaxed and focused. For the first time in my life I was in complete control, I knew exactly what I was doing. A feeling of calm and serenity descended on me in the darkness and I said my mental good-byes to the world and stared at the first batch of pills. I remembered my days at the cottage and the fun we had and how lovely Alison was.

On the way to the woods I'd bought two bottles of the cheapest and most disgusting cider imaginable. I opened a bottle, took a handful of pills and threw them into my mouth. I swallowed them with great gulps of cider that burnt my throat on the way down. I took handful after handful of pills swallowing them down with increased certainty that I was on the way out, leaving this world of pain, misery and hopelessness. As I continued it became harder to keep the pills down as my stomach lurched and heaved trying to remove the poisons. Using all my training at keeping the vomit at bay, I forced my system to obey my command for death.

After I'd consumed what I thought was enough to kill a rhino, I stopped. My head was beginning to swim and things began to get blurry. The world around me started to spin and I felt like I was in the middle of a washing machine. Thoughts whizzed through my consciousness, thoughts of my kids, my family, Criss and Carol, then more random and barely recognisable snippets of my life. I lay down on the bench and closed my eyes, wrapping the coat around me tightly. I wanted to stop the spinning. I began to shiver and remembered I'd brought a blanket.

As I sat up to retrieve it stars spun in front of my eyes and I felt dizzy and sick. I got the blanket and settled down again pulling it up around me. Once under the blanket I felt relaxed and warm and kept repeating to myself, 'everything's going to be alright, it'll be fine in the end.'

The last thing I remember is the smell of the pond, a musty rotting smell and I could visualise the whole scene. I know it sounds strange but that's what it was like. I could see the whole scene, the pond, the mist starting to form, the frost on the grass and me lying on the bench as still as Carol had been the previous morning, only I knew I wasn't meant to die, not there and not then, then blackness.

The next thing I knew I was waking up feeling like I was drowning, which I was, in my own vomit. The cold had penetrated my body to the bones and as I tried to sit up I found my face was frozen to the bench. I had already been sick and the greenish liquid was frozen solid, I had to rip my face off the bench and then sat up. I looked down at the vomit and a sudden dread fell upon me as I put two and two together, I was still alive. I should have be dead. Why wasn't I dead? I felt like I'd been sentenced to a thousand years of painful torture and spewing the remnants of sick from my mouth, I uttered "Please God no more please".

I instinctively felt for the bottle of cider in my pocket and it had frozen round the edges. I took it out and banged it against the bench, I tried to drink some. The pills in my system prevented me from taking any down and I threw up again. I decided to leave the booze for a while, anyway I had more pressing problems. I had to get warm; it felt like my body had turned into an ice pop and I felt more ill than I had ever done in my life. It was one thing to die when you're out of it but quite another to have hypothermia kill you the next morning.

For a few weeks my right side had been numb in the mornings, I had ignored it but now I was almost paralysed. I was stuck. My vision was blurry and my teeth chattered like a hammer-drill in my mouth. I tried to stand up, and the shooting pain returned to my hip as if a sniper was picking me off. I became dizzy and the world began to spin and before I could actively think my legs gave way and I slumped back to the bench. I knew I was in serious trouble, if I didn't find warmth soon I'd die and having lost the control over how it would happen I decided I didn't want to.

I stood again and screamed with the effort as pain reverberated through every sinew. Once on my feet I took a giant breath and at the top of my lungs yelled at the trees, 'HELP...ME...YOU...FUCKERS!' The woods were a quagmire in winter and nobody went into them for any sane reason, especially first thing in the morning. My plea went unheard but the effort had roused me a little. I took a pace forward and the whole world revolved around me, my balance started to go and I felt myself falling but incapable of preventing it. I sprawled sideways staring at the trees from a weird angle as I collapsed. The meeting of hard ground sent more pain vibrating through my body.

I tried and fell a few more times, each time taking more effort to rise. I could see the path I had to reach but it might as well have been over an ocean. Every time I got to my feet the merry-go-round would start and I'd fall to the ground again. I went into a routine, staggering up, taking a few paces and collapsing. It took ages to get halfway up the bank towards the path. I needed a rest and knelt on my knees breathing deeply. The sudden intake of oxygen into my system caused a reaction in my stomach and I heaved and threw up again. I honestly have no idea what was keeping me alive at that point.

I was going into withdrawal badly and I couldn't feel my feet or hands, they'd been turned senseless by the cold. I decided to stay on all fours, as at least I couldn't fall from there. Each limb movement was painstakingly fought for and my hip began to burn. I got three-quarters of the way up the hill, puking periodically. I could see the path and moved forwards. Unfortunately, without my sight on the ground I lost my balance again and I fell to the side, then gravity took hold. I tumbled over and over cascading down the hill I'd just fought so hard to climb. I gathered pace, rolling over and over. I was powerless to stop; I had no energy to break the momentum.

I finally careered through the brambles and crashed heavily through the ice into the pond. I had never been brought round by anything so quickly. The pond was only two feet deep but I had landed on my side and almost gone completely under. The cold forced the air out of my lungs and I sucked it back as fast as I could. Breathing quickly and noisily I stood and tried to take a step. The bottom of the pond was covered with thick sludge and I fell forwards, my face taking another ducking. I clambered feverishly through the water on all fours, breaking the ice as I plunged my hands forwards with each movement. I reached the bank and dragged myself up till my feet were clear of the water. I lay their panting and feeling a warm glow come over me. I knew it was only a reaction to the severe chill of the water but it felt good for the few minutes it lasted. It was soon replaced by a freezing feeling that was colder than anything I'd experienced before.

I was in the second stage of hypothermia, I was shivering uncontrollably and my body was seizing up. I knew I was dying and had to move. As I sat there with my mind convincing me I was mad I thought of death and remembered a bloke I new for a while called Nobby, he was a nice enough bloke, a drunk and a homeless just like me. I saw him a few times down at the Monday night salvation army soup kitchen that was run at a church overlooking the sea. Despair and sadness overwhelmed me again as I remembered why Nobby was stabbed to death before our very eyes, the soup kitchen also gave out sandwiches to take away and Nobby shared his sandwich with his dog Buster, some homeless druggie who was out of his head and hungry took offence to this and started on Nobby, without any provocation Nobby was run through three times, with the last time the most fatal as the blade entered Nobby's stomach and the point came out of his back, Nobby lay there dying whilst we panicked and tried everything we knew to save him. My mate Mick knelt beside Nobby for nearly forty five minutes with his hands inside Nobbys stomach trying to hold his sliced and broken organs together whilst we waited for the ambulance. Nobby died. The thought of death brought me back to my present situation, at least the ducking had achieved one thing the spinning had stopped. That meant I could now stand and walk a little. I struggled back to the bench, my clothes soaking and feeling like armour. I was minus my boots and had lost my cider, the later being the more important. I was covered in a stinking sludge and must have looked like the creature from the black lagoon. I slumped onto the bench and leaned over towards the bin, fishing out old newspapers and rubbish. I used this to scrape off as much of the muck as I could and put the newspaper under my coat to try and dry some of the water. This struggle had been going on for about an hour and a half and I should have been dead. Why wasn't I dead.

I was exhausted but very awake; I had never felt so ill and sick. The thrashing through the pond had made me aware that I wanted to live. Now I had to get somewhere warm or I wouldn't. I sat on the bench for an hour, shivering and banging myself to keep warm. My hands and feet were still numb and the pain in my side had decreased, hiding under an ice anaesthetic. I stared over the pond blankly, my mind empty of thought.

The light was returning and with it a modicum of heat. I stayed on the bench slowly drying out as the sun rose. A gurgling sound and sudden movement stirred me from my state and a flicker in my peripheral vision became my focus. I saw my cider rise from the murky depths like a submarine and surface ten feet or so from the edge of the pond. I looked at it for a while, willing it to move. I needed alcohol badly and knew I'd feel better if I could get some inside me.

With the nearest shops a world away, the cider was my only hope. The consequences of wading through the pond again didn't even cross my mind, all I could think of was getting the booze into my system. It was what I'd relied on for the whole of my life, the only consistent comfort; I knew it would save me now. With the addict powering my movements I walked down the slope like a zombie, my eyes focused on the bottle and my only feelings were of future alcoholic gratification, I felt none of my pain. I waded through the sludge again hardly noticing it till my hands had grasped the bottle and clutched it to my chest.

Only then did I look around and realise what I'd done, I was momentarily horrified before the addict overwhelmed my thoughts with the promise of relief. I waded towards the shore becoming filthier than before and clambered out all over again. I struggled to the bench and collapsed. The morning sunlight had warmed the wood and my vomit was dripping onto the earth below. I put the bottle to my lips and drank. I was swallowing with such conviction that the retching was overpowered, and it tasted like the shitty cider it was.

I drained the bottle and threw it to one side. I sat back and closed my eyes letting the warm glow from the low winter sun bathe my face and I was aware that I had to get back up the slope, onto the path and under a roof.

After what felt like an eternity of staggering, falling and crawling I finally made it to the edge of the wood and could see buildings in front of me. As I passed the last tree I looked back into the woods. I felt like death warmed up. I didn't know where to go at first; it needed to be as close as possible. Walking on flat, hard ground again was bliss although with each step my hip ached and the rest of my body trembled with pain. I wracked my mind for somewhere to aim for and remembered a dealer I had done some 'work' for who lived on the edge of town, it would have to do, my balance was ruined and I was periodically falling over gaining bruise after bruise.

I made it to the front door and knocked as heavily as I could. The door opened and he stood before me looking me up and down, his nose crinkling. I must have looked disgusting. My ripped and torn clothes were covered in mud, pond sludge, blood and vomit. My hair was lank and stuck to the sides of my face and my long beard filled with the same mixture that caked my clothes. I can't even imagine what I smelt like. I tried a grin that was probably more of a sneer and said, 'I need a bit of help, mucker, any chance?'

The dealer took pity on me and ushered me in. He gave me a mug of warm, sweet tea and a can of Special Brew. I was sitting on the floor in the front room, my legs stretched out in front of me because they wouldn't bend and the wall supporting my back; I'd made it, somehow. I drank the tea. 'You look like you could do with a bath,' said the dealer, trying his best not to look disgusted. I could just about manage a grunt of agreement. I finished my tea and walked through to the bathroom clutching my can.

'You got a washing machine?' I asked. The dealer snorted, I guessed not. I asked if I could wash my clothes in the bath and he agreed as long as I cleaned up. I remember feeling fear at this point as I knew my balance had gone and I didn't have a clue what my name was, I could remember loads of other stuff but huge chunks of my memory had been destroyed that night, for the first time in years I felt vulnerable, like I did when I was a child knowing that a hiding from my mum was on its way.

I filled the bath a third full and started to undress. I'd already removed my coat and peeled off what was left. Even *I* was shocked, they were completely filthy and the smells unleashed from their removal made me gag. I tried not to think about the state I was in, threw the clothes into the bath and managed to kneel down wincing from the pain. I picked up the can and gulped back a couple of mouthfuls. My hands were slowly thawing out and putting them into the hot water felt like a hundred pins were stabbing at them.

I swirled the clothes around, took them out and twisted as much of the water out as I could. I placed them on the radiator, drained the bath for a refill and sat down on the toilet to finish my can. When the bath was as clean as I could get it I lay down and opened the taps. The warm water crept up my body and my whole system relaxed. When the water was close to the rim I stopped the taps with my feet and lay back. I took a breath and submerged my entire being in the water. I lay there for as long as I could. I stayed in the bath for hours refilling it twice, and noticing that I had lost a lot of feeling in my right leg and arm and my sense of touch was crap. I had never been this bad before.

By the time I got out, my clothes had dried but were stiff and hard. They felt like card board when I put them on. When I emerged from the bathroom I felt like a new man at least for half an hour. It wasn't long before the pain, withdrawal and truth of my position settled in again. The dealer said I could stay for a bit as long as I pulled my weight. Considering I was losing weight rapidly I thought it was a good deal.

I stayed there for the next month. The first two weeks he took my Giro money and I just stayed indoors. He fed me with booze and little bits of food. I joined him whenever I could in whatever drug he was taking and tried to recover a bit. I was permanently terrified and my paranoia was all encompassing. Looking back now I can see that I was psychotic. When people came round I would hide under a pile of coats and clothes in the corner of the room and wait till they'd gone. I jumped at the slightest sound and was always ready for the fight that I thought was coming every other minute. I had lost a lot of weight and when I made my first journey into the outside world I had lost three stones.

I had a permanent limp in my right leg, my right hand was always numb and the rest of my right side tingled all day. I was more of a target than I'd ever been and wondered if I could last a full fight. Because of this I'd resorted to a 'hit first and ask questions later' routine and God knows how many people got smacked in the face just for glancing at me in the wrong way, my paranoia twisting their harmless gaze into a life threatening situation.

I was still drinking heavily as the pain of withdrawal was too much to take. I was managing a few odd jobs for the dealer, collecting money and cashing in Giro's and I'd always get my cut and he gave me drugs. My addict kept telling me I was fine even though I was periodically pissing blood, puking blood occasionally and continuing to lose weight. Quite clearly I was far from well but I was also insane and that kept me pushing myself further towards total self-destruction.

Even in this state I was still playing the hero and had tried to help a woman down on the front who had got herself into a bit of a predicament. She had got involved with some guy who had kidnapped her and locked her in a squat. Luckily, before he could do anything to her, her husband had stormed into the place and shot the bloke in the thigh. We all thought that that would be the end of it but the kidnapper had other plans. He had become obsessed with the woman and, on crutches and in a desperate state had stolen the woman's front-door key.

I had befriended the woman, mainly to share her booze, and she had told me all this. She was weeping in my arms when the guy on crutches came hobbling along the front. I got up, walked over to him and kicked his crutches away. He collapsed to the ground and started to scream in terror protecting his face. I kicked him as hard as I could in the leg where I'd been told his wound was and demanded the key. He wailed in pain, took it out of his pocket and threw it at me.

I wasn't proud but was glad that I could still take someone out, my twisted mind was not able to fully comprehend that it hadn't exactly been a fair fight. I had left the squat and returned to the streets. I could have found my own squat but I wanted to keep moving, terrified that if I stayed in one place the people who were after me would find me and kill me. I carried around a paranoid list of possible attackers in my head and added to it daily. Each day the madness escalated and was becoming intolerable.

One morning I was drinking on the front and a new face had arrived. He was out of it and was touching up the female drunks and generally causing trouble. He grabbed one woman by the breast, she squealed and I snapped. I ran over and punched him in the back of the neck as hard as I could. He sprawled to the floor and we went at it hammer and tongs. I felt like he represented all the fuckers who were out to get me and went into a furious, violent madness.

I grabbed his head and beat it against the side of the bench, over and over. Blood flowed down his face and the wood turned red. When my arms ran out of energy I stopped and stood back shaking uncontrollably. He fell to the floor and looked up, his face was bloody and bruised. The people around the bench were frozen in horror and I must have looked like a maniac, standing over him, heaving, with my fists clenched by my sides.

During the beating an automatic pistol had dropped out of his pocket and I picked it up. I pulled back the loading mechanism and pressed the nozzle into his cheek. 'Right, you need to fuck off and not come back' I told him. I put the gun in my pocket and walked into the shopping centre losing myself in the crowd. The fight had completely drained me and I felt weak. I promised myself that that was my last fight. From now on there'd be no fisticuffs, I'd just shoot. I was chuffed to pieces; a gun was exactly what I needed. I'd been getting weaker by the day and knew that if someone attacked me with any strength I'd be a goner. The months drifted on and I spent most of my days in the park with the rest of the low life's with whom I belonged now.

Friends were few and far between but one friend that I remember well was Orris and he was a pal, or as close as anyone got to being a pal. He was a huge, soft fella with big hands and a warm podgy face. He was the original gentle giant. He was just less than seven feet tall was always smiling and was mentally retarded; he had a mental age of nine and was a haemophiliac. All in all, Orris hadn't been handed a brilliant deck of cards. He loved his booze and drugs though and abused with the best of us. He had no concept of danger or death but knew that if he bled then it was bad. I tried to look out for him as the more mercenary amongst the street folk used and abused him, as he was an easy target. No one messed with him when I was about and I'd warned as many people as I could that if he was hurt or fucked with, they'd have me to deal with. He also shared his booze and drugs with me.

A few days after my last fight, I walked into the park to find a frightened and angry Orris. He was shouting at a crowd around him to leave him alone and was crying. My hand went to my pocket and felt the gun. I stormed over and asked what had happened. As it turned out Orris had just fallen and cut his head and refused to go to the hospital. Like children sometimes just need to be told and not argued with, I looked directly at him and told him to go home, put a pressure bandage on and wait for me. I had helped him out before by making sure he had gone to hospital by going with him.

I decided to stay in the park just for a little while to catch up with a couple of geezers who I knew there. Time passed quickly and before long night had arrived and I was shit-faced. The group was shuffling off to a party and I tagged along, my promise to Orris buried away deep as my mind became foggier with drugs and alcohol. The rest of the night was spent boozing and getting high. I passed out on the floor of the squat and didn't wake till the following lunchtime. When I did wake and was reasonably sober, the memory of Orris came back to me. "Shit". I said to myself and set off for Orris's flat as quick as I could bloody go, all the way there hoping that he was O K., kicking my self emotionally for not doing what I said I would do, feeling guilty and reaffirming in my mind that Mum was right when she called me a vile pathetic specimen.

As I approached Orris's place I was met with a familiar scene. There were two police cars and an ambulance parked outside the flat. I waited for the police to go and went over to Orris's neighbour. She was a lovely old girl and helped Orris to wash and keep his flat clean. I knocked on the door and she answered, tears rolling down her cheeks. Her eyes were bloodshot and she looked terrible. She told me, through sobs, that she'd gone round to check on him in the morning, like she always did and had found him sitting upright in his chair surrounded by a massive pool of blood.

I was stunned and shocked, I said 'thank-you' and walked away. Orris had relied on me and waited for me to show. I pictured him sitting there for hours, the blood and life slowing seeping from his body. I felt sick, the emotions only able to manifest themselves in physical symptoms. I walked straight to the offie, my addict revelling in the excuse to drown myself with booze. I went and found a smack dealer, scored and sat under the pier smoking myself into oblivion.

I was using the back streets and alleyways to get about, and who did I bump into one day but Criss. She looked quite well, compared to me anyway; She couldn't conceal her shock and put her hand to her mouth although she was good enough not to say anything. She told me she was pregnant again and had the gall to ask if I would be with her at the birth, as she wasn't getting on that well with Bob, was she totally mad?, I was dumbfounded and speechless. I didn't know whether to cry or laugh but being incapable of both just managed to shake my head, indicating a negative response to her.

I was living in self-imposed isolation, drinking and using on my own. I hated being near anyone, as my paranoia would run wild. I had turned to begging in streets away from my usual haunts, something I had promised myself I'd never do. I was just about getting by through a mixture of shoplifting and begging, keeping myself in booze and drugs. One day I was half asleep sitting on a street with my begging bowl out when a fiver dropped into it. I couldn't believe my luck and looked up to see the generous donator my eyes nearly fell out of their sockets, it was Psycho.

He didn't look too mad and suggested we go for a walk. With no alternative I complied. We wandered down to the front and as we walked I tried to explain what had happened again. He started to get agitated and refused to believe me. His eyes took on a mean stare, one which I'd last seen follow the body of a guy he'd just thrown out of a fourth floor window. Once he turned, he was capable of anything and I knew I was in trouble.

We walked past a concrete alcove and he shoved me in. The light was fading and the sea behind his shoulder was grey and stormy. No one could see us or even hear us and I guess he had planned it. He began to rave and shout, yelling all sorts about him not being a man to cross and he had his reputation to think of. His eyes were fierce and bulging and he produced a blade from his pocket. It was an old army knife, about seven inches long. I looked down at it scared; I didn't like the idea of being stabbed again.

There was about a foot between us and I knew what I had to do. It was cold and I had my hands in my pockets, one of which concealed the gun. I slipped off the safety catch and drew it, he lunged forward with the knife, it was him or me, I didn't want to scare Psycho, I wanted to shoot him and aimed for his kneecap. I pulled the trigger and there was a terrible 'bang', the sound magnified in the enclosed environment. Psycho's leg flew backwards; he collapsed to the floor instinctively grabbing his leg, his face a picture of shock. He didn't scream or shout but wriggled feverishly like a snake cut in two.

A cold, calm steeliness settled in my mind. Silently I stepped forwards and put the gun between his eyes, my finger curled round the trigger. My teeth were clenched together so hard they could have shattered. I wanted him out of my life forever and increased the pressure in my finger. Suddenly I had a flash of sanity and looked at myself, I was about to kill a man in cold blood. I froze, lifted the gun and threw it as hard and as far as I could into the sea. I was stunned and in total shock walked off without saying a word. I never saw Psycho again.

13
Gone to the dogs

My mind was fizzing like a firework, thoughts whizzing through it uncontrollably, I thought I was finally going mad. I was loosing grip on myself. Who was I? What was I? I had no idea and with undiluted, pure fear flowing through me like a dam that had burst, I started to walk at a furious pace albeit with a limp. I didn't know where I was going, I just needed to walk, fast and forever.

I had no shoes on and walked in disintegrating socks for miles. I wasn't in my body; I wasn't anywhere but a force was driving me to go somewhere. I walked straight through the night and all the next day, hardly stopping but for some water and a sandwich I stole from a petrol station. I didn't stop till I reached the next big coastal town. Once there I found the pier, collapsed under it and slept for hours. I woke to the familiar sounds of the sea and felt completely disoriented. I staggered up the beach to the front, it was the same but different. It wasn't long before I found the usual band of drunks only this time *I* was the new face.

I felt in my pockets for money and found Psycho's fiver and the events that went with it washed over me like a giant wave. I asked where the nearest offie was, luckily I was able to steel a couple of cans of beer and didn't need to spend my fiver, at least I could buy my puff that night. It was difficult to steal, as my hands never regained their sense of touch. I opened a can and started to drink as I made my way back to the pier. After drinking half the can I started to feel the effects, as my bodies tolerance was now so low and battered that small amounts of booze could get me pissed. I felt like I was starving and looked about for food opportunities. I could see the fabled golden arches of Mc Donald's in the distance and set off down the beach. Before long the wrappers began to appear, scattered on the ground. I started to look in each of the bins dotted along the front and was soon rewarded with the remains of a cheeseburger with a few chips thrown in. After I'd found enough remains to qualify as a meal I sat down on one of the benches and polished off the rest of my can.

I was in a bad way. My feet were bloody and sore with bits of flesh hanging off them, the numbness in my hand had spread to my whole right side, my head permanently ached and God knows what was happening to my internal organs. I scoured the promenade each morning and evening looking in bins for discarded burgers, fish and chips, whatever I could get, reading this you might be asking your self why didn't I buy some decent food with my fiver, the answer to that is that drugs and booze are much more important than food, a starving person would buy food but a starving addict would not, out of my three needs the drugs and booze always screamed loudest. The rest of the day I spent on the street begging and drinking. I had shunned the usual groups of drunks, knowing I wouldn't last two minutes in a fight. I was a stinking shell of a tramp.

I survived like this for about three months, barely existing. I had found a pet shop in the parade near the pier. It had a wire basket outside full of old and dented dog and cat food tins. I used to shuffle along, steal out a can and sit under the pier opening it with a sharp pebble and eking out the contents with my fingers. I was a sorry state and was reaching the end of my road. It was entirely my own fault and I had no one to blame but myself but when you're as sick as I was, it's not that you can't see the wood for the trees; you can't even find the forest.

One night I was sitting in a shelter as a storm had come in and the place under the pier where I usually slept was flooded. I was eating the contents of a tin of dog food with my fingers, I heard someone say once that apparently dog food is quite nice; they had obviously never had to live on it. A figure approached the shelter. It was just some young punk trying his luck on the weakest target he could find; these days that was me. He demanded my booze and money. I had fuck all of either. The one thing an addict would never do is give up his booze. He picked up a bottle, smashed the end on the floor and walked towards me. I managed to stand but didn't even have the strength to punch, without warning he punched with the bottle in his hand, by this time I was so decrepit there was no way I could stop him.

He stabbed me in the chest. Then having what I presume was the same flash of sanity I had had just after I had shot Psycho, looked at me in shock and ran off. I slumped to the ground thinking, 'this is it, I'm finally going to die thank God.' But no such luck, it was a flesh wound and was a couple of inches above my heart. I lay on the ground, completely done in. I expected a line of people to come and lay into me one after the other. I looked down at my chest and the wound was bleeding through my filthy clothes. I lay there for a while thinking. I knew I was dying and if the next punk didn't get me then eventually the cold would. I decided I didn't want to die without seeing my parents and made a decision to go home, don't ask me why, as I haven't got an answer, maybe it was to blame them for my life and try to make them feel responsible for the way I was, I just don't know, but I know I had to go.

Using the bench as support I got to my feet and made a mental plan for my final journey. I swayed, stumbled and fell. I got up and repeated the pattern. I finally got to my feet properly and managed to walk to the station. I got on and hid in the toilet. I peered out at every station until I recognised a name and got out. I walked towards the village I was born in on what felt like my last legs. I had decided I wouldn't go straight to my parents but stop off at my Uncle's first as his house was closer and I was exhausted.

We had been close in the past and I hoped that would count for something when the wreck of his nephew knocked on the door. I needed to be safe, I couldn't look over my shoulder anymore and was burnt out. I had nothing left and wanted to collapse for a hundred years. I made it to the house and knocked on the door. I stood waiting like the waking dead unable to comprehend what reaction I'd get. If I had I wouldn't have been expecting the one I got. My Uncle opened the door, peered at me and as the shock of recognition hit him he began to yell. I know now it was just his fear reacting but at the time it wasn't what I needed. He started to shout all sorts, really tearing strips off me. I didn't have the strength to argue as I barely had the strength to talk.

The one thing I desperately needed was some understanding. I wished I could download all the events from the last decade and beam them into my uncle's head. Instead I stood there, like a zombie, soaking up his horror. The last time he had seen me I had been healthy, sixteen stones and confident. The bedraggled, beaten shell of a man that stood before him now was a world away from that.

I couldn't answer and as he continued I had to agree with him. I did look like a sick stick insect, I did smell like a refuse dump and I was disgusting. My face was bloated and red and covered in sores, scars and filth. My eyes were like piss holes in the snow; my beard was down to my chest and filled with a world of its own life. My clothes had been lived in for months and were tatters of dirt and my feet were bloody and swollen.

He kept looking me up and down and repeating the same words without hearing them. Eventually he got hold of himself and ushered me in shaking his head. He put some papers down on a chair and made me sit. He was a guy from the old school, tough as nails with a heart of gold. He stood over me tutting and said, 'well, are you going to say anything or has someone cut out your fucking tongue?'.

I grasped at the whirling thoughts inside my head trying to string some words together to create a sentence but I kept losing them. I finally managed to get out, 'sorry, I'm so sorry.' As I wasn't able to really speak and was close to passing out it was all I could manage. Jimmy hardened his expression and said, 'Well that's all well and good but sorry ain't going to fix anything is it?' he scowled and wrinkled his face in disgust as he got a waft of how much I smelt.

'What you need boy is a bath, some food and if you weren't so weak a fucking good hiding!' His words were harsh but his eyes were worried and full of pity. He went off to the kitchen and came back with a bowl of soup and a hunk of bread. It was the first time I'd had proper food in months and I wolfed it down hungrily, burning my mouth. He half carried me up the stairs, opened the taps and left me to it.

After a few hours I emerged feeling a bit better. By this time the family loyalty had replaced shock and Jimmy was all concerned and unbelievably helpful. He cleaned my clothes and put me to bed. I was drained of all energy and had no power of thought; I just lay down and immediately fell into a deep sleep.

I'll never forget my Uncle's generosity. Even today I look back and I know that he saved my life. During the following week he sat with me and listened as I poured out my troubles, he fed me and made sure I ate what I was given. It was the first time in years I'd been looked after and I felt safe for a while. He gave me a drink when I needed it, which was often and said very little against me. The couple of times I went out to the pub he came and found me to take me home, once in the middle of the night. His kindness and unconditional love brought me back from the brink of death that week.

However, I hadn't changed, I was still a raging addict and lost in my own world of self-destruction. After my body and mind had recovered from total exhaustion I was back to my old tricks. The booze was never far away and I'd already found a dealer in the local pub and got some puff. I had no self-awareness and the addict inside still raged with need and that need had to be fulfilled at all costs as it was the only identity I had.

One morning Jimmy told me that I should go and see my parents. A jolt of fear, like an electric shock, stunned my body and I looked at him and managed to nod. I hadn't seen my parents for years and the thought of facing them terrified me. No matter how hardened I had made my emotions the reality of my parents seeing how I'd turned out scared me. I was filled with the thought of their disgust and the shame that I'd feel. I hadn't known them for so long that I didn't know if I could ever build a bridge back for us to even talk, and looking back why did I want to talk to people who had abused me as they had anyway, goodness knows what was going through my mad head.

When I'd left all those years before it had been as a hungry young boy determined to go into the world and return a conqueror. I wasn't sure how but I had promised myself that when I next knocked on their door I'd be a great success and not the vile pathetic specimen they had labelled me. The reason I had never contacted them in the passing time had been deep embarrassment and fear. I was totally disgusted with myself so I thought that would be nothing compared to what *they'd* think. I wanted them to be proud of me and be amazed at my achievements. Now, as I contemplated facing them I went through the 'achievements' of the intervening years and shuddered at their consequences.

For more time than I could remember I had buried my feelings for them deep down in a place I could never consciously reach. The only thing I had excelled in was addiction and although I was brilliant at it, it was hardly something to be proud of. I knew I had to see them but I needed a push and Jimmy certainly provided that. He wasn't nasty but was firm. I was in a no win situation, I couldn't run away as I had nowhere to go and the thought of fending for myself on the streets again was worse than whatever would happen with my parents.

As I stood in front of the door that I'd run through so many times as a child, mixed memories flooded my mind. I stayed standing a foot away from the final barrier to a meeting I had dreaded, I wasn't even that pissed. After ten minutes of paralysis I reached forwards and with everything in my body and mind screaming, "No don't do it!" I knocked.

I waited for what seemed like an eternity; my feet nailed to the ground and as the footsteps approached my entire body tensed. The door opened and I saw my father. He hadn't changed a bit. He took a disinterested and disgusted look at me and went to shut the door. He hadn't recognised me and as I instinctively put my foot in the door he looked angry and frightened thinking I was some tramp begging, which in a way I was. I said 'Dad', and his jaw fell open. He stood there shocked and rooted to the spot, his mind trying to work out who was standing there. He looked hard at my face as he finally recognised me.

He couldn't speak and simply opened the door wider indicating that I should come in. It was the first time I'd crossed the threshold of my home in many, many years. I walked through the door and into the lounge. My Mum was sitting in her favourite chair and turned round to look at the person her husband had let in. I was met with the same reaction although I think she knew it was me instantly.

So there I was, standing in the lounge of my family home with my parents on either side, frozen with horror, unable to speak with jaws slack from shock. They both went into automatic pilot mode and my Dad asked me if I wanted a cup of tea. I nodded unable to speak. My Mum pointed to the sofa and I sat down. 'How are you?' she said, as if I popped round every day. 'Not bad', I replied both of us still unable to take in the reality of what was happening.

My Dad came through with the tea and had obviously had a word with himself in the kitchen. He had calmed down and was able to ask me how I had been. From my appearance it must have been obvious that I hadn't been brilliant. The problem I had was that my memory was shot to pieces and I could hardly remember what had happened in the last few years, mum stared at me with an awkward disgust and for the next hour that was all I felt, awkward and disgusted, with me.

I got out of there as quickly as I could and walked back to Jimmy's. I thought it had gone as well as it could as they hadn't said anything nasty and had mostly just sat and listened. However it had shaken me to my roots and I needed security and comfort. I had to retreat into the familiar and that was alcohol. I had found a few drunks in the most run down local in the village and made my way there to get trashed. The onslaught of emotions was far too much for me to deal with. My insanity was raging and I needed to quell it.

That night I got rat-arsed and staggered back to Jimmy's in the small hours. I had successfully blotted out what I needed to, found my bed and passed out. The following morning I was still pissed as my liver was finding it increasingly difficult to process the alcohol. For me this was a result, as the hangover didn't kick in till the afternoon, by which time I was drinking again.

The village was small and like most gossipy. I had already been banned by every place that sold booze and word had filtered back to my parents and Jimmy. Jimmy did his best and tried to help me any way he could, he was a heavy drinker himself so had some understanding, My parents reaction was to do their up most to make me feel uncomfortable and not wanted whenever I was within five hundred yards of them.

The truth was that each day I was slipping further and further from reality into a mad and dangerously self-delusional world. My body had not recovered and my system was slowly shutting down. The blood in my urine was becoming constant, as it was when I threw up. In short I was dying but oblivious to the fact.

I was still stealing as it had become my way of life and without my own children around had taken to nicking clothes, shoes, toys and sweets and handing them to the kids from the rougher end of the village. As always there was something in it for me as the parents paid me in booze, it was my way of getting round my banning from the shops.

I had caught up with some old faces from my past and I now hung out with them in the pubs. They kept me in drinks when I joined them and I could see pity etched into their expressions. I hated it, but I hated the thought of going dry even more. I had lost everything, even my pride. All I lived for was booze and nothing else mattered, my identity erased and replaced with a chemical compound. I was nothing more than that and I couldn't even begin to see it although it was plain for everyone else to watch and discuss.

I was barely holding it together and was slipping towards the final edge. My family looked on in disgust not knowing or wanting to do anything. One day I was in the pub and having lost control of my bladder pissed myself sitting on a stool, the urine soaking into the carpet in a puddle at my feet. I didn't even notice and got confused and angry when I was barred. This is how bad it was; I was a millimetre away from breaking point.

The following day I went in to see my local doctor, trying to scam more pills and potions but something different happened. When the doctor asked me how I was, I wanted to issue forth my usual lie of, 'I'm fine but I could do with....' But instead, the words failed, something snapped inside me and I decided for the first time in my life to not lie to the Doctor.

The doctor was very patient with me and explained that what I needed to do was stop drinking and the only way to do this was through a detox programme. I knew it was what I had to do and agreed and so my name went on the list, the wait was six weeks. Six weeks, I'd never last. As I walked back from the doctors the paranoia wound itself into a tornado and whirled around my mind. I knew I was going to die before the six weeks was up; I convinced myself that someone would find me and kill me. This became the only thought rotating round my head.

The next morning things were the same and I set off to find my old friend Hunger to arm myself. It didn't take long to locate him and for the right price he furnished me with an old Colt service revolver. I kept this within arm's length from that point onwards; the thought of preventing getting killed the only thing that kept me going. I stopped going out unless it was absolutely necessary and when I did the gun went with me. When I was indoors I sat in my Uncle's chair, the gun resting on the arm and when I slept it was under my pillow.

I struggled through the six weeks wait living off a single commanding thought. I became completely disconnected from the world outside my head; in my head I was psychotic. The morning came for my detox visit and my Dad arrived to take me, why he had decided to help me then I don't know, guilt maybe. The addict still controlled my every move and I fought against going, as the bottle of vodka I had left would then go to waste. My Dad got angry and insisted I went so I agreed and grabbing the vodka went to the toilet explaining I had to pee. I sat on the loo and putting the bottle to my lips drank a quarter in one go. I came up for air, breathed as deeply as I could and then had another go at it. Because I was so physically ill at this point that amount of booze should have killed me, but then again many things over the last few years should have. I walked to the car and collapsed into the back seat. By the time we arrived the vodka had been round my system and I was totally shitfaced. I couldn't walk or talk and was out of it. The doctor looked at me through the window and sighed. He refused to accept me and walked off. My Dad was livid and spat swear words at me. I don't remember any of this, I'm just telling you what Jimmy told me.

The following day when I sobered up a bit it was explained to me what had happened. Jimmy couldn't believe what I was doing to myself and found the situation unbearable. He had done all he was capable of and was faced with the only option I had left him with, to give up.

That afternoon a few drinking buddies turned up and brought a case of booze with them. My Uncle was out at work and we tucked into the bottles of beer. I had only managed to drink two when I began to feel dizzy. I was sitting in the chair and felt the room spin. As it spun faster I tried to make it stop but couldn't. The room started to go dark and I found I couldn't think. The darkness enveloped me and I was suddenly scared. I tried to stand to shake the darkness away but it took over. I passed out, collapsed to the floor and stopped breathing.

I came round to find one of the drunks, John, who was trained in first aid, straddling my chest, saying, 'It's alright he's breathing.' I opened my eyes but couldn't move. I whispered something and John leant forward. He shouted to the someone not to call for an ambulance but to get the doctor instead. Twenty minutes later the emergency doctor arrived and examined me. By this time I had sat up and was propped against the side of the sofa.

Just my luck, the emergency Doctor turned out to be my own doctor and as she walked into the room her face was a mixture of anger and serious concern. She prodded and poked me for a good five minutes and examined the notes she had brought with her. She went into the hall to speak with someone on her mobile and I reached up to the coffee table, grabbed a glass and downed the dregs of a whisky, my addict in full control.

She returned looking grave and knelt next to me. She told me I couldn't drink another drop of booze and that I was going back to the detox the following morning. I thought I had another six weeks to wait and reacted with a mixture of relief and annoyance. She put three pills on the coffee table and told me to take them instead of drinking. I looked at her and said, 'I'd rather have a drink if it's all the same.' The look on her face shocked even me.

She brought her face to within a few inches of mine and said slowly and deliberately, 'You have a maximum of three weeks to live.' The words managed to pierce through my insanity fog and struck home as I realised I had reached my limit. 'Your next drink could kill you,' she said and I instinctively looked at the empty whisky glass and wondered if it was too late.

She pulled back and I looked at her, I knew she wasn't lying; this was it, my absolutely last chance. She waited for a reaction and it took a while as the news spread throughout my mind trying to find a point where it would register. When I finally realised what was happening I reached out and took the first tablet. I looked at it, held between my fingers and knew that the innocent little white pill was what stood between my booze and me. I put it on my tongue and instinctively reached for the nearest beer bottle. I checked and looked at her, she got some water and I waited, watching the bottle, thinking that a few bubbles and fermented hops might kill me. She returned from the kitchen and I swallowed the pill.

She left, repeating her solemn warning and I struggled to get into the chair. I asked the drunks to leave, put the two pills on the arm of the worn out chair next to me and settled in for the biggest battle of my life.

Vile Pathetic Specimen

14
Hanging in there

I woke in the early hours. It was still dark. My Uncle had put a rug around me and refreshed my glass of water. My body ached and I desperately needed a drink. As I started to think of obvious sources, the memory from a few hours earlier hit me as if I'd walked into a lamp post. The doctor's words rang in my ear, one more drink and I might be dead. I looked down at the little white pill and chucked it down my throat. I desperately wanted a pint of rum but I couldn't have it, the fight for sobriety had begun.

I drifted off into fitful sleep, going through the usual routine although without booze it was much worse. My body twitched relentlessly and the cramps in my stomach were agonising. Each time I woke I yearned for liquid relief. I imagined the booze sliding down my throat and filling my veins with comfort and release from the pain. I became obsessed and started to fantasise about all the different forms of alcohol I could swallow down, vodka, rum, whisky, beer, wine, cider and so on.

Every time I woke to reality, the room seemed more depressing. I hugged myself closer and shivered with pain and anxiety. I had one pill left and my addict told me they weren't working, trying to convince me to drink. I swallowed it and held on to my knees praying I wouldn't let go, knowing if I did I'd be straight on the hunt for booze. I sat like this for hours, waiting for the light to return. As the sun came up and I knew I'd have to go to the hospital, the cravings grew increasingly acute. I had to have a drink. I let go of my arms and the fear of death rushed through me and I grabbed on again as if I were on the edge of a mountain and if I let go I'd fall.

I drifted off to sleep again and was woken by my uncle shaking me. My insanity told me it was my attacker and I went for my gun, which was down the side of the chair cushion. As my hand reached metal my eyes opened and I saw my uncle's face. I relaxed and even managed a smile;

it was not mirrored. He didn't look happy and was scowling at me. I think his patience had run out.

Evidently my doctor had phoned him first thing and told him the previous day's tale. He had got straight into the car and come over. 'Have you had a drink?' he asked fiercely. 'No ', I whispered, my throat almost closed and dry. The cramps were crippling me and I was sweating profusely. My system was screaming for booze and it was taking all my effort not to scream out with it. I'd have killed for a shot of vodka but it would have killed me and I held onto that thought with my fingernails.

I grasped the mug of tea Jimmy brought me with both hands and whilst shaking half of the contents onto my lap I drank it down. I tried to gain some control over my fizzing mind and focused on a clock on the wall. The time was almost ten and I had to go. I tried to get to my feet and my legs buckled, I slumped back into the chair. With Jimmy on one side I was hoisted up and supported. I bent forwards my guts cramping like mad and dry retching.

I managed to stand straight again and winced with the pain. Jimmy's face scared me, as he looked petrified, the truth of what the doctor had told him now fully apparent. After a few minutes the shakes returned and my body convulsed and twitched violently. Sweat was running down my face and making its way through my beard. I must have looked appalling. I took a step and retched again. Getting to the car was a mission in itself and when I finally made it to the back seat I was panting with the effort.

Experience had taught me that I had about four hours before I began fitting and without the booze I needed, the only thing that would prevent it were the drugs I'd get at the hospital. This thought became the eye in the middle of the hurricane of madness swirling round me. It was all I focused on although the flashes of fear, pain, anxiety and terror kept on overwhelming me.

I was way beyond being in trouble. I was dying and the journey to the hospital was my only salvation. A part of me knew this and battled with the thoughts of booze. I felt like civil war had broken out in my head. I had no control over who was winning and hung on to any solid thought with all my will. In one moment all I knew was the need for a drink and in the next all I wanted was the pills. The fires of war burned in my head and I knew I was going mad.

Jimmy passed me a bottle of water and I clutched onto it and swallowed the contents down furiously. It bounced in my stomach and I heaved up a little blood. I tried again and managed to keep a small bit down. Jimmy opened the window and breathed through the gap.

The rest of the journey was just as horrific, the crippling sensation of my cramping guts combined with dry retching left me in permanent agony and any minute respite I got was spent wiping the sweat from my eyes. Once again the desire for booze was triggered and the need became overwhelming. It was like this for the whole journey, thoughts linking together using random bits of knowledge but always leading to the same result: Booze and my need for it.

The miles trickled by, the pain unrelenting and when we turned the final corner and saw the imposing Victorian grey building that was to be my home for the next few days I was swamped by an overwhelming desire to run for the hills. However I was dying and needed relief, it could only come in the form of the drugs waiting for me behind the doors of the hospital. Jimmy parked as close to the entrance as he could and opened the back door. I was still doubled-up, my joints welded in place.

With great effort he dragged me out and I fell to the side of the car. With my uncle helping me I stumbled and wobbled towards the entrance, we were quite a spectacle. The doctor came to meet us and strode purposefully towards me. He stopped a foot away and bent down to my line of sight.

'You have three weeks to live!' he barked into my face. I had heard this before but the repetition from someone new doubled the impact on the tiny bit of receptive brain I had left. Almost immediately the thought of future death was replaced with the need for relief from my pain and I began the battle that was to become a constant element of my conscious hours, booze versus life.

The two of them manhandled me through to the waiting room and left me there whilst they filled out paperwork. I sat slumped in a cold, white and terrifying space. I couldn't fully comprehend what was happening, my ability to make sense of reality was shot to pieces. Paranoid thoughts filled my mind. Had I gone mad and was I about to be strapped into a straightjacket? Was I in prison? Without a link to reality through a face I knew, the world I sat in was becoming anything my mind could create. The tension built steadily and bubbled away as thoughts became increasingly more ludicrous.

I bent forwards, the cramps attacking with a vengeance and taking great handfuls of hair grabbed my head between my hands holding on for dear life. I sat in the room rocking.

Outside of my reality, two Irish doctors were talking to my uncle. They were explaining procedure but to me they were plotting. Jimmy came into the room and at the sight of something familiar the paranoia calmed down. I looked up at him hoping he had got the pills I needed and we were going home. His face was set in stone as he told me he'd call later and with that turned on his heels and left. I was alone in a place I didn't know with a mind I didn't want; I was fucked again. Only this time I couldn't physically fight my way out, this fight was going to be something altogether new.

So there I was, sitting with my chin in my knees my arms now wrapped round my legs, shaking and shivering knowing that it wouldn't be long before I began to fit uncontrollably. I found it impossible to ground any thoughts and tried counting in my head to give focus to my mind. I reached three before the madness returned. One of the doctors walked into the room and the reality of another human being snapped me out of my thoughts. He looked down at me and said, 'Ahh, are we feeling a bit tearful?' Was he fucking kidding?

Another staff member joined him and they gently lifted me onto my feet and guided me down a long corridor. I had no strength to resist but inside was fighting for all I was worth. I was mumbling, dribbling and desperate for booze, I felt I was losing my grip and choked out the words, 'help me, I need drugs, I think I'm dying.' There was no response. I could hear wailing and screaming from behind the doors we passed. I tried to work out if they were real or just in my head and the questions brought me to the brink of breakdown.

The geezer on the right told me his name was Hugh and as we went into a small room with a bed in it he told me he would go and get the medication I needed. I lay on the bed curled up trying to speed up time so the drugs would arrive immediately. Hugh returned and sat me up, gave me the pills and a glass of water. I swallowed them down with difficulty, each retch like a ratchet working them towards my stomach.

With the pills inside me I relaxed. With the drugs on their way the pain would soon decrease, at least to a bearable level. Hugh explained that the screaming I could hear was coming from patients with wet brain. In great detail he told me that wet brain was a condition I had to look forward to if I didn't stop drinking. It's when the addict reaches a point of insanity where they have no control over their mental or physical functions. It is so severe that the poor individual has to be strapped down to a bed or chair and wear incontinence pads. They wail through their living hell getting only fleeting glances of sanity. This is their life; there is no recovery, only death. With that thought placed in my mind I grabbed the remaining pills and forced them down as fast as I could.

I spent the next forty-five minutes on the edge of my bed holding my cramping guts and praying for relief. I was still shaking and sweating and it felt like I was never going to feel any better. My addict threw memories of booze at me, reminding me that a vodka would quell the pain within minutes. I fought hard against the thoughts, the screaming a constant reminder of the consequences I faced. Over the next hour the pain receded at a desperately slow pace. However, I was soon able to unwind my body and the cramping became sporadic and controllable.

Hugh returned and gave me some water. I sipped it slowly and it was the first liquid I'd taken down for a long while. I moved to the back of the bed and stretched out my legs. I was still shivering and shaking but felt a hundred times better than I did an hour before. Hugh started to tell me the programme outline and I managed to catch bits of it but mostly it passed over my head. The one thing that stuck was his insistence that I spend as much time as possible with the other patients when I wasn't in therapy, as social isolation was a killer. My paranoid mind didn't want to be around people at all. All I wanted was to curl up in a room without having to worry about being attacked and sleep until all the pain and problems had been taken away.

Hugh left me and I stayed in my room wishing the pain away for a couple of hours. I couldn't really get a handle on my situation as each time I tried to follow a single line of thought I was bombarded by an unruly mass of others. It was excruciating. The cycle would begin with an idea of how to escape and find the nearest booze outlet followed by reminders of dying and interspersed with memories of the last few years, all backed up by the constant screaming. I desperately wanted peace, peace from the noises around me, peace from the never-ending shouting in my head and peace from the struggle to live through each tortuous minute without booze.

The hours passed very slowly, each cycle of mental torture becoming harder to control. The anger swelled inside me, I wanted to lash out at someone, hold them up against the wall and repeatedly punch them over and over, blaming them for all the pain I was feeling. I clenched my fists, the knuckles turning white and clenched my teeth, trying to force the rage away. After this, my body would relax and my mind would take over, lashing me with horrendous thoughts. I couldn't sit still and fidgeted, rocked and moaned with the effects of the storm raging inside.

Hugh returned and asked how I was feeling. The shakes and cramps had died away but I felt awful. Although a part of me knew where I was I felt I was in the wrong place. I didn't want to be there, I wanted to be holed up in my

Uncle's front room nursing a bottle of whisky. 'How do you think I fucking feel?' I replied. 'Well, that's what you're here to work out.' He said calmly. All I wanted was a load of drugs to keep the pain at bay and be on my way. However, a tiny bit of me said "Come on you can do this". Hugh looked down at me and said bluntly, 'You stink and before you do anything else you need a bath.' I was shocked. I looked up and simply said, 'OK'. I was struggling to keep pace with reality. I had to follow the instructions I was given and knew that by trying hard to do so meant I'd soon be able to leave having fooled the doctors into thinking I was well enough to be released.

My thoughts were mixed up, one minute I would jump from paranoid addict with no way out and the next minute to clear thoughts telling me I could beat this. Each side took it in turns to control my thoughts.

I stood up and gasped with pain as my seized-up joints came unstuck from their positions. I was bent over and my right side was numb, I felt like a ninety-year old man. Hugh took my arm and I accepted the help without complaint slowly standing up straight. Although the cramping had stopped, my stomach muscles were sore and ached. I began to walk forwards very slowly, dragging my unresponsive right leg behind me. The corridor, like everywhere else was white, bright and sterile. I half closed my eyes and focused on each step hoping it wasn't far.

We turned into a huge room with a giant bath standing in the middle, I shuffled towards it, my eyes still watching the floor in front, and making sure I didn't fall. Hugh said he'd leave me to it and after turning the taps on and making sure the temperature was OK, left the room. I looked up and found myself staring at a disgusting figure at the end of the room.

The far wall was one massive mirror and it took me a second to work out the figure I was staring at was me. It had been a long time since I'd seen myself without the aid of some sort of substance. The sober reality of the man who faced me now took my breath away. I was transfixed; I couldn't believe it was *me*. I painfully shrugged off my clothes and looked at my reflection.

I slowly studied the man in the mirror starting at the head and working my way down. His beard and hair were filled with bits of vomit and dirt. His face was covered in filth and scars, his expression haggard and worn. He was painfully thin with ribs protruding through pallid, yellowy-green skin, a scar on the right of his chest weeping with fresh pus and blood. His legs were bowed and bent at a strange angle and ended with bloodied rags of feet.

I itched my chin and watched the arm opposite me move too. I waved it up and down and then looked away from the mirror and down at my body, I was repulsed, shocked and confused. It *was* me but I couldn't make the connection.

I looked at my hands and watched them turn off the taps. As I tried to comprehend the truth that it was really me living in the horrendous body I had seen. I began to panic as I was exposed to flickers of self-awareness, the first for far too long. My fear response kicked in loud and clear. I turned round, desperately and foolishly looking for booze. I wanted to drink and drink to block out what was happening, it wasn't me, it couldn't be me.

The shock subsided and was replaced with disgust and despair. I wondered how I had let myself get to this point and suddenly closed down. I couldn't think about it anymore and blocked it out, looking away and closing my eyes. I stood there in self-imposed darkness breathing deeply, trying to calm down. After a while I opened my eyes and turned my back to the mirror and got into the bath.

I wanted to feel and if pain was all I could manage then that would have to do. I deserved it. When the pain dispersed I lowered my body into the water and winced, the pinpricks of heat stabbing my wounds. When I was finally submerged I tensed my body with all my strength till the heat became bearable and then sighed loudly as relief flooded through me, after seeing myself in the mirror I wanted to be clean.

I scrubbed myself clean trying to remove the dirt and desperately wished that this simple effort could clean my insides as well. I stayed until the water turned cold then got out, and stood once again in front of the mirror. With the dirt gone and feeling refreshed I examined the reflection anew. Although I still had an unsightly appearance I felt better and knew that I was going to turn my situation around, the sight of myself cold sober shocked my mind into action, I still had some fight left in me, looking back this was a big turning point.

Some clean clothes had been put on the only chair in the room. I walked over; feeling completely strung out and climbed into them. They were soft and clean and once dressed I felt like a new albeit knackered man. I left the bathroom and ambled up the corridor to the common room. I found a comfy armchair and collapsed into it. I was too tired to think anymore and all I wanted was to sleep, my eyes already closing. I sat back, shut my eyes and instantly faded away.

Someone shaking my shoulder brought me out of deep sleep and as I began to become conscious, my mind suddenly exploded into readiness, expecting the threat I was always awaiting. I jumped up, fists clenched and looked around for someone to attack. Hugh came into my vision and before I could register who he was or where I was I drew back my fist and threw out a punch. It glanced his shoulder as he effortlessly moved out of the way.

I became fully awake and remembered where I was. I stood there panting and madly looked around for confirmation that there was no imminent threat and once satisfied, calmed down and apologised to Hugh, who just shrugged. I was to wake from sleep like this for the next few years and still do today unable to let go of the fear provoked defence mechanism burnt like a brand into my subconscious.

I sat back down, still trembling with suspicion and paranoia. I stared around and found myself in a circle of chairs containing a mixture of people, all looking edgy. I had no idea what was going on and stayed tense, ready for battle. Hugh called my name and I looked at him. He asked, 'How do you feel?' I didn't have time to think and simply said, 'Nervous'. He snorted and said loudly, 'That's bollocks!' and turned to the person next to me. I was stunned. It was my first honest answer to a direct question in ages and I'd basically been called a liar. I now know that he was right, as at the time I had no idea what feelings were and only understood fear and anger.

The first of the many groups I would become part of were strange and new. It was something I had never done before in my life, open honest discussion, and I didn't know how to handle it. Staying silent and cursing the other members in my head was the only way I could deal with it. I had no ability to understand my feelings as my range went from fear to anger, all the intricate and complicated feelings in-between were lost to me.

I was frustrated and thought the losers around me were pathetic and sad, never once, in the early days did it dawn upon me that I was one of them. I stayed aloof and separated from what was going on trying to find other things to think about, refusing to take responsibility for who I was, thinking I was above it all, when in fact I was merely finding a new way to hide from it.

Without this first and vital step, the groups were pointless, because without giving in to the problem I faced, I was still fighting myself and lying to convince myself that it wasn't me that needed help, *I* was fine. All that happened was I flushed with anger stemming from a simmering resentment and would stare coldly at whoever was talking, wishing we could just have a straight fight to sort out the discussion. I would sit and fume. Occasionally this anger and resentment would bubble over, and a string of angry swear words would leave my mouth and enter the room.

The detox I was part of was renowned as one of the toughest but to me it was bliss, I had a comfy bed, as much tea and coffee as I could manage and the luxury of three meals a day. The internal fighting for booze still raged in my head but, as I had no access to any it began to decrease, along with the drug-controlled withdrawal symptoms. That's not to say I was having a good time, I hated it and had built up an internal personal vendetta against everyone there. I despised them all. I wanted to get back at them for making me stay and blamed everyone for my own feelings.

In the end I did get a bit of revenge but not in my normal way. I managed to infect everyone with head lice. One afternoon we all had to be treated with a liquid that smelt like off petrol and sat in the group session with multi-coloured turban like towels wrapped round our heads looking like we'd joined an Indian cult. That afternoon I had my first true belly laugh for years, even the counsellors had to have it done.

As the days passed, the tiny piece of me that wanted to recover and get well strengthened and grew. My mind began to clear and I got glimpses of whom I really was. This was terrifying, as it was someone I didn't recognise, let alone know. Every time I caught an accurate sense of self-identity it was a stranger to me and I threw it away hiding it somewhere in a box in my mind with all the other truths I never wanted to face. Usually I'd have then drunk myself stupid to help the process but without drink a piece would remain, the piece I had to face. With time it grew until I had no choice but to deal with it.

During these times I'd have to contend with a thousand other thoughts. I longed for my trusty booze to take the madness away but each time my addict told me to drink I found I had a new part of me that said, 'NO!'.

The first time I heard myself say this loudly inside my head I was shocked, as it didn't feel like me. I thought I *wanted* to drink but now I was beginning to fight against it. It was very tiring, as there was no respite. Without the booze or drugs to help me escape and blanket the noise, the fighting raged inside my head. Without anything to dull the madness I had no choice but to sit in the middle of the madness, frightened and weak, powerless to stop it. At times it became almost unbearable and I would look around for an outlet: Substance, violence, anything, but instead I held on to the new spark of hope that shone faintly, deep in my being. It became my focus and with all my future hopes pinned on it I prayed for peace, over and over, rocking like the madman I was.

With each group my resentment and fear, was being balanced and overtaken by curiosity and hope. I desperately struggled to understand what feelings were and then search within myself to see if I could find any. It was nearly impossible, as I didn't know what I was looking for. As I struggled for understanding, tiny blocks of solid sanity were being laid down inside my head. They were small, but they were the first foundations of my new life and I protected them fiercely.

One morning I was due to meet with a doctor and sat in the common room waiting and thinking about my 'new' self trying to work out who it was and how I could become it. It is a constant battle as finding the quiet space inside to gain perspective and peace is like trying to get dry whilst swimming in a lake.

I went through to a consultation room to meet the doctor, desperately trying to subdue my usual anger and resentment. It was all I knew and the new bit of me was still fresh and weak but hungry and fought with all the courage I was slowly building. I wanted to learn, I wanted to get well and I wanted to win.

I sat down and we began our discussion. He asked me how I was getting on and I was honest and told him how much of a struggle it was, fearing the same response as I got from Hugh. It was a risk but I knew I had to take it, I had become frustrated with myself, always answering, 'fine' to any questions about my state of mind. The doctor nodded slowly as I spoke and then he told me that he was an ex-addict himself and spoke the most important words that have ever been said to me, "You do realise you have a choice, you choose every action you take."

I was stunned and shocked and felt like a fish taken out of water. I sat there in silence, the possibilities of his words bouncing off the sides of my mind. It seems the most obvious thing but to me it was an entirely revolutionary idea. I'd never been told I had a choice and I'd never felt that I had one. Now, I was faced with the possibility that I could control my actions for the first time in my life by choosing whether or not to follow up the preceding thoughts.

The importance of this staggeringly simple fact cannot be overestimated. It became the starting point from which my recovery really began. I had finally found the path I had been looking for and my spirits soared.

I walked back to the common room in a daze, feeling happy and hopeful. It was the turning point in my life. I was determined to become all I could be and destroy the part of me that wanted to destroy itself. The road would be hard, painful and at times test me to my very limits but I knew I was going to win. I had turned the corner and the mountain I had to climb loomed in front of me but for the first time I actually *wanted* to climb it.

I got myself a coffee, rolled a cigarette and started to think clearly about my future. I now had a focus and a reason to live. For the foreseeable future my only reason to exist was to beat my addict, take control and stay in control. With this decision made I had to find ways to make it happen. I was still severely messed up. From the beginning of my life, the 'normal' feelings and reactions to life had been warped and slowly over the previous years my identity had been broken down till I became a vessel for substance abuse and that alone. This had clouded all other decisions and made it impossible to form sensible, balanced ideas about the choices I made.

Now I had been told that those choices were mine and mine alone to make. I had been in the control of something else all my life, the booze and drugs had ruled my mind and decisions and I look at where it had got me. I wondered what life would be like without them and knew it was going to be difficult. I had been stumbling through life, falling from one thing into another and never really *thinking* about what I was doing. Now I would try and make my life choices with proper thought but that meant changing everything I had become and starting from scratch. Unfortunately, it's not like rubbing out a picture and restarting, the mess that was in my head was ingrained and my patterns of behaviour and thought so familiar that I thought undoing them might be impossible.

That night I went for my medication got myself some water and went to my room. I sat on the bed and thought deeply about my task. I knew I could do it. I had always thrown myself into whatever lay in front of me with all my power and now I had to do this with recovery. I promised myself I would never drink or take drugs *ever* again and with that thought lay down for sleep.

I woke with the usual pain and my pillow and bed were wet from the night sweats. I felt awful and my first thought was of booze. I remembered my last thought from the night before and the day's battle began, I had only been awake for seconds. My body was still trashed and each day although I felt a bit better, the pain constantly reverberated through my system. I went for some breakfast. The ability to eat three proper meals a day was still such a novelty for me that at each meal I ate until I felt ill but one thing I didn't do was nip out to the toilet and start making myself sick as I had done not so many years before.

I joined my first group of the day determined to listen and understand. At times the people around me might as well have been speaking German but I persevered, the recovery side to me solid and determined. Frustration was to become a constant theme of my early recovery as I floundered around trying to turn the words I heard into sense. I often felt angry and rage would smoulder away inside as I tensed my muscles struggling to stop myself from lashing out. I can remember some moments when I gripped the chair sides so hard my fists would ache, it was the only way I could prevent myself from hurting someone, my old habits a breath away. At moments like this the battle inside took all my energy and concentration and the outside world melted away into insignificance. It wasn't that I didn't *want* to listen; it was simply impossible, as my internal rowing prevented me from hearing the conversation around me.

The group was made up of a number of different characters. There was a 'flash Harry' type called Mike, who wore designer clothes and talked at a million miles an hour. He was a real wide boy and told countless tales of wheeling and dealing to anyone who'd listen, he was hooked on booze. There was a girl whose mother had been a Satanist and along with other cult members had abused her severely as a child, she was stuck on heroin and her eyes were dead, although bizarrely I remember fancying her. There was another guy, old for an addict at 41, he had been on heroin for most of his life and looked like a walking skeleton. Another bloke there I warmed to and tried to listen to as he talked a lot of sense. He lived by the twelve steps AA/NA (Alcoholics/Narcotics Anonymous) programme and knew it all by heart. The others I can't remember, as I was full of a cocktail of drugs, (prescribed), at the time and certain memories of people have fallen by the wayside.

There was another important thing I had to learn. In the group, everyone talked a great game and an outsider would have listened in, impressed, thinking they were watching a genuine group of recovering addicts. From the inside, everyone was playing the game, going along with the discussions and regurgitating what they had heard, some even believing what they were saying. But a day off the programme and most would be using again, within the month they all would and within a few years they'd be dead. I didn't know this at the time though and struggled to focus on everything that was being said. Each night I would return to my room a little stronger than I'd been in the morning.

The eleven days passed slowly but soon the last day approached and my fear returned. I was terrified of leaving the centre and having nowhere to live, the thought of returning to the streets a fate worse than death. I was to ashamed to go back to my uncles and any way he was a drinker. I went to ask the centre staff for advice but they were unable to help. I was pinning my hopes on getting a bed at a rehabilitation house but I was told flatly that there was no chance; there wasn't even a space for me on the day programme.

It was day seven of my stay, a week into the three weeks I had been given to live, although hopefully I'd now extended that, and I was faced with the prospect of returning to the world that had almost destroyed me. I couldn't believe it and the anger and resentment I'd been sitting on all week threatened to overflow. I stamped down the corridor, fell into one of the beaten old chairs and rolled a cigarette, fuming.

One of the other patients came over and asked me what was wrong. She was a lovely lady, always ready to help, brilliant at focusing on other people's problems whilst systematically failing to address any of her own. She listened patiently as I spat out my reaction to the centre's housing procedure and when I'd finished she told me about a local landlord that provided homes for DSS tenants. I thanked her, handed her my unlit fag and rushed down the corridor to the phone.

I held the scrap of paper, on which she had written the number and dialled. It wasn't easy to sort out Even though I had come a long way the reality of it was I was doped up to the eyeballs, physically half dead and mentally exhausted. I managed to get an address. I felt like a huge weight had been lifted from my shoulders and I returned to the common room, my hope extended a little further into the future.

The last of my days were spent trying to formulate a plan for my return to the outside world. I had come a long way from where I started, slumped in the chair of the waiting room on my first day, close to disintegration, however in reality I had a long way yet to travel. If my recovery was a single mile then I had only walked the first few yards. I was weak, vulnerable and anxiety ridden. My paranoia, anger, resentment, violent and addictive impulses were all just being kept at arm's length and threatened to overwhelm me at any time. I had only been sober for a few days and they were in an unreal environment. I was full of trepidation about the days ahead, the prospect of walking in a new and unfamiliar world, the world of sobriety frightened me shitless. Regardless of that today was the day I was leaving, I stood in the doorway of the detox unit, the door open and me looking out, it was sunny and the day looked promising, I took my fist step into this new world and wondered what would happen next.

That was seven years ago now and it's been rocky at times but well worth it, to me it seems like I have lived my life twice, once as an addict and now as a therapist helping other addicts and their families. I'm not the vile pathetic specimen as I was told so many times by my parents; I am a family man bringing up my children and I have a wonderful wife. I have peeled away the labels I was given in the past and have sworn never to label my children. Instead I nurture them and we enjoy life. I have a life worth living and I am going to live it. I still have my dark days but on the whole I am happy. My wife was also sexually abused by her father and we both struggle sometimes but we support each other and appreciate the words of this last quote as I am sure anyone who has suffered abuse will.

Death is not the greatest loss in life, the greatest loss is what dies inside us while we live.

Vile Pathetic Specimen